D0299499

HOW TO COOK FOR
FOOD ALLERGIES

HOW TO COOK FOR
FOOD ALLERGIES

A GUIDE TO UNDERSTANDING INGREDIENTS, ADAPTING RECIPES AND
COOKING FOR AN EXCITING ALLERGY-FREE DIET
LUCINDA BRUCE-GARDYNE CO-AUTHOR OF THE AWARD-WINNING *LEITHS TECHNIQUES BIBLE*

MACMILLAN

First published in 2007 by Rodale Ltd
an imprint of Pan Macmillan Ltd
Pan Macmillan, 20 New Wharf Road, London N1 9RR
Basingstoke and Oxford
Associated companies throughout the world
www.panmacmillan.com

ISBN: 978-1-905744-04-6

Photography by Ian Greig Garlick
Food styling by Lorna Brash
Edited by Jillian Stewart
Illustrations and original design concept by Simon Daley
Designed by Emma Ashby

1 3 5 7 9 8 6 4 2

A CIP record for this book is available from the British Library

Printed and bound in Great Britain by Butler and Tanner

Notice: This book is intended as a reference volume only, not as a medical manual. The
information given here is designed to help you make informed decisions about your health.
It is not intended as a substitute for any treatment that you may have been prescribed by
your doctor. Neither the author nor publisher shall be liable for any loss or injury arising as
a result of information in this book. If you suspect you have a medical problem, we urge
you to seek competent medical help.

Visit **www.panmacmillan.com** to read more about all our books and to buy them. You will
also find features, author interviews and news of any author events, and you can sign up
for e-newsletters so that you're always first to hear about our new releases.

RODALE
LIVE YOUR WHOLE LIFE™

We inspire and enable people to improve their lives and the world around them

This book is dedicated to my mother,
Margie Monbiot, whose health would have benefited
hugely from the improved understanding and wealth of
information on food allergies that we have today.

Acknowledgements

A special thank you to my husband, Hew, for his constant support, guidance and involvement through all stages of this book, and to my three sons, Angus, Robin and Otto, for inspiring me to write it in the first place. I am also immensely grateful to Penny Webber, my oracle at the start of this project, Lucie Nason for introducing me to Websters, to Millie Scott-Dempster for being a wonderful child minder to Otto, to Dorothy Bruce-Gardyne – Granny – who has held the fort on a regular basis, and to Mary Stansfeld for her gluten-free cooking tips. Thank you also to my friends and family without whose support this book would have been much harder to write.

I would also like to thank the team at Websters, namely Anne Lawrance, Jillian Stewart and Emma Ashby, for the thought and sheer hard work they have put into producing this book. Thanks also to Ian Greig Garlick and Lorna Brash for taking such care over the photographs.

CONTENTS

Part iii   THE RECIPES

INTRODUCTION

The diagnosis of a food allergy is at once a blessing and a source of anxiety. It is a blessing because it often comes after a long and frustrating search for the cause of the debilitating symptoms from which you have been suffering. And the anxiety? That is inevitable, as you now face changes in your lifestyle or circumstances to accommodate or overcome the problem. At first it may feel as if your 'can eat' list would fill no more than a Post-it note in comparison to the tome that is your 'cannot eat' list and, if you allow it to, this can quickly impact on the rest of your life. After all, many of the things we enjoy in life – celebrations, birthdays, get-togethers with friends – revolve around food and when you see food as a problem, it dampens your enjoyment of life.

In a funny way, we were lucky. Our eldest son was a tiny baby when we discovered he was acutely allergic to both dairy and egg. Because he was so small we had time to adjust as a family and we adapted and grew together. He has never known the taste of dairy products and so does not 'miss' them and, because his reaction was so severe, there was no decision to be made: we had to go dairy and egg free as a family and that was that.

That was seven years ago. We now have three boys who, between them, cannot eat dairy, eggs, anything containing gluten and, bizarrely, potato. Yet despite these restrictions we manage to have an interesting, varied diet, using the wide range of ingredients that we can eat. Our experience is that allergies can be conquered without the need to adopt the sort of 'hair-shirt' approach that necessitates living on a limited range of foods. How? The answer is simple: cook your food yourself using fresh ingredients.

When you cook your own food from scratch, you'll find that there are surprisingly few restrictions as to what you can eat. Gone are the days of worrying about the traces of allergens in all those ready-made meals. In addition, you'll find that your food is fresher, purer, tastier and will become a focus of family life. And if that conjures up images of hours spent slaving over a hot stove, think again. Contrary to what you might believe, cooking 'from scratch' doesn't have to be time-consuming or difficult. By taking a few minutes to plan the week's menu, writing out a shopping list, cooking in advance in batches and freezing, it is possible to eat an exciting, healthy and varied diet without spending all your time in the kitchen. There is also no reason why eating this type of diet should be more expensive. In fact, it can be cheaper to buy fresh basic ingredients rather than processed versions or the few ready-made meals that will cater specifically to your dietary requirements.

More importantly, being able to cook for yourself will help you cope better in everyday life. If you understand the ingredients to which you are allergic and how they are used in food, you will be able to anticipate problems when eating away from home and hence avoid them before they arise. It will help you to be more confident in suggesting easy alternatives to friends and family who would like to cook for you. An understanding of how food is cooked will also help you identify 'safe' foods on the menu when eating in a restaurant and the right questions to ask to check that your needs are understood by the staff. In short, it will give you far greater control over your life.

I have had to find out how to do all of this over the last seven years. Even as a professionally trained chef, I have found this challenging and I have been surprised that I haven't been able to find a book that approaches food allergies from the perspective that food can and should be normal and enjoyable – naughty even (after all, everyone needs a treat now and then). With this book I hope to fill that void – it's full of delicious real food; it's food that we eat all the time and it's the stuff we really enjoy.

The book is divided into three parts. The first part, Living with Food Allergies, looks at the key rules that will help you cope with food allergies in daily life, such as how to avoid cross-contamination of food in the kitchen, preparing for travelling, and eating away from home. There's also plenty of help for those with children, including how to help your child's nursery or school cope with their allergy and how you can ensure your child enjoys birthday parties without feeling excluded or 'different'. The section also covers the basics of nutrition and balancing your diet. When you have to cut things out of your diet, you may well be missing a key source of nutrients, minerals or vitamins and Chapter 3 provides a checklist of alternative sources of these nutrients. It is by no means an exhaustive guide but it will help point you in the right direction.

In Part Two you will find out why ingredients are used and the general rules for using substitutes for the foods you can't have. The most common food allergens – dairy, wheat, egg, nuts and soya – are also some of the most common and versatile ingredients and in order to be able to adapt a recipe successfully you must first know the purpose that the food is serving in the recipe. Armed with this knowledge you'll find that food will come alive for you. Rather than look at a recipe in a book and think 'I can't have that because it contains …', your response will be 'That looks delicious – I'll just use … instead.'

Of course, you have to walk before you can run, so before you launch yourself into adapting your own recipes, familiarize yourself with the cooking techniques and recipes in Part Three. In all of the recipes I have aimed for simplicity. Firstly, as far as possible I have used normal ingredients that you can find in your local supermarket. If you are on a gluten-free diet, you may need to visit a health food shop to get some of the gluten-free flours, but even these are gradually becoming more widely available. Secondly, I have kept the methods as simple as possible. After the formal testing process for the recipes, I gave them to my husband, Hew, to try – to make sure that the instructions were sufficiently clear and complete for the novice cook. He was really pleased with the way they turned out and how much he learned in the process. If he can cook them, anyone can (sorry Hew!). Lastly, I have tried to be realistic. There are limits to what can be adapted. The more a recipe relies on an ingredient that you cannot have, the harder it will be to effect a workable substitution. While it is important to recognize these limitations, don't beat yourself up over the food you can't eat: look at all the delicious things you *can* enjoy.

If you haven't cooked – seriously – before, this book will get you up to a very good level of proficiency. It's not as hard as you might imagine, and the rewards – in terms of conquering your allergies, regaining control over your life and improving the healthiness and taste of your diet – are definitely worth the effort.

USING THE RECIPES

Before you begin cooking any of the recipes please note the following:
- Many of the recipes in this book are suitable for all the featured food allergies, without any adaptations. Where a recipe is not suitable for a particular allergy and cannot be adapted, this is made clear in the introduction – although in many instances I have provided an alternative, similar recipe.
- The flagging system that is used in the recipes indicates the ingredients you need to subsititute in order to make the recipe suitable for your particular allergy (or to alert you to an ingredient that potentially could be a problem). Where no quantity is given for the alternative ingredient the quantity is the same as the standard ingredient.
- At the start of each section you will find guidance on preparation techniques and the suitability of that particular cooking method or food for each of the food allergies – it is helpful to read this information before making any of the recipes that follow. The techniques are covered in much more depth at the beginning of each chapter, as it would be impossible to include detailed guidance in every recipe.
- Unless the recipe states otherwise all spoon measures are level, all eggs are medium (as are vegetables) and onions, garlic, shallots and ginger are peeled.
- All stock featured in the recipes is made using the recipes in Chapter 9.
- Sunflower, corn and olive oil are used as cooking oils throughout the book as they are free of nut and soya oils. If you have a nut allergy and are also allergic to seeds, cook with corn oil or olive oil.
- Use one set of measurements – i.e. metric or imperial – as they are not interchangeable.

For news, updates and additional information see:
www.lucindabrucegardyne.com

Part I

LIVING WITH FOOD ALLERGIES

Chapter 1 | AVOIDING PROBLEM FOODS IN DAY-TO-DAY LIFE

When you – or your child – suffer from food allergies, you need to make some very basic changes not only with regard to what you eat but how you store, prepare and cook food. This might sound daunting – and there's no doubt food allergies make life more challenging – but you and your family can lead a full life, by planning ahead and taking time to explain to friends and family how food allergies can be managed. As well as avoiding unsuitable foods in the diet, contamination of safe foods with unsafe foods must be prevented by storing and preparing them separately, and by using clean hands and clean utensils. Mealtimes away from home need to be planned and your condition explained to anyone who prepares food for you. You will also require the cooperation of your colleagues at work, and, if it is your child who has an allergy, the staff caring for your child at school. Food allergies have a bearing on the restaurants you choose to eat in, the holiday accommodation you choose to stay in and how you plan to travel.

EATING AT HOME

At home you are in control of the food you prepare, and control is the key. Allergic reactions to food are caused by eating or coming into contact with the foods you must avoid. To prevent allergic reactions occurring at home you therefore need to:
- know what you are eating
- keep safe and unsafe foods separate
- ensure you and your food do not come into contact with contaminated surfaces, utensils, tableware and people eating or preparing unsafe food.

Before eating or preparing food, take time to read the ingredients lists on food labels (see box opposite and the 'What to Look for on Food Labels' sections in chapters 4 to 8).

KEEPING SAFE AND UNSAFE FOODS SEPARATE

- Store safe foods separately from allergy-causing foods. For example, store wheat flour and gluten-free flours on separate shelves.
- Prepare foods separately to reduce the risk of cross-contamination via hands, utensils or work surfaces.
- Prepare safe foods before unsafe foods so that your hands, work surfaces and utensils are free of traces of unsuitable foods.

Making life easier for yourself

If you are cooking for a family, there is no reason why you should always go to the trouble of preparing separate meals for allergenic and non-allergenic members – why not make the same safe food for everyone? This saves time and means no one will feel different or left out. This book is full of familiar recipes that are easily adapted for dairy-, gluten-, egg-, soya- and nut-free diets – they taste great, too.

Understanding food labels

To avoid exposure to food allergens always check the list of ingredients on the label of packaged foods before buying or eating them. The latest European Union food labelling rules have made food labels much easier to understand. They require manufacturers of packaged food to state clearly in the ingredients list when food products contain ingredients that are derived from the 12 major allergenic foods: milk, eggs, cereals containing gluten, fish, crustaceans, tree nuts, peanuts, soya beans, celery, mustard, sesame and sulphur dioxide, at levels of 10 mg/kg or 10 mg/litre.

Food products containing any of these allergenic ingredients must clearly list them next to or after the list of ingredients so it is clear at a glance whether a product contains a particular allergen. This labelling method prevents the purchaser from having to read through long lists of ingredients, and is also easier for children to read and understand. Continue to check products you buy regularly as manufacturers change their recipes and may, at any time, add ingredients you are allergic to.

For terms used on food labels to describe ingredients derived from gluten, dairy, egg, nuts and soya, see the information about food labels at the end of each of the 'Substituting for…' chapters.

AVOIDING CONTAMINATION OF SAFE FOOD

In the kitchen
- Always wash your hands, and make sure the work surfaces, pots, pans and utensils are clean before using them to prepare food.
- Use separate cloths or disposable kitchen paper to mop up spills containing food allergens, for general cleaning and for wiping the hands and face of allergic children.

At mealtimes
- Make sure the table is clean before people sit down. Traces of food left on it may cause a reaction.
- Wash your hands before laying the table and serving food, to prevent contaminating cutlery and serving spoons with traces of unsafe foods.
- Keep safe foods and allergy-causing foods away from each other on the table.
- Serve safe and allergy-causing foods with separate spoons.
- If you have a small child who is allergic, put them in a clean high chair (invest in a portable one that can be taken to other people's homes, and restaurants).
- Keep serving dishes and serving spoons used for unsuitable food out of the reach of allergic children.
- Sit allergic children out of reach of other children eating unsuitable foods.
- Before cleaning an allergic child's face and hands after a meal or snack, make sure both your hands and the face cloth are clean.

EATING AWAY FROM HOME

Visiting friends and family should be an enjoyable event and not a source of stress or anxiety. Provided you take time to discuss your dietary requirements beforehand, it is possible to maintain the level of control necessary to ensure you eat safely and enjoy your time away from home. If you explain which foods have to be avoided but also offer to bring your own food, your host can decide to cook or ask you to provide food without embarrassment. By mutually agreeing to take your own food you may both feel relieved and more relaxed knowing that your food will not contain any allergens.

VISITING FRIENDS AND FAMILY

Whether your hosts would like to cater for you or would prefer you to bring your own food, the following points are worth discussing to make your visit 'allergy free' and enjoyable.

When your hosts would like to cater for you
- Ask what they are planning to serve. The menu may be perfectly suitable or easily adapted. To be certain, ask whether the recipes contain any of the ingredients you cannot eat.
- If the menu is not suitable, help them by listing the foods you can eat and suggest safe dishes that are familiar and enjoyed by everyone.
- Alert your hosts to allergy-causing ingredients on food labels they may not be familiar with.
- If you are staying overnight or for longer, offer to bring key foods that you rely on, such as gluten-free bread, dairy-free milk and suitable snacks and drinks. This will save your hosts time and effort when shopping for your visit. If they offer to buy these products for you, give all the details they require to buy the right product: this is particularly important if you have allergic children, who may not eat unfamiliar products. It also makes shopping easier for the hosts.
- While you are visiting, offer to help your hosts prepare the food and to serve at mealtimes. This may be a relief for your hosts and reduces the risk of contamination.

When the hosts are nervous catering for you
It is perfectly possible to take easy-to-prepare ingredients or ready-prepared meals and snacks for a day or so. For longer, it is best to take staples with you and shop for basic ingredients nearby. Ask the host what she plans to cook so that you can plan a similar meal or menu for yourself.

WHEN YOUR ALLERGIC CHILD IS IN THE CARE OF OTHERS

If you have an allergic child, controlling their diet can be difficult once they are outside the home. Inevitably, as your child grows, and he or she visits friends and family or begins nursery or school without you, you will need to trust other people to ensure your child does not come into contact with allergy-causing foods. However, in spite of having dietary restrictions, it is important that your child learns to enjoy periods of time away from you, with trusted friends and members of the family, and feel normal and included at nursery or school. This section outlines ways of ensuring your child is safe when he or she is in the care of others.

Family and friends may be unused to dealing with food allergies. When they first invite your child to play, or to a party, explain that certain foods and food containing those ingredients make him or her allergic and offer to supply suitable snacks and meals. Depending on how daunting the hosts regard your child's dietary requirements, they may be happy to provide suitable food for your child or ask you to supply your child's food. Discuss the following points so that you all feel confident that your child's visit will be safe and allergy free.

When friends and family would like to cater for your child
Although the same guidelines apply here as for 'When your hosts would like to cater for you' opposite, other precautions must be in place for allergic children. As toddlers and small children are mobile and are prone to eating anything within their reach, suggest that the snacks, meals and drinks served are suitable for all the children present (see page 219). This way, if the children share beakers, swap food or wipe it on each other it doesn't matter.

When friends and family are nervous catering for your child
For your allergic baby or small child, supply purées, snacks, drinks, milk, bibs, dishes, spoons and a portable high chair with a tray and face cloth. This way, you can be assured that your child is unlikely to come into contact with unsafe foods while he or she is eating. If possible, provide a meal similar to the meal served to other children present so your child does not feel different and tempted to try unsuitable foods on the table.

Irrespective of whether the host or the parent has provided the food, the person looking after the child should be able to recognize the symptoms of an allergic reaction and treat them swiftly and correctly. In order for them to do so:
• Supply and explain how to use any medicines in the event of an allergic reaction.
• List any early signs or symptoms of an allergic reaction so that the carer can quickly recognize and deal with the reaction before it has time to escalate into something serious.
• Make sure the carer can contact you easily.
• Ask them to ring for an ambulance immediately, if your child suffers from anaphylactic reactions to food.

You may have taken all the precautions possible regarding your own child, but other children there may present a risk:
• Ask the carer to explain to any other children, old enough to understand, that they must not hand food to your child.
• When your child is old enough to understand, teach him or her to be responsible for what he or she eats (see page 18).

Children's parties

Invitations to parties for very small children are usually extended to one or both parents too. This arrangement means you can take your own food, keep your child away from unsuitable food and inform other parents present of your child's allergies so they can make sure their child does not pass food to or wipe sticky hands on your child.

Parties for children aged between 4 and 7 often do not include parents, and can instil dread and anxiety in parents of allergic children. You may not know the parents hosting the party very well; traditional party food including sandwiches, pre-packed snack food, cakes and biscuits are likely to contain food allergens; and sweets that may also be unsuitable for your child are often given as small prizes and included in party bags. It is also inevitable that the parents will be busy during the party and cannot watch your child's every move.

There are many ways that you and the parents hosting the party can make the party safe, inclusive and enjoyable for your child. Accept an invitation to a children's party by speaking directly to the parents hosting the event so you can discuss your child's dietary requirements.

When food will be provided for your child

- Once the parents have decided on the menu, go through it carefully to agree which foods are safe and which are not.

- Suggest how birthday cake, other home-baked foods and sandwiches may be adapted using alternative ingredients. Offer to give them ideas and recipes for simple, safe party foods (see page 219) or provide food that may be difficult to find in the supermarket or is difficult for the parents to make.

- Offer to provide suitable sweets for games and party bags.

When you are providing your child's food

Discuss the menu and if possible provide similar food, birthday cake, snacks and any sweets for games and your child's party bag.

Other ways of making a party safe for your child

- When you arrive at the party, confirm that the food the hosts say is suitable is OK.

- Ask the hosts to show your child which foods he or she can and can't eat on the table.

- Suggest that safe foods are assembled on a party plate, ready to serve. The parents then need only place the plate of safe food in front of your child when he or she is seated at the table. This means the child will not stand out as different and both you and the host parents will feel confident that your child is eating safely.

- Ask that unsuitable food is kept out of reach of your child.

- Explain the symptoms of an allergic reaction so that the parents will recognize the condition if it occurs.

- Provide all necessary treatments for your child's allergies and explain how to administer them.

- Give contact phone numbers so that you can be reached immediately in an emergency.

- If you are worried that your child may eat the wrong foods, or requires an Epipen to treat allergic reactions, ask if you can stay to help.

- Ask the parents to mark foods that are safe and unsafe by placing safe foods on paper plates of a particular colour so that your child can choose his food without drawing attention to himself.

CHILDCARE AND SCHOOLING

It can be a worrying time when your allergic child starts nursery or school, as it involves trusting virtual strangers to keep your child safe and happy during mealtimes and throughout the day. The organization may or may not have dealt with your child's particular food allergies and a detailed discussion regarding your child's requirements is essential before he or she begins there. When you first visit the nursery or school, talk to the staff who will teach, care and cater for your child, to ascertain how much experience they have of dealing with food allergies and how much additional information they require to ensure your child is safe in their care. By talking to the staff, you will also gauge how adaptable, creative and sensitive they are to your child's requirements.

Ask the teachers or staff responsible how they guard against children with food allergies feeling different and isolated during mealtimes. Children with special dietary requirements are often seated together or amongst older, more responsible children who are more aware of not touching and swapping food. Provided your child is out of arms reach of the other small children, sticky fingers, scattered food and spilt drinks, your child can enjoy a sociable meal. It is also worth asking how they plan to prevent your child from feeling excluded from any classroom activities using allergy-causing foods. For example, are they prepared to adapt recipes used in cooking activities so your child can take part?

If you are confident that the nursery or school will make every effort to make your child's life in their care as happy and as 'normal' as possible, make another appointment to discuss the specific details of your child's diet and medication before the term begins. If you are not impressed with the general attitude it may be advisable – in extremis – to look at another nursery or school in the area.

When the nursery or school is happy to cater for your child
- Provide a clear list of the food and drinks your child cannot eat. This list must also include a list of all the terms for unsuitable ingredients used on food labels.
- Provide an extensive list of the foods that your child can eat, as this will help the catering staff enormously when they plan lunch menus for your child.
- Arrange to meet the head of catering to go through the weekly menus. You may both be pleasantly surprised and encouraged to see how many dishes can be made suitable with simple adaptations to recipes.
- Offer suggestions for other lunch dishes that would be practical for them to cook.
- Suggest products they can order in, such as dairy-free milk, yogurt and ice cream or gluten-free flours.
- Ask how they will cater for your child on school outings. Would they prefer you to provide food?

If the nursery or school does not have the facilities to cook for your child
- Ask to see their weekly menus and provide similar food where possible.
- Find out what other food and drink they would like you to provide – such as suitable dairy-free milk, biscuits, gluten-free bread and cakes – so your child does not feel left out, for instance when it's snack time or when birthday cakes are brought in by other children.

Teaching your child responsibility

By the time children reach school age they usually have a good understanding of the foods that make them ill and can be given more responsibility in ensuring they do not eat unsuitable food. They will be fully aware of how ill they feel when they become allergic and this should be enough to persuade them to be careful. Ensure they are aware of the following:

• Exactly which foods they need to avoid and the various terms used for those foods on labels.

• They must read food labels carefully before eating something they are offered. Teach them to ask 'Does this contain ?' before accepting any food, even from an adult.

• They must not help themselves to food unless they know it is safe to eat.

• They must not swap food with other children in the playground or at mealtimes unless they are sure it is safe for them to eat.

HELPING STAFF RECOGNIZE AND TREAT ALLERGIC REACTIONS

In the event of your child having an allergic reaction, it is vital that the staff know what to do. Before your child starts:

• Confirm that all staff dealing with your child are aware of and understand your child's dietary needs.
• Provide a list of initial symptoms of your child's food allergy so that they can recognize the first stages of an allergic reaction. Although it is very obvious to you when your child is suffering an allergic reaction, the staff in a busy classroom may not notice.
• Provide all necessary medicines and clear instructions for administering them if a full allergic reaction occurs. If your child carries an Epipen, the staff may require training to use it.
• Provide contact numbers and ask that they contact you immediately if a reaction occurs.
• Confirm that medicines will be taken on school outings.

Chapter 2 | EATING OUT AND TRAVELLING

At home you are in control of the way in which food is stored, prepared, served and eaten. When you are eating at restaurants, travelling or on holiday, you are less able to protect yourself or a member of your family from allergy-causing foods. The knowledge that you are no longer in control is powerful and can be debilitating to such an extent that you may feel confined to your home. Although food allergies make eating out and travelling more complicated, it is still possible to lead a normal and fulfilling life by:

- planning mealtimes
- choosing carefully where to eat
- being prepared to ask questions about the food available to buy in shops or on menus
- taking food with you.

In this chapter you will find advice on selecting restaurants and safe food from menus, travelling and flying safely, and choosing appropriate holiday accommodation.

EATING OUT

For most people, eating out is a treat, providing an opportunity to try new foods and to relax with friends, with no clearing up afterwards. However, for those with food allergies, it can be an anxious, frustrating experience. Unless you visit a particular restaurant, café or fast-food outlet regularly, you have no established relationship or connection with the people running it and no way of knowing how food is stored or prepared. You must either take your own food, or place your trust in waiters, managers and chefs. You will need to be confident that they will communicate your requirements to each other, check their dishes for the ingredients that could make you ill and take care to prepare and serve safe and unsafe foods separately. Many people have suffered serious allergic reactions as a result of traces of unsafe food present on unwashed or carelessly washed pots, pans, utensils and hands.

CHOOSE YOUR RESTAURANT WISELY

In order to eat out safely and for the experience to be enjoyable, it is vital to choose your restaurant wisely, book well in advance and plan your menu with the restaurant manager and/or the chef before you eat there.

If possible, choose restaurants that have experience of dealing with food allergies and are careful to prepare your food on clean work surfaces with clean utensils and hands. The safest restaurants are those that prepare food from scratch and offer roasted, grilled or pan-fried meat, poultry or fish cooked to order. This way, you can choose simple ingredients, cooked plainly in suitable oil and served simply with their cooking juices. When restaurants rely on ready-made food, which will almost certainly contain the common food allergens, there is very little they can do to cater for your needs.

It also makes sense to choose restaurants serving food that does not rely heavily on the ingredients you are allergic to. For example, Asian cooking uses very little dairy but frequently includes soya and nuts in sauces and garnishes, and nut oil for frying; in contrast, the cuisine of northern France uses dairy products, wheat flour and eggs in many dishes.

PLANNING AHEAD
If possible, book your table at least two to three days in advance. This gives you the opportunity to talk to the restaurant manager – and, if necessary, the chef – to establish whether the menu includes dishes you can eat. If it doesn't, ask whether the chef could prepare a suitable dish for you. If they don't understand your requirements or are not helpful then choose another restaurant.

If the chef is happy to cater for you, help him to plan your menu by telling him what you can eat as well as the ingredients you can't. Ask him to contact you to run through the ingredients in the proposed menu to confirm the food is safe for you to eat. It is also a good idea to contact the restaurant the day before you are due to eat there, to confirm with the restaurant manager and head chef on duty that they haven't forgotten about you, and to run through the dishes they are planning to serve you, to double check they understand your requirements.

CHOOSING SAFE FOOD FROM A MENU

If the restaurant has prepared a special menu for you, run through the ingredients with the waiter, manager or chef once more before ordering. Even after the efforts both you and the restaurant staff have gone to, food allergens in basic ingredients may slip through the net. If the dish turns out to be unsafe for you to eat, do not take the risk. Most restaurants will be very apologetic and will make every effort to provide you with a safe alternative.

When you have not had the opportunity to book ahead, if possible explain to the manager or waiter on arrival how serious your food allergy is and run through the menu with them to look for suitable dishes or simple adaptations that could be made.

Self-service restaurants

These are generally too risky for those with a serious food allergy. While some of the foods may be suitable, it is too easy for them to become contaminated by food from other dishes falling into them or by serving spoons that are used for a number of dishes.

If they are not confident they can provide a suitable meal for you, it is safer not to eat there. Once you are confident they can cater for you, look for a familiar, simple dish that is normally safe for you to eat and can be freshly cooked to order, such as plain grilled, pan-fried or roasted meat or fish, cooked with a suitable fat and served with its cooking juices. Ask for a plain salad with oil and vinegar, served separately, to make your own dressing, or plain boiled or steamed vegetables. Desserts, more often than not, are made with dairy products, wheat, eggs and nuts, as they add richness, flavour and help to lighten delicate foods. Avoid rich desserts and look for those made with fresh fruit, such as poached fruit, fruit salads, sorbets, water ices and fresh strawberry or raspberry coulis, as they tend to be the safest options. Your meal may not be as interesting as you would like it to be but you will have chosen safely.

If you have a dairy allergy

- Does the sauce, gravy, soup, casserole or braised dish contain butter, milk, cream, yogurt or cheese? What are they garnished with? Soup is often garnished with croutons or croutes, often made with butter, or topped with a swirl of yogurt, soured cream, cream or crème fraiche. If the sauce is unsuitable, ask for olive oil and wedges of lemon to moisten and flavour plainly cooked food.
- Is the food roasted, baked, pan-fried or grilled with oil or do they use butter or ghee (a clarified butter used in Indian food)? If so, can they prepare food for you cooked with a suitable fat?
- Has the food been marinated before cooking? If so, check the ingredients in the marinade – it may contain dairy products.
- Are the vegetables served plain or are they cooked or tossed in butter? If the vegetables are buttered, could they prepare you a salad or plain boiled or steamed vegetables to order? Roasted, baked and grilled vegetables are normally cooked with oil but always check. Puréed vegetables, such as mashed potatoes, are best avoided as they normally contain milk and butter.
- Does the salad dressing contain dairy products? If so, ask for oil and vinegar as a simple alternative.
- When ordering pizza, confirm the dough is dairy free and ask the chef to make a cheese-free pizza. Before eating your pizza, drizzle with olive oil, or an oil flavoured with garlic or chilli, to moisten it.

Other tips for eating out gluten free

If you are going to an Italian pizza restaurant, ring the restaurant manager in advance to ask if you can bring along a gluten-free pizza base for them to top or gluten-free pasta for them to cook; ask for a gluten-free sauce such as fresh Italian tomato sauce.

If a dish is normally flavoured with soy sauce, ask if they can use the gluten-free equivalent, Tamari instead – if necessary, take your own bottle with you.

Ground white pepper can contain flour to bulk it out. To be sure, ask for a pepper mill to grind fresh pepper on your food.

Don't forget that there are a number of drinks you must avoid, too. Many alcoholic drinks such as beer, lager, ale, stout and whisky are made from malted barley, which contains gluten. Some soft drinks served in restaurants are also questionable: tomato juice may be thickened with wheat flour, while cloudy fruit squashes and fizzy drinks may contain wheat starch.

If you have a gluten allergy

- Are the sauces, gravy, braised dishes, soups and casseroles thickened with flour? If the restaurant uses stock cubes or gravy granules to make sauces, these may contain gluten.
- Is the meat, poultry or fish in pan-fried dishes coated in flour before frying? Meat and fish seasonings can also contain wheat flour.
- Are other fried dishes floured, battered or crumbed?
- Do the sauces contain soy sauce, barbecue sauce or Worcestershire sauce (all are common sources of hidden gluten)?
- Has the food been marinated before cooking? If so, check the ingredients in the marinade – some of them may contain wheat flour or wheat derivatives.

- Do sausages, stuffing and terrines contain flour or breadcrumbs? Bought meat products often contain 'rusk', or dried breadcrumbs.
- Are bulgur wheat, couscous, semolina, barley, oats or rye used in the dish (all of these contain gluten)?
- Is the salad dressing freshly made or bought in (manufactured salad dressings are often thickened with wheat flour)? If they are not sure, ask for an undressed salad with oil and vinegar served separately, to make your own dressing. Also choose plain new potatoes, baked potatoes, rice and plain cooked vegetables.
- Which desserts contain wheat flour? Many desserts, including some manufactured ice creams, contain wheat flour. To be safe, choose plain fresh fruit or fresh fruit salad, meringues, poached fruit, cheese and fruit or homemade sorbet.

If you have an egg allergy
- Do the salad dressings contain egg (restaurant salad dressings often contain a small quantity of egg to emulsify and thicken them or are made with a mayonnaise base)? If they are unsure ask for oil and vinegar so that you can make your own salad dressing.
- Which of the sauces contain egg? Avoid egg-based sauces such as hollandaise and béarnaise sauce.
- Are fried foods battered or crumbed? If they are they will contain egg. Are baked foods glazed with egg?
- Do your hamburgers, meatballs, sausages and fish cakes contain egg? Foods made with processed or minced meat or fish are often bound with egg to prevent them crumbling when cooked.
- Does the pasta or noodles contain egg?
- Do any of the stir-fried dishes contain egg? If you ask for stir-fried food without egg, confirm they will be frying your food in a clean pan and not in an unwashed one previously used to cook a dish containing egg.
- Most baked goods and desserts contain egg. To be safe, ask for a fresh fruit salad with a fresh fruit coulis. Homemade sorbets may also be suitable, provided they do not contain egg white.
- Do any of your drinks contain egg? Egg is often added to hot drink mixes, including hot chocolate and cappuccino, to make them frothy.

If you have a nut allergy
- Are there any nut oils in the salad dressing (they are sometimes added to give flavour)? If they are unsure, ask for vinegar and olive oil to make your own dressing.
- Are oils containing nut oil used for frying? If so, could they fry your food in a suitable oil in a clean pan?
- Are nuts and seeds used to garnish salads and other savoury dishes?
- Are nuts and seeds present in the bread?
- Are there nuts present in any of the stuffings, meat terrines, sausages (Mortadella is one example) and processed meats?
- Are ground nuts used to thicken and flavour sauces? Be especially aware of curry sauces, satay sauce and pesto.

- Many desserts, including ice cream and baked goods, may contain nuts and are not safe to eat in restaurants. Also avoid marzipan and nougat.
- Be aware of nut syrups and nut liqueurs (Amaretto and Frangelico) added to coffee and hot chocolate.

Be especially careful with Japanese, Malaysian, Thai, Chinese, Indian, Middle Eastern and vegetarian dishes (nuts are often used in vegetarian 'meat').

If you have a soya allergy

- Does your chosen dish contain the soya-based flavouring ingredients soy sauce, Tamari, shoyu or miso? Also ask about salad dressings, spreads, dips, marinades and sauces (including Worcestershire, barbecue sauce and mayonnaise), as these often contain soya.
- Which dishes contain tofu or tempeh (which are soya-based)?
- Do they use soya bean oil or vegetable oil, which contains soya bean oil, for frying? Can they use an alternative cooking oil such as corn or olive oil?
- Are soups, stews and sauces flavoured with stock cubes? Stock cubes often contain soya-based ingredients. Canned soup and dried soup can also contain soya.
- Are baked foods, such as pastry and cakes, homemade or bought? Manufactured baked foods may contain soya flour and margarine made with soya bean oil.
- Is the tuna canned or fresh? Canned tuna is often stored in soya bean oil.
- Which dishes contain beansprouts (as they are likely to be soya beansprouts)?
- Are breaded foods homemade or bought (manufactured breaded foods often contain soya)?
- Are the desserts manufactured rather than homemade (homemade desserts are much less likely to contain soya)? If homemade desserts are available, ask if margarine containing soya bean oil has been used to make them. Otherwise choose a simple dessert made with fresh fruit, such as poached fruit or fresh fruit salad.

Be especially careful with Japanese, Malaysian, Thai, Chinese, Indian and vegetarian dishes, as soya in various guises is a common ingredient.

SHOW YOUR APPRECIATION

When restaurant staff have been helpful during your visit and you have eaten well and safely, it is worth returning. Tip them well and let them know how pleased you are. They will appreciate your comments and are more likely to remember you next time you book. When you book another time, be just as careful to discuss and plan your menu as the first time. And remember, menus and staff change and your second experience could be different.

Take your medication with you

Always take your medication with you when you go out to eat, especially if you carry an Epipen. If you become allergic despite the precautions you have taken, immediately stop eating, tell the people you are with and take your medication. If the allergic reaction is becoming serious, ask your friends to ring for an ambulance.

TRAVELLING

When travelling for the day by car, boat or train make sure you take satisfying and nutritious meals and snacks to last the journey, as the majority of foods available for you to buy on the way may not be suitable. Although travelling by air is also perfectly possible for people with food allergies, it is made more complicated by restrictions on luggage and carrying medication, the limited range of food available on board, sitting in such close proximity to fellow passengers and the risk of delays.

TRAVELLING BY PLANE

Plan your journey carefully in order to give yourself and the airline an opportunity to plan for your food allergy, so that you can travel in safety and comfort. The following guidelines will help.

BOOKING YOUR FLIGHT

- Book your flight directly with the airline as early as you can. This gives you the opportunity to discuss your food allergy with a member of the airline staff.
- Let them know if you or a member of your family have a serious food allergy.
- If you suffer from peanut allergy, request a flight when peanuts are not served on the aeroplane. Morning flights are usually nut free.
- If your allergies are easily managed with medication you may like to request a special meal if the airline is able to provide it.
- If you feel safer taking your own food, find out how much luggage you can take on board. You will want to take your maximum allowance for long journeys to ensure you have sufficient food to last until you get to your final destination.
- Ask what documentation is required from your doctor to enable you to carry your medication on board. Airlines usually request that all medicines are stored in their original containers that show dosages and clearly identify the drugs for customs officials. If you carry an Epipen, airlines also ask you to carry a letter from the doctor confirming the drug and an explanation of why it is essential you carry it.
- If possible book your seat. A window seat means you have a passenger on one side only and food will not be passed above you as it is served and cleared away.

PREPARING FOR YOUR FLIGHT

- Visit your doctor to discuss which medication you should take with you. Ask them to prescribe more than you would normally need and to prepare the documentation required by the airline to enable you to carry the medication on board.
- Contact the airline 24 hours before your flight to confirm that you have all the medical documentation you need; that they have special meals in hand if you have ordered them; the volume of luggage you can take on board; and, if you have arranged to travel on a nut-free flight, confirm it will be so.
- If you are away for a few days, pack staples you may not be able to find at your destination in your 'checked'/hold baggage.
- Store delicate foods that squash or crumble easily in airtight containers. Pack containers of satisfying, filling foods – and avoid anything that is likely to deteriorate on a long journey. Allow for delays and provide for yourself as generously as your hand luggage allowance permits.

Flying with allergic children

Taking lots of food on the plane is a great way to keep children happy. If your children are old enough, give them a small rucksack to carry filled with safe snacks. This way you can take more food on board. Keep them busy with small packets of dried fruit, small boxes of raisins, apples, carrot sticks, rice cakes, bread sticks, suitable fruit and cereal bars and biscuits. These are all ideal snacks for travelling.

Keep a close eye on your child for symptoms of an allergic reaction during the flight. Treat any symptoms at the earliest opportunity to avoid complications.

- Even if you have ordered special meals, take satisfying snacks with you in case of delays or to tide you over if the special meal does not materialize.
- Pack your medication where it is easy to access.
- Take a small packet of wipes for wiping down trays and arm rests.
- Arrive at the airport in plenty of time. This will allow you to advise check-in staff you will be carrying medication on board, confirm that they have special meals for you and reserve your seat (choose a window seat or an aisle seat so that you are not sandwiched

between people who may be eating food that could cause an allergic reaction). Reconfirm the above with the cabin staff at the gate.

ON THE PLANE
- If you are allergic to nuts and they are likely to be served on the flight, request that they are not served to people sitting around you.
- Wipe the food tray and arm rests to remove any traces of food allergens.
- Explain your food allergy to your fellow passengers. Their cooperation is essential if you are to have a safe, stress-free flight.
- Inform the flight crew that you suffer from food allergies, that you have ordered special meals and explain you have all necessary medication with you.
- If you have ordered a special meal, run through the ingredients with a member of the cabin crew before you eat it.

CHOOSING HOLIDAY ACCOMMODATION

Accommodation that has self-catering facilities is usually the best option for those with food allergies. Even if you only have a small fridge to store fresh ingredients, some basic cooking utensils and a hot plate to cook on, it means you are in control. By cooking for yourself or your family, you may not be trying local specialities in the restaurants every night but you will still have the chance to purchase and prepare local produce (though do exercise caution with anything you are unfamiliar with, unless you are sure it is safe to eat).

Although hotels are in theory more relaxing than self-catering accommodation this does not necessarily follow when you or someone in your family suffers from food allergies, as you are forced to rely on restaurants or the hotel kitchen.

If you choose to stay in a hotel
- Stay in a hotel that has experience of catering for food allergies or provides self-catering facilities too, so you are not totally reliant on the hotel kitchen.

- Help the hotel plan your stay. Send a list of foods that you can and can't eat to the catering manager in advance. Follow up with a call to make sure he understands your restrictions.
- When you arrive at the hotel, introduce yourself to the catering manager or head chef so they know who they are catering for.
- Choose a region where the local cooking does not rely on the ingredients you are allergic to. For example, eating in hotels and restaurants in northern France can be very limiting for someone on a dairy-free diet, as many of the local dishes contain butter, cream and cheese. However, in southern France, the diet is lighter and relies more on olive oil, fruit and vegetables, offering a wider range of suitable dishes.

Useful ingredients to take on holiday

As there is no guarantee that you will be able to find the products you rely on back home, it is advisable to take essential basic ingredients and snacks with you. You can then supplement these with suitable local ingredients.

FOR A DAIRY-FREE DIET: It is possible to live without dairy-free spread and soya yogurt for a short period of time but milk is difficult to live without, particularly when you are travelling with children. Get in touch with the resort and find out whether your favourite brand of dairy-free milk is available – children get used to one variety and may refuse to drink other brands. Alternatively, calculate the minimum quantity of dairy-free milk you require and buy it in small cartons of UHT dairy-free milk to limit the volume of milk that is open at one time (milk will go off more quickly in warm countries). Use a water bottle for carrying milk once the carton is opened. Dairy-free biscuits and other snacks are also useful to have.

FOR A GLUTEN-FREE DIET: Take gluten-free flour for thickening sauces and flouring food for frying, as well as gluten-free pasta, breakfast cereal and biscuits. If bread is an important part of your diet, take ready-mixed gluten-free flours, sachets of dried yeast and a loaf tin to make your own bread.

FOR AN EGG-FREE DIET: Take egg-free biscuits and snacks you are unlikely to find while you are away, to keep you going between meals.

FOR A NUT-FREE DIET: Take nut-free snacks and breakfast cereals you are unlikely to find while you are away. You may also want to take a trusted brand of nut-free cooking oil for cooking and salad dressings.

FOR A SOYA-FREE DIET: Take soya-free biscuits and snacks you are unlikely to find while you are away, to keep you going between meals. You may also want to take a trusted brand of soya-free cooking oil with you for cooking and salad dressings.

Chapter 3 | EATING A BALANCED DIET ON A RESTRICTED DIET

Dairy products, wheat, eggs, nuts and soya products are more than just simple ingredients. Due to their availability, low cost, high nutritional value and versatility in the preparation of homemade and manufactured food most of the world's population rely upon them to provide basic nutrition. This chapter outlines the nutritional role of these core ingredients and the wealth of alternative food sources that provide the same nutrients and can help ensure your diet is balanced and varied.

THE COMPONENTS OF A HEALTHY DIET

A healthy, balanced diet is achieved by eating good quality, fresh ingredients, prepared from scratch, that are collectively rich in the essential nutrients: carbohydrate, protein, fibre, fat, vitamins and minerals. Specific sources of these nutrients are outlined in the tables at the end of this chapter.

- **Carbohydrates** are produced by photosynthesis in plants and are stored as sugars in fruit and vegetables, or as starch in tubers, such as potatoes, and seeds. Starchy ingredients make food more satisfying and filling to eat, while sugary ingredients enhance the flavour of food that would otherwise be bland. Both starch and sugars are converted by the body into glucose, which is used to generate energy or added to our fat stores in the liver and muscles.
- **Protein** provides the building blocks for our bodies to create, maintain and repair skin, hair, bones, organs, muscles, enzymes, hormones and genes. Foods high in protein are richly flavoured and make food more satisfying to eat.
- **Fats and oils** provide us with energy, enable the absorption of fat-soluble vitamins and are broken down into essential fatty acids that cannot be made by the body. Fatty acids are essential for utilizing the energy contained in the fat stores of the body, for normal growth, behaviour and maintenance of cell membranes, the skin, a working immune system and balanced hormone levels. Ingredients rich in fat add flavour and richness, moisture and succulence to a whole variety of basic ingredients including meat, fish, fruit, vegetables and starchy foods, and are used widely to make both savoury and sweet food interesting and delicious to eat. Used in moderation fat has an important place in our diet.
- **Fibre** remains relatively unchanged as it passes through our digestive system, assisting the carriage of food through our gut and regulating the absorption of nutrients such as glucose and cholesterol. Fibre derived from both gluten-rich and gluten-free whole grains, wholemeal flour and bran, nuts, pulses, fruit and vegetables gives a hearty flavour and texture to the foods we eat.
- **Vitamins** are organic substances required in small amounts in the diet. They enable the body to use proteins, carbohydrates and fat to produce energy for growth, maintenance and repair of healthy tissue. It is essential that we consume the correct

levels of vitamins as most vitamins are either produced in limited quantities by the body or not at all. Some vitamins are only found in animals, others only in plants, so we have to eat a wide variety of foods to obtain the nutrition we need to be healthy. A number of basic foods such as milk, bread and flour are fortified with vitamins to improve their nutritional value, as a large proportion of their nutritional content is lost during processing and refining. The principal vitamins are the water-soluble vitamins, B and C and the fat-soluble vitamins A, D, E and K. Vitamins B and C are not stored in the body so rich sources of both must be eaten daily. To maintain the levels of fat-soluble vitamins, stored in the liver and body fat, rich sources of these vitamins must be eaten regularly.

- **Minerals**, like vitamins, are essential for regulating and building the cells that make up the body. To maintain good health, calcium, phosphorous, potassium, sodium and magnesium are required in quantities exceeding 100 mg a day. Iron, manganese and zinc are required in lower amounts and trace minerals such as selenium and copper are required in minute quantities. Plants and products derived from plants, including fruit, vegetables, grains, pulses, nuts and seeds, are the richest sources of minerals, as plants absorb minerals directly from the soil through their roots. Animal products including dairy products, eggs, meat, poultry and fish contain slightly lower levels of minerals, derived from plants eaten by the animals.

All these nutrients are found in a diet that regularly includes fresh meat, poultry, dairy products, eggs, fish, fruit, vegetables, nuts, pulses and whole grains. Milk, from which all dairy products are derived, and egg (often eaten as a meal in its own right) are both complete sources of protein, fat, minerals and vitamins, designed by nature to support new and growing life. Similarly, wheat grain, soya beans and nut kernels are the seeds of plants where carbohydrate, protein, fat, vitamins and minerals are stored to provide energy for the germination and growth of new plants. Soya bean products such as soya milk and tofu are as rich in protein as foods derived from animals.

When you are allergic to one or a number of these highly nutritious ingredients it is essential to eat other foods that are collectively rich in the same nutrients, in order to provide the energy and materials that keep your body healthy (and, in the case of children, promote growth). For example, milk and dairy products are a principal source of calcium in the Western diet, hence those with a dairy allergy must turn to other calcium-rich foods, such as green leafy vegetables, nuts and calcium-fortified dairy-free milk, in order to obtain sufficient calcium. This is especially important for growing children. The following tables show which foods contain the nutrients you may be lacking as a result of omitting dairy, gluten, eggs, nuts or soya from your diet.

MAIN NUTRIENTS

IF YOU CUT OUT...

DAIRY	EGG	WHOLEGRAIN WHEAT	WHITE WHEAT FLOUR	SOYA	NUTS	You may be missing	What it does	Rich sources include
X	X	X	X	X	X	Carbohydrate (starch)	Provides the main energy source in the diet. Carbohydrates are split into sugars, which are then broken down to release energy	Gluten-rich and gluten-free breakfast cereals, grains, bread, pasta, pulses, potatoes and bananas
X			X			Carbohydrate (sugars)	Sugars are broken down to form the simple sugar glucose, the primary source of energy used by the body and brain	Fruit and sweet vegetables, milk, whole grains, honey, white and brown sugar, syrups
X	X	X	X	X	X	Protein	Provides the building blocks for our bodies to create, maintain and repair skin, hair, bones, organs, muscles, enzymes, hormones and genes	Red meat, offal, poultry, fish, seafood, eggs, dairy products, glutenous and gluten-free grains, pulses, soya products, nuts and seeds
X	X			X	X	Fat	Provides a source of concentrated energy, fatty acids and enables the body to absorb fat-soluble vitamins A, D, E and K	Red meat, poultry skin, oily fish, eggs, dairy products, nuts, pulses, seeds, vegetable oils and margarine
		X		X	X	Dietary fibre	Indigestible skins, husks and hulls of plants aid digestion and absorption of nutrients and passage of food through the gut	Pulses, fruit and vegetables with thin skin that can be eaten, nuts, seeds, whole grains, wholemeal bread, brown rice, soya bran, green leafy vegetables, dried fruit, bananas

VITAMINS

IF YOU CUT OUT...

DAIRY	EGG	WHOLEGRAIN WHEAT	WHITE WHEAT FLOUR	SOYA	NUTS	You may be missing	What it does	Rich sources include
X	X	X		X		Vitamin A	Keeps the skin and immune system healthy, and is important for bone growth and night vision	Liver, eggs, dairy products, soya, green leafy vegetables, dried fruit, orange foods (carrots, mangoes, sweet potatoes, apricots, pumpkins), fish oils, pulses
	X	X	X	X	X	B vitamins*	Break down carbohydrates, proteins and fats into energy for growth; help repair of skin, and ensure a healthy nervous system and red blood cells	Red meat, offal, poultry, fish, seafood, eggs, dairy products, fortified dairy-free milk, soya, fruit and vegetables, pulses, fortified cereals, whole grains, wholemeal bread, brown rice, dried fruit, nuts, seeds, yeast extract
X	X	X	X	X	X	Folic acid B12	Enables the formation of red blood cells; necessary for growth and a healthy nervous system	Red meat, offal, poultry, eggs, dairy products, soya, green leafy vegetables, pulses, cereals, bread, brown rice, citrus fruits, dried fruit, potatoes, bananas, nuts, seeds
						Vitamin C**	Maintains healthy skin, teeth, gums, tendons, bones, immune system; necessary for wound healing, energy production and growth	Most fruit and vegetables (especially citrus fruits), green leafy vegetables, green peppers, strawberries, broccoli, cabbage, potatoes, tomatoes, melon
X	X			X		Vitamin D	Enables the absorption of calcium to maintain healthy bones	Produced by the skin when exposed to the sun. Also in white fish, oily fish, shellfish, molluscs, eggs, dairy products, soya milk
	X			X	X	Vitamin E	Maintains good muscle control	Eggs, soya, green leafy vegetables, cereals, bread, nuts, seeds, olives, corn, fish oils and vegetable oil, pulses
	X			X		Vitamin K	Aids blood clotting	Red meat, offal, poultry, eggs, dairy products, green leafy vegetables, strawberries, pulses, beans and lentils

* The B vitamins include B1 (thiamine), B2 (riboflavin), B3 (niacin) and B6 (pyridoxine) ** Vitamin C intake is not affected by cutting out any of the common food allergens, but it is an important part of the diet so it is vital to get an adequate daily intake.

MINERALS

IF YOU CUT OUT...

DAIRY	EGG	WHOLEGRAIN WHEAT	WHITE WHEAT FLOUR	SOYA	NUTS	You may be missing	What it does	Rich sources include
X	X	X	X	X	X	Calcium	Maintains healthy bones and teeth, and muscle function	Milk and fortified dairy-free milk, dairy products, tofu, fish with fine bones that are eaten (i.e. sardines and whitebait), green leafy vegetables, pulses, apricots, nuts, seeds, eggs
X	X	X	X	X	X	Phosphorous	Maintains, with calcium, strong bones, teeth and muscle function, and is a vital component of cells	Red meat, offal, poultry, fish, seafood, eggs, dairy products, soya, green leafy vegetables, cereals, bread, pulses, dried fruit, nuts, seeds, rice
X	X	X	X	X	X	Potassium	Maintains, with sodium, the water balance of the body by controlling the composition of blood and other body fluids	All meats, fish, seafood, eggs, dairy products, fruit and vegetables, soya, cereals, bread, nuts, seeds, pulses, rice
X	X			X	X	Sodium*	Maintains, with potassium, the water balance of the body by controlling the composition of blood and other body fluids	Salt, red meat, offal, poultry, fish, seafood, eggs, dairy products, fermented soya products, salted nuts and seeds, processed foods
	X	X	X	X	X	Magnesium	Maintains the function of nerves and muscles in artery walls and reduces the risk of diabetes	Red meat, offal, poultry, fish, seafood, eggs, dairy products, soya, green leafy vegetables, cereals, bread, pulses, dried fruit, nuts, seeds
	X	X		X	X	Iron	Forms haemoglobin in red blood cells to transport oxygen in the blood around the body	Red meat, offal, poultry, fish, seafood, eggs, soya, green leafy vegetables, cereals, bread, pulses, dried fruit, potatoes in their skins
	X			X		Zinc	Enables growth and development	Red meat, offal, poultry, fish, seafood (particularly oysters), cereals, bread, peas, pulses, dried fruit
	X	X	X	X		Selenium	A potent antioxidant that strengthens the immune system to help protect the body from bacteria, viruses and cancer	Red meat, offal, poultry, fish, seafood, eggs, cereals, bread, pulses, cabbage, broccoli, green peppers

*Very few of us lack sodium in our diets, because of the amount of salt added to processed foods. High sodium intake is more of a problem and is linked to disorders such as high blood pressure. It is not recommended that you consume lots of salted products. Only those who eat a very pure unprocessed diet and avoid a number of food groups are likely to need extra sodium in their diet.

Part II

HOW TO SUBSTITUTE INGREDIENTS

Chapter 4 | SUBSTITUTING FOR EGGS

The properties of egg provide versatility in cooking unmatched by any other ingredient. Whole eggs are rich in fat, protein and colour, constituents that enhance a wide range of foods, from sauces, pastry and fresh pasta, to cakes, tarts and puddings.

Because egg seems ubiquitous in many dishes it may, at first glance, appear very limiting to try and cut it from your diet. However, although there are some foods, such as meringues and whisked sponge cakes, which cannot be made without egg, there are many more where egg can be replaced with other ingredients or even left out entirely. For example, egg is often used to glaze the tops of pies and breads, and is not included in the main recipe. In this case the pie or dough can just as easily be brushed with milk to add shine and colour.

Due to its versatility, there is no single 'egg substitute'. This means that in order to adapt a recipe successfully, you first need to understand why egg is being used. This chapter will help you understand what purpose the egg component of any recipe is fulfilling and how to substitute for those properties.

Egg is used in cooking to:
- Make cakes
- Bind or hold ingredients together
- Lighten, add volume and enable mixtures to rise
- Thicken custard sauces and custard-based ice creams
- Set custard puddings and custard fillings in tarts
- Emulsify and thicken sauces
- Soften the texture of sorbets
- Glaze or add shine to baked foods

By looking at the type of food you are cooking and how egg is handled in the recipe, you should be able to recognize which of these eight roles the egg is fulfilling:

Form of egg used	Preparation/Recipe type	Role of egg
Beaten whole egg or white and yolk whisked separately	Cake	**Binding and lightening** see Making Egg-free cakes, page 37
Beaten whole egg	Stuffing mixture or other foods made from minced meat or fish – such as beef burgers or fish cakes, anything with a breadcrumb or batter coating, batter cakes such as brownies, pastry, biscuits, pancakes	**Binding** see page 37
Whisked egg whites only	Meringue or a mousse	**Lightening** see page 38
Egg yolk only	Mixed with milk or cream, and stirred over low heat Custard-based sauce or ice cream	**Thickening** see page 38
Egg yolk only	Mixed with milk or cream and baked gently Custard tart or a quiche	**Setting** see page 38
Egg yolk only, raw, beaten	Mixed with oil and vinegar Mayonnaise or a mayonnaise-based sauce	**Emulsifying** see page 39
Egg white only, used raw, not whisked	Sorbet	**Softening** see page 39
Whole egg, egg yolk or egg white, beaten	Brushed onto the surface of food before baking	**Glazing** see page 39

Egg substitute	Quantities needed to replace 1 egg in recipe	Comment
Custard	50 ml/2 fl oz thick cold custard (made with 1 tbsp custard powder and 290 ml/10 fl oz milk or dairy-free milk) + ½ tsp baking powder added to the flour. Add the custard to flour, fat and sugar and beat together. Mix self-raising flour with the extra baking powder to ensure the cake rises	Gives the cake a moist consistency and delicate, sweet flavour **Useful for:** Sponge cakes, fruit cakes and muffins
Apple purée	50 ml/2 fl oz apple purée (see page 166) + ½ tsp baking powder added to the flour Sift the baking powder with the flour; add the purée to the flour, fat and sugar and beat together	Gives cakes a delicate fruity flavour **Useful for:** Sponge cakes, fruit cakes and muffins
Apricot purée	50 ml/2 fl oz apricot purée (see page 166) + ½ tsp baking powder added to the flour Sift the baking powder with the flour; add the purée to the flour, fat and sugar and beat together	Adds a pleasant yellow colouring and rich fruity flavour **Useful for:** Rich flavoured sponge cakes, fruit cakes and muffins
Mashed banana	1 small mashed banana or ½ a large banana	Makes a moist binder for light cakes and muffins, but strongly affects the flavour **Useful for:** Banana cakes, muffins and bread
Milk, self-raising flour and baking powder	50 ml/2 fl oz milk, replace plain flour with self-raising flour and add 1 tsp baking powder for every 110 g/4 oz flour in the recipe	Best used in strongly flavoured, moist cakes where the flavour of raising agents is masked **Useful for:** Fruit loaves and batter cakes
Arrowroot powder	1 tbsp arrowroot, ½ tsp baking powder + 1 tbsp water per 140 g/5 oz flour. Sift the arrowroot powder and baking powder into the flour. Add the water to the butter, flour and sugar before beating	Arrowroot is flavourless, but can leave a 'dry' taste in the mouth **Useful for:** Sponge cakes, fruit cakes and muffins

| MAKING EGG-FREE CAKES | While whisked sponge cakes cannot be made egg-free because they consist mainly of whisked egg foam (plus sugar and a little flour), richer, heavier cake mixtures can be successfully adapted. Sponge cakes, fruit loaves, fruit cakes and batter cakes contain a higher proportion of butter, sugar and flour and egg is usually beaten in to lighten, moisten and hold the cake ingredients together. This is a role that can be filled by egg-free binding ingredients, such as milk, cornflour-thickened custard and fruit purées, along with wheat flour mixed with chemical raising agents (see opposite). In the home baking chapter you will find examples of how to use egg substitutes to make delicious cakes. |

MAKING EGG-FREE CAKES

While whisked sponge cakes cannot be made egg-free because they consist mainly of whisked egg foam (plus sugar and a little flour), richer, heavier cake mixtures can be successfully adapted. Sponge cakes, fruit loaves, fruit cakes and batter cakes contain a higher proportion of butter, sugar and flour and egg is usually beaten in to lighten, moisten and hold the cake ingredients together. This is a role that can be filled by egg-free binding ingredients, such as milk, cornflour-thickened custard and fruit purées, along with wheat flour mixed with chemical raising agents (see opposite). In the home baking chapter you will find examples of how to use egg substitutes to make delicious cakes.

BINDING FOODS

Beaten egg is added to a wide variety of mixtures to hold ingredients together, for example stuffing, burgers, sausages and fish cakes. It also helps stick breadcrumb coatings to fish or meat for frying. By binding ingredients together, beaten egg also enriches the flavour and improves the texture of coating batters, pancakes, biscuits and pastry by making them less crumbly and dry. But there are alternatives …

EGG-FREE BINDING AGENTS

To make...	Use substitute binder...	Recipe example
Pancake batters	Tapioca flour and arrowroot powder blended with plain wheat flour	Egg-free Pancakes (page 197)
Coating batters	Cornflour/self-raising flour + sparkling water or lager	Battered Cod (page 102)
Breadcrumb coatings	Coat moist foods such as fresh fish and meat in fine, fresh breadcrumbs only	Crispy Fish Ribbons (page 104)
Stuffing	Replace each egg with 1 tbsp fine white breadcrumbs	Stuffings
Beef burgers and sausages	Provided meat is very fresh and cold it will bind together well without egg	Burgers with Tomato and Corn Salsa (page 92)
Fish cakes	Mashed potato: before frying, roll fish cakes in seasoned flour or breadcrumbs to prevent them breaking up while they cook	Salmon Fish Cakes (page 89)
Rich shortcrust pastry	Extra 15g/½ oz butter rubbed into flour + 1 tbsp cold water per egg to be replaced	Rich Shortcrust Pastry (page 152)
Biscuits	Replace each egg with 50 ml/2 fl oz milk and use self-raising flour in place of plain flour	Chocolate Chip Cookies (page 180)

REPLACING THE LIGHTENING PROPERTIES OF EGG	There are a number of egg-free ingredients that can be used to add volume and lightness to dense mixtures. Whipped cream is often used to add volume and lightness to rich mousses and other light textured creamy puddings (see Rich Chocolate Mousse page 190).

There are a number of egg-free ingredients that can be used to add volume and lightness to dense mixtures. Whipped cream is often used to add volume and lightness to rich mousses and other light textured creamy puddings (see Rich Chocolate Mousse page 190).

When whisked egg foam is folded into mixtures it helps them to rise when baked, as the air bubbles in the foam expand in the heat. Once the egg foam reaches a given temperature, it sets to support the risen mixture so that it remains light and bubbly once cooked. Yeast or chemical raising agents, present in baking powder and self-raising flour, are frequently used with or in the place of egg, to lighten and add volume to baked foods by filling the mixture with bubbles. If eggs are not included in the recipe then other binding ingredients must be used in the mixture to trap the bubbles that lighten and enable the mixture to rise in the oven (see Yeast and Chemical Raising Agents page 183).

THICKENING CUSTARD SAUCES

A rich, smooth cream sauce, very similar to egg-rich crème Anglaise, can be made with double cream, milk, sugar, vanilla and a small quantity of custard powder. The custard powder contains cornflour, which helps to stabilize and thicken the cream and milk as the mixture is heated, and its yellow hue adds subtle colour to the sauce to enhance its appearance (see Vanilla Cream Sauce page 208).

SETTING TARTS AND PUDDINGS

Savoury custard tarts normally contain other ingredients in the filling to add flavour and texture and the creamy custard holds them in place. Egg is central to savoury baked custards as it is the only setting agent that sets liquids in a hot oven, necessary to develop the flavour and brown the surface of the filling to an appetizing golden colour. (Gelatine and agar agar are used to set chilled liquids.)

Egg-free tarts with a creamy filling similar to savoury custard tarts can be made using an equivalent quantity of Rich White Sauce (page 74) to bind the ingredients. Provided the sauce is seasoned well it can be used as it is or flavoured with herbs or grated cheese. Unlike egg custard, it does not set firm while the tart bakes but browns well and sets as the tart cools. So the tart filling is firm enough to slice, allow the tart to cool down and set then gently warm it through in a low oven just before serving.

Sweet custard tarts are baked very gently to lightly set the custard. If custard is baked for longer it loses its sweet creamy consistency and takes on unwanted colour and a stronger baked flavour. As the eggs are used only to set the custard they can be replaced with gelatine. To make lightly set creamy puddings without egg, substitute 1 heaped teaspoon of gelatine for every three eggs in the recipe. Eggs are liquid ingredients and the volume of egg in a recipe must be replaced with an equivalent volume of water, milk or cream to ensure the gelatine does not set the mixture too firmly.

One beaten egg measures approximately 50 ml/2 fl oz. Measure out the equivalent volume of water required to replace the volume of eggs used in the recipe and use it to soak the

Using egg replacers

Egg replacers, developed to replace the binding, rising and setting properties of egg, are made from a blend of potato starch, tapioca flour, raising agents and natural gums. Although egg replacers can be whisked to a foam they are unsuitable for lightening mousses or making meringues. Read the label carefully when buying egg replacers as some are made for people on cholesterol-free diets and contain egg derivatives.

gelatine before melting it and adding it to the cream mixture. Alternatively, if liquid ingredients such as lemon juice or coffee are used to flavour the pudding, use it to soak the gelatine and add extra cream to replace the volume of egg (see Lemon Tart page 162).

EMULSIFYING
SAUCES

Although manufactured egg-free mayonnaise is available in good health shops, there are no other ingredients available that can replace egg successfully for making mayonnaise at home. Instead there are many ingredients and recipes that can be used instead. Mustard Cream Dressing, for example (see page 85) provides an egg-free creamy dressing for salads. To accompany cold fish and meat make Horseradish Cream (page 85) and make creamy dips with soured cream or natural yogurt (see Mayonnaise Based Dips and Sauces, page 84). Sandwiches can be spiced up and made more interesting with chutneys and mustard.

REPLACING EGG
WHITE IN
SORBETS

Sorbets do not need egg white in them to make them smooth and soft textured. Churn the half-frozen sorbet mixture to the consistency of softly whipped cream and return to the freezer. Once it is frozen, remove it from the freezer 15 minutes before serving and its texture will be soft and smooth (see Raspberry Sorbet page 202).

GLAZING BAKED
FOODS

Although the shine will not be as great, replace egg with milk or soya milk, mixed with a pinch of salt or sugar. Alternatively, enhance the appearance of bread and scones by sprinkling the top with flour before baking. Sweet pastries and biscuits look lovely sprinkled with granulated or Demerara sugar.

WHAT TO LOOK FOR ON FOOD LABELS

Whole egg, egg white, egg yolk and isolated proteins – obtained from egg white and egg yolk – are used to enrich, add colour, bind, emulsify, coagulate, flavour and thicken processed foods. Food manufacturers in the European Union are now required to display 'contains egg' when egg or ingredients containing egg are used in a product. In addition to obvious sources of egg, these less familiar terms indicate some form of egg:
• Albumin lysozyme conalbumin
• Livetin simplesse (a fat substitute made with egg white and whey)
• Ovalbumin
• Ovoglobulin
• Ovomucin
• Ovomucoid
• Ovovitellin
• Ovotransferrin
• Lecithin vitellin

Chapter 5 | SUBSTITUTING FOR WHEAT AND OTHER GLUTEN-RICH GRAINS

This chapter deals with two different but inseparably linked issues: allergies to wheat or other similar grains and allergy to gluten. Since it is impossible to remove the gluten entirely from wheat, the task is the same: remove the wheat and other gluten-containing grains from the diet. In order to remove it, you must first know where to find it.

The most commonly used gluten-rich grains in the Western diet are wheat, barley and rye. These three grains must be avoided by those with a gluten allergy. Oats are also off limits as they contain a protein that is similar to gluten and, as they are usually processed and stored in the same mills as wheat, are therefore often contaminated with gluten. In order to eliminate these grains from the diet it is important to recognize the many forms they take in foodstuffs.

Barley is used to make breakfast cereals, and is added to hearty soups and casseroles. Fermented, it is used to make beer, whisky and malt, a flavouring found in a whole host of products. Rye and oats are less widely used. Rye is used in cereals and to make bread and crackers. Oats are mainly used to add texture to baked goods – such as biscuits and flapjacks – and to make oatcakes and porridge.

Wheat, however, is by far the most widely used grain. It features in an astonishing array of foodstuffs because it has many useful properties and has a versatility unmatched by any other grain.

It is used in a number of forms. Whole wheat grain is rolled to form wheat flakes used in cereals or cracked to make bulgur wheat and couscous – starchy staples in the Middle East and North Africa. It is also ground to make nutty flavoured wholemeal flour. To produce white flour, the starchy centre of wheat grain is ground once the fibrous outer layers have been removed. Both wholemeal and white flour form the basis for bread and other baked foods, pasta and noodles.

White flour is also used widely in both manufactured and homemade food to thicken sauces, soups, casseroles and batters.

Wheat and other gluten-rich grains feature very widely in the food we eat, however they can be replaced with gluten-free substitutes in most cases or omitted from recipes altogether. In order to replace gluten-rich ingredients with gluten-free substitutes it is essential to understand how and why they are used so you can make the right substitution. Choosing the right gluten-free substitutions becomes progressively more important as the proportion of gluten-rich ingredients used in a recipe increases. For example, almost any gluten-free flour can replace wheat for flouring food before frying but gluten-free flours must be carefully selected and blended in the right proportions to produce a light, open textured bread.

GENERAL RULES
FOR COOKING
WITH GLUTEN-
FREE FLOURS

• Ready-mixed gluten-free flour is not necessarily the best substitute for wheat flour. Wheat flour has many properties and the importance of each property varies when flour is used for thickening sauces, coating food, and making batters, cakes, pastry and biscuits. By blending specific flours for a specific purpose, foods made with gluten-free flour can closely rival – and sometimes even better – foods made with wheat flour.

• Gluten-free mixtures require binding ingredients to make up for the lack of gluten in the flour. Without binding ingredients, gluten-free mixtures are likely to taste dry and fall apart.

• Most gluten-free flours do not absorb liquid as readily as wheat flour and often produce baked foods that taste dry and crumble easily unless extra egg or liquid is added to the recipe.

• Baked foods made with gluten-free flour dry out more quickly than those made with wheat and are best eaten on the day they are made (alternatively, sliced bread, scones, biscuits and cakes can be frozen and defrosted as required).

THE ROLES OF
GLUTENOUS
GRAINS IN
COOKING

This chapter will allow you to work out what role the wheat component of any recipe is fulfilling and how to substitute for each of these properties. It provides alternative ingredients and methods, and outlines their limitations.

Wheat and other grains are used in food and cooking:
• as a carbohydrate to add bulk – for example as pasta, couscous, bulgur wheat etc.
• to thicken sauces, casseroles and soups
• as bread or breadcrumbs, rather than flour, often to add bulk
• as a coating for food before frying
• to thicken and bind pancakes and batters
• to provide body and to bind pastry and biscuit dough
• to bind and give structure and body to cakes
• as the principal ingredient in bread.

By looking at the type of food you are cooking, in what form the ingredient appears and how that ingredient is used in the recipe, you should be able to recognize which of these roles it is fulfilling:

Form of ingredient	Preparation/Recipe type	Role of grain/gluten
Whole grains, flakes or pasta	Main constituent of recipe	See Substitutes for Whole Grains opposite
Plain flour	Soup, sauce or casserole	**Thickening** see Thickening Sauces, Soups and Casseroles below
Breadcrumbs or bread	Sausage or stuffing mixes; using bread directly e.g. in croutons	See Bread as an Ingredient (page 43)
Plain flour and/or breadcrumbs	Dusted onto the outside of food before frying	**Coating** see Coating Food for Frying (pages 43–44)
Plain or self-raising flour	Mixing a batter for pancakes or coating food for frying	**Battering** see Coatings box (page 44) and Pancakes
Plain or self-raising flour	Making biscuits or pastry	**Binding** see Binding Agents (page 46)
Plain or self-raising flour	Cakes, muffins or scones	See Cakes (page 47)
Strong bread flour	Bread	See Bread (page 48) or go straight to the Gluten-free Bread recipes from page 184–87

COOKING WITHOUT GLUTEN

Once you understand why wheat and other grains containing gluten are used in a recipe, the next step is to see if there is a gluten-free ingredient that will do the same job. Although there are no other grains with the same properties as wheat, one or a number of gluten-free grains, flaked grains and gluten-free flours can be used instead to similar effect. See box opposite for substituting gluten-rich whole grains and pasta.

THICKENING SAUCES, SOUPS AND CASSEROLES

Plain white wheat flour is used to thicken many savoury dishes as it is rich in starch, which swells and absorbs boiling liquid, thickening the consistency of the dish. Its bland flavour also means that it can be used to thicken both delicate and robustly flavoured sauces. The colour is important, too, as it doesn't affect the appearance of white or pale coloured sauces. In addition, the soft and fine texture of white wheat flour gives a smooth consistency to sauces. The starch contained in wheat flour remains stable and does not break down and thin the sauce when it is cooked or kept warm for a period of time. This is a great advantage for dishes that are bound with flour-thickened sauces and then baked in the oven.

Most gluten-free flours are also rich in starch and have the ability to thicken liquids. However, some are gritty in texture, producing grainy sauces or are dark and strongly flavoured and overpower the flavour and colour of sauces.

Recipe	Usual grain content	Recommended substitutes
Boiled whole grain wheat for salads or with Middle Eastern food	Cracked wheat (bulgur wheat) or couscous	Brown rice, quinoa and millet grain, boiled (see page 136)
Winter soups and casseroles	Pearl barley	Brown rice, reconstituted dried haricot or borlotti beans
Flapjacks	Wheat flakes or rolled oats	Buckwheat flakes or gluten-free puffed rice (see Chewy Syrup Squares page 178)
Muesli	Rolled oats, wheat flakes and wheat bran	Buckwheat flakes, millet flakes and brown rice flakes, rice bran (see Gluten-free Muesli page 141)
Porridge	Rolled oats	Millet flakes, rice flakes, buckwheat flakes or risotto rice (see page 141)
Pasta	Durum wheat	Gluten-free pasta e.g. millet and rice pasta or corn pasta

Substitute plain flour with an equal quantity of fine cornflour or rice flour. Cornflour produces the smoothest gluten-free sauces. However, the starch in cornflour is not as stable as the starch in wheat flour and tends to break down. Sauces thickened with cornflour must be eaten soon after they are made (see box on page 74).

BREAD AS AN INGREDIENT

White wheat bread and good gluten-free white bread are largely interchangeable in recipes that use breadcrumbs, croutons and croutes.

Breadcrumbs are often added to homemade sausagemeat and fine stuffing mixtures to bind and add bulk. Breadcrumbs also absorb the juices of sausagemeat and stuffing ingredients, which helps to keep the cooked mixture moist and full of flavour. Replace wheat-based breadcrumbs with an equal quantity of gluten-free breadcrumbs, which are just as suitable for the purpose.

For croutons, small cubes of bread fried in oil, and croutes, thin slices of bread fried or baked with oil, substitute white wheat bread with gluten-free white bread (see Garlic Croutons, page 70).

COATING FOOD FOR FRYING

Food is coated with flour, breadcrumbs or batter to protect it and to add crispiness and colour to the finished dish. The chart overleaf explains how best to use gluten-free alternatives to wheat flour coatings, crumbs and batters.

Coating	Uses	Recommended substitutes
Plain flour on its own	Slices of meat, small fish or fillets, food made with minced meat, e.g. burgers	Cornflour, buckwheat flour or soya flour. Avoid using potato flour and rice flour as they become mushy
Breadcrumb coating on fried food	White meats such as pork, veal, chicken and white fish; sliced vegetables	For pan-fried crumbed food, use bland gluten-free flours such as cornflour or rice flour, seasoned with salt and pepper, to flour fish or meat before coating in egg and gluten-free breadcrumbs. For deep-fried crumbed food use gluten-free breadcrumbs
Batter for deep-fried food (made with self-raising flour)	Small pieces of fish, chicken and vegetables	To make gluten-free coating batter, use 50 per cent potato flour and 50 per cent cornflour plus 1 teaspoon baking powder for every 110 g/4 oz of flour used (see Battered Cod page 102)

PANCAKES   Batters traditionally made with flour, egg and milk are used to make pancakes as well as to coat food before deep-frying. As the ingredients of pancake batter are stirred together, the small amount of gluten in the flour develops which helps, with egg, to bind the ingredients together so that the pancakes do not fall apart when cooked. Gluten-free pancakes rely on egg and fine flours with binding properties including potato flour, tapioca flour, arrowroot powder and buckwheat.

Use	Comment	Recommended substitutes
French pancakes/crêpes	These require plain flour that swells and binds in liquid to form the smooth tender texture of pancakes	Use 50 per cent fine rice flour, 25 per cent arrowroot powder and 25 per cent tapioca flour mixed with egg and milk (see French Crêpes page 195)
Buckwheat pancakes	These are made with an equal quantity of wheat flour and buckwheat flour (which is gluten free)	Buckwheat binds pancake batter in a similar way to wheat flour. The batter therefore does not require other binding flours such as tapioca flour or arrowroot powder so simply substitute rice flour for the wheat flour (see Buckwheat Pancakes with Caramelized Cinnamon Apples page 196)

BINDING
INGREDIENTS

Plain wheat flour is used to make crisp biscuits and pastry. When mixed with butter or margarine and a small quantity of liquid, such as water or beaten egg, it helps bind dough so that it holds together but is sufficiently 'short' to crumble in the mouth.

Gluten-free plain flours

Gluten-free flours with binding properties include potato flour, tapioca flour, arrowroot powder, cornflour and buckwheat flour. Bland tasting, fine rice flour is used to provide bulk. Other useful flours include cornmeal, ground rice and soya flour. Cornmeal and coarsely ground rice flour can make food gritty, and soya flour and buckwheat flour darken the colour of food and add their own characteristic flavours to it.

THE MOST USEFUL GLUTEN-FREE FLOURS

Coating	Uses
Potato flour and tapioca flour	These flours readily absorb liquid, lightly bind mixtures and retain moisture in cooked foods. They are especially helpful where binding and moistening properties are required in gluten-free batters and bread dough. Food made with them tends to be heavy unless they are mixed with cornflour or arrowroot powder, which lighten the consistency of mixtures, and rice flour, which forms the bulk of mixtures
Arrowroot powder	This has binding properties when mixed with liquid, it lightens the consistency of baked goods and is used to thicken clear sauces. It is best suited for use in batters as it tends to leave a dry, powdery taste in the mouth
Rice flour and cornflour	These are used to make light textured baked goods such as cakes, biscuits and pastry, where binding properties of flour are less important. As baked goods made with cornflour and rice flour tend to be dry and powdery, they are blended with ground almonds or potato flour to provide added moisture
Ground almonds	Rich in oil, ground almonds enrich and moisten, hence often make up 25 per cent of the flour content of gluten-free biscuits, cakes, sweet and savoury pastry dough and bread. Only use more than 25 per cent ground almonds in foods that are meant to taste of almonds. Ground almonds used in larger quantities will strongly flavour and coarsen the texture of baked foods
Soya flour	Due to its strong beany flavour and tan colour, use in moderation. When mixed with bland white flours, soya flour retains moisture to produce soft crumbly biscuits, and pastry that is tender and rich to eat
Buckwheat flour	Buckwheat flour also has binding properties but is dark and strongly flavoured. It is therefore best combined with bland white flour and used for specific purposes, most notably in buckwheat pancakes
Cornmeal and ground rice	Cornmeal has a pleasant delicate flavour. Both cornmeal and ground rice add a crisp, gritty texture to biscuits and pastry

Gluten-free pastry

When replacing gluten-rich flours in pastry:

- Use 50 per cent rice flour, 25 per cent cornflour and 25 per cent ground almonds for simple, neutral flavoured shortcrust pastry (see Rice and Almond Pastry page 155).
- Use 50 per cent rice flour and 50 per cent cornmeal for a coarser textured, neutral flavoured, nut-free shortcrust pastry (see Rice and Cornmeal Shortcrust pastry page 156).

Wholemeal plain flour is used to make a coarser textured, nutty flavoured pastry for hearty savoury and sweet pies and tarts. Used on its own it tends to produce heavy pastry so it is usually mixed with equal quantities of white plain flour to lighten the end result. For gluten-free wholemeal pastry, use 50 per cent brown rice flour, 25 per cent cornflour (for lightness) and 25 per cent finely ground whole almonds (with skin on – to add moisture and richness). For every 225 g/8 oz of this flour mixture, add 1 tablespoon of rice bran to add extra fibre and colour. (See Wholemeal Rice and Almond Pastry page 155.)

Pastry dough is bound with the fat in the mixture and a small quantity of cold water or a mixture of beaten egg and water. Mashed potato can also be used to bind pastry as it gives pastry a savoury flavour and flaky texture. The quantity of binding liquid required to bind pastry dough depends on the flour. Wheat flour absorbs liquid more readily than gluten-free flours so if you're adapting a wheat flour recipe to make it gluten free it may require more liquid than the recipe states before the dough will hold together.

BINDING AGENTS FOR GLUTEN-FREE PASTRY

Binding agent	Usage/Quantities	Comment
Cold water	Pastry dough made with 225 g/8 oz flour requires 2–3 tbsp cold water	Used to make simply flavoured, pale coloured pastry with a crisp but crumbly texture
Beaten whole egg	Pastry dough made with 225 g/8 oz flour requires 1 egg, beaten with 1 tbsp cold water	Gluten-free pastry is less likely to crumble when bound with whole egg mixed with water. Egg white in the whole egg binds the pastry more firmly. The yolk softens the texture of the crumb, enriches the flavour and deepens the colour of the pastry
Beaten egg yolk	Pastry dough made with 225 g/8 oz flour requires 2 yolks, beaten with 2 tbsp cold water	Beaten egg yolk enriches and colours gluten-free pastry but mainly relies on the water to bind the pastry
Mashed potato	110 g/4 oz mashed potato binds 170 g/6 oz flour	Mashed potato produces rich tasting, flaky pastry ideal for savoury pies and tarts

CAKES   Cakes are characteristically tender and spongy in texture. In order to achieve that spongy texture they require just enough gluten, along with binding ingredients such as eggs, to trap small bubbles of air incorporated into the mixture by whisking or by the use of chemical raising agents. For this reason, cakes require the strong binding properties of either gluten or egg: cakes can be gluten free *or* egg free but *not both*.

In order to adapt a cake recipe to make it gluten free you need to take the following steps:

- substitute a suitable gluten-free flour or combination of flours
- add extra egg to bind the mixture and to ensure the cake is not too dry and crumbly.

GLUTEN-FREE FLOURS FOR CAKES

Flour type	Gluten-free alternative	Comment
Plain	For light sponge cakes use 50 per cent rice flour (for bulk), 25 per cent cornflour (for lightness) and 25 per cent ground almonds (for richness and moisture). For heavier cakes such as scones use 50 per cent rice flour, 25 per cent potato flour (for a soft, moist texture) and 25 per cent ground almonds. For moist batter cakes, such as chocolate brownies, simply substitute plain flour with potato flour	These flours are bland, white and fine in texture
Self-raising	Use the same flour mixtures as listed above and add 1 teaspoon of gluten-free baking powder for every 110 g/4 oz flour	Mix thoroughly by sifting the flours and baking powder together 2 or 3 times
Wholemeal	Use 50 per cent brown rice flour, 25 per cent cornflour and 25 per cent finely ground whole almonds	Use for gluten-free wholemeal scones and for wholesome gluten-free cakes such as carrot cake

Gluten-free cakes often require a different method from standard cake making: see the gluten-free cake recipes in Chapter 16 before you attempt to adapt your own recipes.

Gluten-free binding agents for cakes

Without the binding qualities of gluten, gluten-free cakes rely solely on the binding properties of egg to trap the bubbles of air and produce a light spongy texture. Eggs are therefore invaluable in gluten-free cake making. Egg in the mixture forms the bubbly structure of the cake by trapping and stretching around air bubbles and steam, enabling the dough to rise before it sets in the heat of the oven. Egg also moistens, colours and enriches the flavour of cake. Cake recipes containing dried fruit, fruit purées and mashed banana are ideal for adapting with gluten-free flours as all these ingredients add moisture to the cake mixture.

BREAD   Bread is characteristically chewy in texture with an open, bubbly structure. In gluten-rich breads this structure is provided by strong flour, the rising agent yeast, sugar, salt, oil and water. When strong flour is mixed with water, elastic strands of gluten develop which bind the mixture, enabling the dough to trap and stretch around large bubbles produced by yeast, causing it to rise and develop its characteristic structure.

In order to produce a gluten-free bread with a similar texture, a gluten-free substitute with strong binding and elastic properties is required. Unfortunately, the properties of strong bread flour and gluten-free flours are so vastly different it is not possible to simply substitute a gluten-free flour for strong wheat flour. Gluten-free bread is made by an entirely different method to take account of the lack of gluten in the mixture. When making gluten-free bread:

- gluten-free flours are carefully selected and blended
- a small quantity of xanthum gum is used as a gluten substitute to bind the mixture
- to distribute the yeast, gluten-free bread dough is mixed rather than kneaded
- gluten-free bread is not left to rise before it is baked. Gluten-free dough, even with added xanthum gum, is less able to trap the bubbles produced by yeast. If left to 'rise' the bubbles produced by yeast would be lost and the bread will 'collapse'.

Since the method and ingredients are so different for making gluten-free bread, a straight substitution of wheat flour with gluten-free flours is not possible. Refer to the recipes given in the bread section of Chapter 16.

WHAT TO LOOK FOR ON FOOD LABELS

Packaged foods in the European Union have to show clearly on the label if they contain cereals containing gluten, or if one of the ingredients contains gluten. However, it is good to familiarize yourself with the many different guises that gluten can go under. Obviously you need to avoid all products that mention wheat or wheat flour – whether it's described as bleached, unbleached, white, whole wheat, all purpose, enriched, farina, graham, durum, high gluten or high protein flour, it contains gluten. So too do products containing semolina, rye, barley, triticale, kamut and spelt.

Meat products, including sausages, often contain 'rusk' (white bread crumbs used as a bulking agent). Foods containing soy sauce and the Japanese flavouring miso must also be avoided as they are both made by fermenting soya beans with wheat.

The use of starch and proteins derived from wheat, and other grains containing gluten, is also widespread in processed foods.

Here are the most common forms of starch and protein that may be derived from wheat:

Starches
- Edible starch
- Farina vegetable starch
- Food starch
- Gelatinized starch/hydrolysed starch

- Modified food starch, modified starch
- Wheat starch
- Malt sugar or maltose
- Dextrin
- Maltodextrin

Proteins
- Vegetable protein (often derived from wheat protein)
- Wheat protein (derived from gluten)
- High-gluten flour, high-protein flour
- Flour protein
- Hydrolysed plant protein (often derived from wheat)
- Hydrolysed vegetable proteins (often derived from wheat)
- Hydrolysed wheat protein
- Monosodium glutamate
- Natural flavouring (can be obtained from wheat protein)
- Cereal protein (obtained from cereal grains including wheat, barley and rye)
- Cereal extract (concentrated protein, extracted from malted cereals)
- Vegetable gum (often derived from wheat)

Wheat-free and gluten-free products

Wheat-free products are not the same as gluten-free products as they may contain other gluten-rich grains such as rye and barley, or oats, and are not suitable for gluten-free diets.

Conversely gluten-free products may not suit those on a wheat-free diet as they may contain other wheat proteins, including albumins, globulins and starch granule proteins.

Other ingredients that may contain wheat flour

Be aware that some powdered ingredients can contain wheat flour, as it is a good bulking agent. These include baking powder, mustard powder, instant coffee, icing sugar and cocoa. Also be careful with ground spice mixtures, such as garam masala and mixed spice. It is best to buy a well-know spice brand in a sealed container, rather than buy from a bulk supplier.

Chapter 6

SUBSTITUTING FOR DAIRY PRODUCTS

Avoiding dairy products in the diet can be a daunting task as milk and the products derived from it – cheese, butter, cream and yogurt – are integral to both home-cooked and packaged foods. Despite this, many recipes can be adapted successfully using one of the many good alternatives to dairy produce now available. These include products based on rice, almonds and oats. However, the majority of dairy-free products are based on soya, as it is an outstanding source of protein, oil, minerals and vitamins, and produces dairy-free milk, yogurt, cream and margarine with a mild flavour, creamy consistency and cooking properties similar to that of dairy products.

DAIRY-FREE MILKS   There are a number of very good dairy-free milks on the market. The best are fortified with vitamins and minerals found in cows' milk, including vitamin D and calcium, and are subtly sweetened to match the natural sweetness of dairy milk. Unsweetened dairy-

Substitute	Nutritional content	Not suitable for
Soya milk	High protein content, vitamins B and D and calcium	Adding to tea or coffee – it tends to curdle. Unsuitable for soya-free diets
Rice milk	Low in fat and protein. Available fortified with vitamin D and calcium	Foods needing a rich creamy flavour
Oat milk	High in fibre, protein and fat, vitamins and minerals	Delicately flavoured sauces and custards. Unsuitable for gluten-free diets
Almond milk	High in fat, protein, omega fatty acids, vitamins and minerals including calcium and vitamin D	Savoury dishes. Unsuitable for nut-free diets

free milk tends to make food taste flat and uninteresting. The most common dairy-free alternatives to milk are generally available chilled or as UHT long-life milk.

Soya milk: Soya milk is most commonly recommended by doctors as the best alternative to dairy milk as it is an excellent source of high quality proteins, vitamins and minerals. Mild and rich in flavour, it has the consistency of whole milk and is very versatile in cooking. It is suitable for drinking, pouring on cereal, making fruit smoothies and milk shakes, and in recipes for soups, savoury and sweet milky sauces, desserts and baked goods.

Rice milk: Light and aromatic, rice milk has the subtle, slightly sweet flavour of rice and the consistency of skimmed milk. Chilled rice milk tastes very pleasant and refreshing drunk on its own, poured on cereal, puréed with frozen soft fruit in smoothies, and in desserts, sweet milky sauces and in home baking. Due to its low fat and protein content, food made with rice milk is not as rich in flavour or consistency as food made with dairy or soya milk.

Oat milk: Oat milk is rich tasting with a consistency similar to semi-skimmed milk. It is mild and oaty in flavour and pleasant to drink chilled from the glass, poured on cereal, in smoothies and milkshakes and used in baking.

Almond milk: Almond milk has a light, sweet flavour, the consistency of skimmed milk and is high in nutritional value. Chilled almond milk tastes very pleasant and refreshing drunk on its own, poured on cereal, and used to make smoothies, desserts and sweet milky sauces.

Other dairy-free alternatives to milk

Fruit juice can be used to add moisture and fruity sweetness to sweet baked foods. Water may also be used instead of small quantities of milk in baked goods such as cakes and breads. If a larger proportion of milk is required in a recipe, water is not a suitable substitute as it will dilute the flavour and affect the overall texture and appearance of the dish.

DAIRY-FREE CREAM

Soya cream: Soya cream is the best alternative to dairy cream. It is made of emulsified and stabilized sunflower oil, soya protein and a small amount of wheat syrup and is available as a pouring cream or in a whipped consistency. Soya pouring cream resembles single cream in fat content, appearance and consistency and cannot be whipped. Due to its mildly beany flavour, soya cream is not suitable for pouring over desserts but is great for giving a creamy consistency to soups, sauces, custards and homemade ice cream, where its beany flavour will be masked.

Whipped-style soya cream has a less pronounced beany flavour and is slightly sweet. Although its consistency, appearance and flavour do not resemble whipped cream it is appreciated by those who cannot have standard whipped cream on desserts and in cakes and pastries.

Soya soured cream: Cultured dairy cream such as soured cream and crème fraiche are made by adding cultures of bacteria to cream. The bacteria convert lactose sugar (milk sugar), present in cream, into lactic acid, which thickens cream and gives it its characteristic sour, fresh flavour. Soya soured cream is very similar to dairy soured cream in appearance, consistency and flavour and makes a very good dairy-free alternative. It can be used in place of crème fraiche, for example to add a creamy, tangy flavour to sauces, or as a soured cream substitute, spread onto blinis, in dips and in Mexican food.

DAIRY-FREE YOGURT

Soya yogurt: Soya yogurt is the closest alternative to dairy yogurt in appearance, flavour and consistency – it is also the most readily available. It is made in the same way as dairy yogurt, by thickening and souring the flavour of soya milk by adding bacterial cultures. Soya yogurt is fortified with calcium and vitamin D and is a good source of protein.

Plain soya yogurt has the same consistency and sourness as natural dairy yogurt and a rich, delicate beany flavour. It can be used very successfully to make Indian raita and Greek tzatziki, sour cream-style dips and adds creaminess and body to Indian curries. Sweetened yogurts are available in a smooth style or with pieces of fruit and are great for adding creaminess to smoothies.

DAIRY-FREE ALTERNATIVES TO CHEESE

Soya cheeses: Soya cheese is made from an emulsion of soya milk, soya milk fat or vegetable oil, salt, colourings and flavourings. The enriched and flavoured milk is soured and curdled with bacteria to produce the semi solid 'soya curd' and liquid 'soya whey'. The curd is used to make two styles of cheese: cream cheese and hard cheese. (Check the labels of soya cheeses as they sometimes contain dairy-based casein and caseinates to give it a flavour and texture closer to dairy cheese.)

Soya cream cheese, available flavoured with herbs or garlic from health food shops, is very similar in appearance, taste and consistency to dairy cream cheese. It is not suitable for cooking purposes but is good for spreading on bread and crackers.

Hard soya cheese is made by pressing the curds to squeeze out the whey and comes in various styles ranging from mozzarella and cheddar to blue cheese flavour. In my view, hard soya cheese is not a viable alternative to dairy cheese. It is very dense and putty-like in texture, and bears very little resemblance to dairy cheese. It has an unrefined sharp acidic flavour and is very rich.

Margarine: Margarine is made from one or more vegetable oils such as soya, corn and sunflower. Many people assume that by definition margarine is dairy free, but many margarines, particularly the soft, spreadable ones in tubs, contain milk solids to soften them and give them a creamy flavour. Foods made with dairy-free margarine (or any type of margarine for that matter) do not taste as rich as those made with butter, but it provides the fat and pale yellow colour essential for making light, moist, appetizing baked products.

Dairy-free soft margarines and spreads: Soft, spreadable margarine is made by partially hydrogenating oils to turn them from a liquid to the consistency of softened butter at room temperature. They are bland and mildly oily in flavour and are best used for spreading thinly on bread, as dairy-free fat for making cakes, scones and soft icings, and as an alternative to the small quantity of butter used in flour-thickened sauces. Due to the soft consistency of dairy-free margarines and spreads, biscuit and pastry dough made with it can be too soft and difficult to roll out. It is also unsuitable for frying foods, as it separates and scorches at high temperatures.

Oil as a dairy-free alternative

When to use olive oil in place of butter: Butter and olive oil are used in dishes where their flavour adds character to the finished dish. Although butter is traditionally used to flavour British and Northern French dishes and olive oil flavours dishes from the Mediterranean, North Africa and the Middle East, they are largely interchangeable. The style of the dish may be altered by using olive oil in place of butter, but provided the ingredients are cooked and seasoned correctly the end result will be just as delicious.

When used on its own to fry food, olive oil, like butter, will scorch at high temperatures. For frying, mix a light olive oil with an equal quantity of a neutral flavoured oil that is stable at high temperatures. Light olive oil can also be used in place of butter or neutral flavoured oils for basting meat, poultry or fish as it roasts, bakes or grills.

When to use neutral flavoured oil in place of butter: Due to its rich but neutral flavour, butter is normally used to make a roux, the flour and fat paste used to thicken delicately flavoured sauces. Olive oil is unsuitable for this purpose as it is too strongly flavoured. Instead use 2 tablespoons of neutral flavoured oil, such as sunflower or corn, in place of 40 g/1½ oz of butter.

In stews, soups, sauces and other dishes where fat is skimmed off during cooking, use neutral flavoured oils to fry ingredients, as it would be a waste to use olive oil.

When oil and margarine cannot replace butter: Delicately flavoured savoury and sweet sauces, and fruits caramelized in butter and sugar, rely on the rich, creamy flavour of butter and would not taste the same made with dairy-free alternatives. Oil as a substitute is wholly unsuitable and although dairy-free margarine and soya cream can be used in the place of butter they give the food a disappointing oily flavour.

Dairy-free hard baking margarine: Hard baking margarines are made by a process involving the complete hydrogenation of vegetable oils to solidify liquid oil to the consistency of hard butter when chilled. Hard baking margarine, as its name suggests, is designed specifically as an alternative to butter for baking. It is normally dairy-free and is sold, like butter, in blocks, wrapped in foil or wax paper. Although its flavour is neutral, uninteresting and slightly oily, its firm consistency is ideal for making moist light cakes and dairy-free pastry, biscuits, crumble topping and other baked goods where chilled fat is rubbed into the dry ingredients. Pastry and biscuit dough made with hard baking margarine is also sufficiently firm and supple to roll out easily. The consistency of hard baking margarine is also ideal for making spreadable but firm butter cream icing for decorating cakes.

Hard baking margarine is also a very good substitute for butter in flour-thickened sauces. However, due to its oily flavour, it is not suitable for frying purposes or buttering cooked vegetables.

DAIRY-FREE ICE CREAM Ice cream is traditionally made with dairy milk, cream, eggs and sugar. Milk, cream and eggs are rich in both fat and protein and soften the consistency of ice cream by preventing large ice crystals forming as the mixture freezes. To make rich and creamy dairy-free ice cream, use egg yolks and a mixture of soya milk and soya cream. Both soya milk and soya cream are rich in protein while soya cream also contains sufficient fat to produce a smooth, creamy result (see Rich Chocolate Ice Cream page 204). Puréed banana and soya cream also provide a rich, smooth base for dairy-free ice cream with a fresh, fruity flavour (see Banana Ice Cream page 205).

Soya-based ice cream is also available from good supermarkets. It is made from a blend of soya and non-hydrogenated vegetable oils and comes in many flavours and on sticks, coated in plain chocolate. And don't forget sorbets, they are always a good alternative to ice cream (see page 202).

WHAT TO LOOK FOR ON FOOD LABELS

Packaged foods in the European Union have to state clearly when they contain milk, cream, butter and yogurt. As well as the obvious culprits that will appear on the label watch out for the following:

- Caramel colouring and flavouring (this is lactose sugar)
- Casein
- Caseinate
- Sodium caseinate
- Calcium caseinate
- Lactose
- Lactalbumin
- Lactalbumin phosphate
- Lactoglobulin
- Lactic acid
- Simplesse (a fat substitute made from egg and whey protein)
- Whey
- Whey powder
- Hydrolysed whey protein

| # SUBSTITUTING FOR NUTS

Nuts that most commonly feature in manufactured foods and recipes include peanuts (also called groundnuts), which are actually a variety of pea from the pulse family, and the tree nuts, almonds, Brazil nuts, cashews, chestnuts, hazelnuts, macadamia nuts, pecans, pine nuts, pistachios and walnuts.

Obviously manufactured foods containing nuts must be avoided, but in many home-cooked dishes nuts can be omitted or substituted, particularly when they are used in small quantities in a recipe. Recipes containing nuts need only be avoided when nuts are used as the principal ingredient, for example in a recipe such as almond cake or in satay sauce, where there is no suitable ingredient to take the place of nuts. The table on the following pages lists the principal uses of nuts and, where appropriate, suitable nut-free substitutes.

WHAT TO LOOK OUT FOR ON FOOD LABELS

Nuts feature in a wide range of manufactured foods, particularly in baked goods, sweets, snack foods, breakfast cereals and Chinese, Thai and Indian food. Nuts are also used to flavour nut syrups, blended to make nut butters, pressed for oil and strongly flavoured essences such as almond essence. Peanuts are often used as a substitute for pine nuts in foods such as pesto, so always read the label.

When packaged food sold in the European Union is made with nuts or uses ingredients containing nuts, the food label must clearly state 'contains nuts'. 'May contain traces of nuts' must also be stated when traces of nut may be present in one or more of the ingredients used to make a product or because the food, or ingredients used to make it, may have come into contact with traces of nuts during the production process. Always check the label for nuts each time you buy packaged food, even when you regularly buy a product, as recipes change.

In addition to the obvious listings that indicate the presence of nuts, the following ingredients may be derived from nuts:
• Hydrolysed plant protein
• Hydrolysed vegetable protein
• Vegetable fat and vegetable oil – may contain peanut oil
• Natural flavourings – can be derived from nuts as well as a plethora of other ingredients

Use of nuts	Substitute ingredient	Comment
Coating food before baking or frying	Dried breadcrumbs, cornmeal polenta or rolled oats	Drizzle with oil before baking to make the coating crisp and to give a golden brown colour
Garnishes for Oriental food, esp. stir-fries and curries	Crunchy vegetables, e.g. peppers, beansprouts, chopped spring onion or diced cucumber	Add a handful of prepared vegetables to the pan to heat through just before serving so they remain crisp
Adding texture to homemade muesli	Add an equal quantity of extra dried fruit, cereal flakes (e.g. rolled oats, rice flakes) or sunflower seeds	Add extra crunch by toasting cereal flakes in a dry pan. Add chopped fresh fruit just before eating
Adding crunch and texture to cake mixtures and biscuit dough	Omit the nuts and use equal quantities of dried fruit. Although dried fruit does not add crunch it adds chewiness, flavour and moisture	Also try roughly chopped chocolate, especially for biscuits
Decoration for biscuits, cakes and pastries	Omit and decorate with sugar, chopped or dried fruit. Avoid marzipan as it is made with ground nuts	Decorate baked rich fruit cakes with dried fruit and glaze with apricot jam
Adding texture and flavour to bread dough	Simply omit or replace with other ingredients e.g. garlic cloves, softened onion, herbs, stoned olives or dried fruit	
Adding texture to stuffings, pies terrines and pâtés	Nuts are included mainly to add 'bite'. Replace with finely diced celery	The texture of stuffing can be made coarser by adding cooked brown rice or bulgur wheat
Ground nuts used in small quantities in cake mixtures, biscuit and pastry dough to add flavour and richness	Replace ground nuts with extra flour	
Ground nuts used as the main ingredient in baked foods	Flour will not replace the rich flavour and moist texture of baked foods based on ground nuts	Choose an alternative recipe

Use of nuts	Substitute ingredient	Comment
Garnishes in salads and other savoury dishes to add bite and protein	Instead try salted, plain or garlic croutons for crunch; cooked chickpeas, beans or diced meat, poultry or fish for protein. Soya nuts can also be used as an alternative	Other raw vegetables work well too – diced celery, cucumber, peppers, onion or beansprouts
Peanut oil or groundnut oil is used in Asian cookery for stir-frying and deep-frying due to its neutral flavour and stability at high temperatures	Other vegetable oils, e.g. soya bean oil, blended vegetable oil (provided it does not contain groundnut oil), rapeseed oil, corn oil, grapeseed oil, safflower or sunflower oil	These substitutes have a neutral flavour and are stable (do not burn) at high temperatures
Flavoured nut oils used in salad dressings and to flavour hot dishes	Use sesame oil to flavour Asian food, extra virgin olive oil or light olive oil flavoured with garlic, chilli or herbs	Butter and olive oil can also be mixed with neutral flavoured frying oils to add flavour
Ground nuts used to thicken and add flavour to sauces in Asian cooking	No substitute	Choose an alternative recipe that does not rely on nuts for its consistency and flavour
Nuts ground and blended with oils to make nut butter	No substitute	Choose an alternative nut-free spread
As a snack food	Soya nuts	Although they are not 'nuts' as such they are the closest in texture and flavour and are a delicious alternative. Soya nuts are made with whole soya beans that have been soaked in water then baked until crisp and golden brown. They are available plain or flavoured with salt or paprika

Chapter 8

SUBSTITUTING FOR SOYA

Due to their outstanding nutritional content, mild flavour and versatility, soya beans are the most widely grown and utilized pulse in the world. Soya comes in many forms, including soya flour, soya protein, soya oil and the emulsifier soya lecithin. It is used in around 60 per cent of processed foods – including baked goods, ready meals, salad dressings, baby foods and an increasing number of dairy-free products – to thicken, enrich, soften, add nutrition, emulsify and stabilize. As a result of its widespread use, allergy to soya is increasing. Unfortunately food manufacturers have not kept up with this and the range of ready-made foods available for those allergic to soya is limited.

However, although the majority of manufactured foods contain soya, only a handful of soya-based ingredients are used in freshly prepared home cooking. These include soy sauce, vegetable oil (containing soya bean oil), soya-based margarines and chocolate (containing soya lecithin). While there is no exact substitute for soy sauce, recipes and cooking methods for dishes where soya is normally used can be altered to ensure they are richly flavoured and coloured. Soya-free cooking oil, margarine and chocolate are also available. Always read the label on packaged products before using them in your recipes to ensure they do not contain soya.

SOY SAUCE

Soy sauce is the collective name for thin, dark brown sauces, with a characteristic rich salt-sweet flavour, made from fermented soya beans. The three main varieties of soy sauce include all purpose, rich and dark Shoyu (or soya) sauce, thinner aromatic Tamari and sweet teriyaki sauce. They are used to season and add colour to Oriental soups, stews, stir-fries, marinades, dressings for grilled food and are used in dipping sauces.

Soya-free alternative to soy sauce

Although there is no such thing as a soya-free soy sauce, a rich brown sauce with a sweet-salt flavour can be made to replace it in stir-fry dishes:

- Brown your fish, meat or seafood quickly and evenly in hot oil to add rich colour and flavour to the dish.
- As the food is frying, mix together $1/2$ teaspoon of salt, 1 teaspoon of dark brown sugar and 1 tablespoon of rich chicken stock per 1 tablespoon of dark soy sauce in the recipe. Just before the ingredients are cooked, stir the mixture into the food. To make a substitute for 1 tablespoon of light soy sauce, mix $1/4$ teaspoon salt and $1/2$ teaspoon of dark brown sugar with 1 tablespoon of rich chicken stock; stir into the food just before it is cooked.

SUBSTITUTES FOR SOYA OIL

Soya oil, an amber coloured oil extracted from soya beans, is mild in flavour, stable at high temperatures and a versatile cooking oil for frying and using in salad dressings and mayonnaise. Vegetable oil, a generic term, is usually 100 per cent soya oil or a blend of soya oil and other vegetable oils. Other general purpose cooking oils that have similar properties to soya oil include sunflower oil, grapeseed oil, rapeseed oil and safflower oil. Light olive oil can also be used for gentle frying.

SUBSTITUTES FOR SOYA MARGARINE
Due to its mild taste, availability and low cost, soya bean oil is one of the most common oils used to make margarine. Margarine is also available made with mild flavoured vegetable oils including rapeseed, sunflower and corn oil or tropical oils such as palm oil – but check the label to ensure they have not been emulsified and stabilized with soya lecithin.

SOYA IN CHOCOLATE
Soya lecithin, an emulsifier and stabilizer, is often added to conventional chocolate to reduce the quantity of expensive cocoa butter required to produce smooth, even textured chocolate. More expensive, high-cocoa-content chocolate, is usually made without soya lecithin and is widely available in good supermarkets and health food shops.

FOOD PRODUCTS MADE FROM SOYA
Whole soya beans are liquidized to make soya milk, dried and ground to make soya flour, fermented to make soy sauce, miso and Tamari sauce and cultured with bacteria to make yogurt, cheese, tofu and tempeh. Soya flour is used to make noodles, to improve the texture and add protein to baked products, to thicken milk drinks, sauces, dressings and ice cream. It also adds bulk to meat products, cereals, baby food products and diet foods. The list on page 60 outlines the most common soya products and ingredients that can be used to replace them.

WHAT TO LOOK FOR ON FOOD LABELS

When packaged food sold in the European Union is made with soya, or uses ingredients containing soya, the food label must clearly state 'contains soya'. However, refined soya oil, the main component of vegetable oil, is regarded by the medical profession as safe for people with soya allergies (though not everyone agrees) as the proteins that cause the soya allergy are removed during the refining process. For this reason, soya oil is not labelled individually when used in blended vegetable oil. Remember that recipes sometimes change so always check the label for soya each time you buy a packaged food. In addition to the obvious ingredients that indicate the presence of soya – such as soya protein, soya lecithin, soya oil and so on – you may find the following terms on food labels:

- Hydrolysed vegetable or plant protein (may be made from soya)
- Natural and artificial flavouring (can mean soya)
- Textured vegetable protein, or TVP (made from soya granules)
- Vegetable starch (a purified starch often obtained from soya beans)
- Vegetable gum (a soluble vegetable fibre, sometimes based on soya)

Canned and frozen vegetables

Surprising as it may seem soya can also be found in some canned and frozen vegetables. Soya-based hydrolysed vegetable protein is added to enhance the flavour of some canned and frozen vegetables, so check the label and use brands free of soya or use fresh vegetables instead.

Soya product	Soya-free substitute
Soya flour	Wheat flour and gluten-free flours
Soya nuts	Nuts
Soya milk	Dairy milk or rice, almond or oat milk
Soya cheese	Dairy cheese
Natto (fermented soya cheese used in Japanese cooking)	No soya-free substitute
Okara (soya bean pulp remaining after soya milk is squeezed from the beans). Used in Japanese cooking	No soya-free substitute
Yuba (made from the skin that forms on heated soya milk). Used in Japanese and Chinese cooking	No soya-free substitute
Soya yogurt	Dairy yogurt
Soya desserts	Creamy desserts made with milk, rice or almond milk
Soya cream	Dairy cream
Soya custard	Custard made with dairy, rice or almond milk
Soya sprouts (beansprouts)	Mung sprouts and alfafa sprouts
Edamame (young soya beans)	Peas or other beans
Soya bean granules or curds	Minced meat
Tofu (made from soya milk curds)	Cheese or meat
Miso (paste made from fermented soya beans and grain). Used to flavour Japanese food	No soya-free substitute
Tempeh (made from fermented whole soya beans)	Meat, poultry
Soy sauce, Tamari	Brown food well, use richly flavoured stock and season food with salt and dark brown sugar
Teriyaki sauce	As above and add a small quantity of vinegar
Soya oil (neutral flavoured oil used in vegetable oil blends)	Grapeseed oil, rapeseed oil, safflower, corn and sunflower oil

Part III
THE RECIPES

Chapter 9

STOCK, SOUPS AND SAUCES

STOCK

Homemade stock, when prepared properly, adds depth and a freshness of flavour to risottos, soups, casseroles, poached dishes and flour-thickened sauces that is simply not possible even with the best quality stock cubes. Unlike stock cubes, homemade stock is also dairy, egg, gluten, nut and soya free. It is made by poaching fresh or browned meat, poultry or fish bones with herbs and aromatic vegetables – such as celery, onion and carrot – in water.

There are two main varieties of stock: white stock and brown. White stock provides a delicately flavoured, pale coloured liquid that can be used in both richly flavoured and subtle dishes. It is made by poaching fresh carcasses of white poultry (usually chicken), veal bones or the fresh bones and heads of white fish in water flavoured with vegetables and herbs. The bones left over from roast chicken or turkey can also be used, however this produces a stock with a thinner flavour, as much of the flavour in the bones is lost in the cooking juices during roasting.

Brown stock is a richly flavoured, dark caramel coloured liquid that enhances full flavoured dishes. Brown stock derives its colour from first browning chicken carcasses or chopped beef bones and vegetables in a hot oven, or in a frying pan with some oil, before poaching in water.

GENERAL RULES FOR MAKING STOCK

- Use a pot large enough to cover the ingredients with water. Exposed ingredients will not flavour the stock.
- Do not season stock with salt. The natural salts derived from the bones and vegetables provide all the flavour stock needs. Salted stock tastes overpowering.
- Use very fresh vegetables and bones for the purest and freshest flavoured stock. Choose meaty bones to make richly flavoured stock.
- Before making fish stock, remove the gills from fish heads as they contain a large quantity of blood, which will make the stock cloudy and bitter.
- Avoid using vegetables that fall apart, such as potatoes and tomatoes, or green vegetables, such as broccoli, cabbage and green beans, which become strongly flavoured when cooked for a prolonged period.
- Dice vegetables so that their flavours are readily extracted. To prevent vegetables

NOTES FOR FOOD ALLERGY SUFFERERS

The pure flavour of homemade stock is achieved by using the simplest ingredients. Stock made with bones, vegetables, herbs and water makes an ideal liquid base for dairy-, gluten-, egg-, nut- and soya-free sauces and dishes. For nut- and soya-free diets, use a suitable soya- and nut-free neutral flavoured oil to brown vegetables and bones.

falling apart during cooking, dice them according to the length of time the stock is cooked for: 1 cm/⅓ inch for stock that takes 30 minutes or less to cook; 2.5 cm/1 inch for stock requiring 3–4 hours; 5 cm/2 inches for stock that requires 6 hours to cook.

- Avoid using burnt bones or vegetables in brown stock as they will spoil the flavour of the stock.

Stock should be perfectly clear. To avoid stock becoming fatty and cloudy:

- Trim the excess fat from bones.
- Submerge stock ingredients in cold water and slowly bring to a gentle simmer. This way fat on the bones gradually melts and blood gradually congeals to form scum, which floats to the surface, where it can be skimmed off. If fat and scum are not removed the stock becomes cloudy and tastes fatty.
- While the stock is cooking, use cold water to top up the water level so that the ingredients remain submerged. Adding cold water encourages fat and scum to rise to the surface, where it can be skimmed off.
- Maintain stock at a gentle simmer to ensure scum and fat gently rise to the surface and are not bubbled through the liquid, as this makes it cloudy and greasy.
- Once the stock is made, strain through a fine mesh sieve to obtain a clear, fragment-free liquid.

USING STOCK Once stock is made, it can either be used as it is in soups, delicately flavoured sauces, casseroles and so on, or reduced to half its original volume (by boiling in a wide pan) to strengthen its flavour and colour, making it suitable for adding depth to richly flavoured and coloured sauces. As stock is reduced it should be skimmed regularly to remove any remaining fat and scum.

STORING STOCK Stock must be stored in the fridge as it is highly nutritious and provides an ideal breeding ground for bacteria. To store stock in the fridge or freezer it is more space efficient to reduce stock by at least three-quarters its original volume. The stock becomes thick and syrupy and sets to a firm jelly when chilled, which keeps for up to three days in the fridge and up to one year in the freezer.

RECONSTITUTING JELLIED STOCK Jellied stock is very strong in flavour and is reconstituted with water before it is used in recipes. To make a light stock from jellied stock, add 1 heaped tablespoon of jellied stock to 290 ml/10 fl oz of water. To make a richer stock add 2–3 heaped tablespoons of jellied stock to 290 ml/10 fl oz water.

WHITE CHICKEN STOCK

White chicken stock can be used to enhance the flavour of almost any savoury dish as it is light in colour and delicate in flavour. **Makes 1 litre/1¾ pints**

INGREDIENTS

1 chicken carcass

1 onion, cut into wedges

1 large carrot, cut into 2.5 cm/1 in dice

1 celery stick, cut into 2.5 cm/1 in dice

1 handful button mushrooms

1 sprig thyme

4 parsley stalks

a grind of black pepper

1 bay leaf

1 Place all the ingredients in a large stock pan, cover with cold water and bring slowly to a gentle simmer. Simmer for 3–4 hours, uncovered. Do not allow the stock to boil.

2 Keep the water level topped up with cold water and lift off any melted fat and scum that rises to the surface.

3 Once the stock is cooked, pass it through a large sieve and use as required (see Using Stock page 63).

VARIATION

BROWN CHICKEN STOCK

Roast a chicken carcass at 200°C/400°F/gas mark 6 for an hour, or until golden brown. Meanwhile, brown the stock vegetables, listed above, in 2 tablespoons of oil in the stock pan, making sure they do not burn. Add the browned bones, herbs and ground pepper to the vegetables, cover with water and continue as above.

FISH STOCK

White fish stock is colourless and delicate in flavour, and is used in sauces served with fish, in fish soups and fish casseroles. **Makes 1 litre/1¾ pints**

INGREDIENTS

450 g/1 lb white fish bones, skin, tails and heads (gills removed)

1 small onion, thinly sliced

1 small carrot, cut into 1 cm/⅓ in dice

1 handful button mushrooms, thinly sliced

1 celery stick, cut into 1 cm/⅓ in dice

1 sprig thyme

4 parsley stalks

4 black peppercorns

1 bay leaf

1 Place all the ingredients in a large stock pan, cover with cold water and bring slowly to a gentle simmer. Simmer for 20 minutes. It is essential that fish stock does not boil or cook for longer or it will become cloudy and bitter in flavour. Lift off any scum that rises to the surface with a large metal spoon.

2 Once the stock is cooked, pass it through a fine mesh sieve. Ensure all fish bones have been removed and use as required (see Using Stock page 63).

BROWN BEEF STOCK

Ask the butcher to cut beef bones into small pieces for you. Brown beef stock has a stronger flavour than brown chicken stock and is used mainly in dishes containing beef, venison or lamb, and in richly flavoured and coloured sauces served with red meat. **Makes 1 litre/1¾ pints**

INGREDIENTS

1 kg/2¼ lb chopped beef bones

2 onions, cut into wedges

2 large carrots, cut into 3 chunks

2 celery sticks, cut into 3 pieces

2 tbsp sunflower or corn oil

2 handfuls button mushrooms

1 sprig thyme

4 parsley stalks

a grind of black pepper

1 bay leaf

1 Preheat the oven to 200°C/400°C/gas mark 6. Place the chopped bones in a roasting tin and bake for 1 hour, or until evenly browned.

2 Meanwhile, in a large stock pan, brown the onion, carrots and celery in the oil, stirring frequently to prevent the vegetables from burning.

3 When the bones are caramel brown, add them to the pan, along with the remaining ingredients, cover in cold water and bring to a simmer.

4 Gently simmer the stock for 6 hours, to extract all the flavour from the bones. Spoon off the fat and scum from the surface and top the pan up with cold water every hour. Once the stock is cooked, strain it through a fine mesh sieve and use as required (see Using Stock page 63).

VEGETABLE STOCK

Vegetable stock is used mainly in soups and vegetarian dishes. It is also a nutritious cooking liquid for baby food (see Chapter 18). **Makes 1 litre/1¾ pints**

INGREDIENTS

2 onions, finely sliced

2 carrots, cut into 1 cm/⅓ in dice

1 leek, cut into 1 cm/⅓ in dice

1 celery stick, cut into 1 cm/⅓ in dice

4 button mushrooms, finely sliced

4 parsley stalks

1 sprig fresh thyme

a grind of black pepper

1 bay leaf

1 Place all the ingredients in a large stock pan, cover with cold water and bring to a simmer.

2 Simmer gently for 30 minutes, skimming regularly, then strain through a sieve and use as required (see Using Stock page 63).

VARIATION

BROWN VEGETABLE STOCK

This stock is suitable for richly flavoured and coloured soups, puréed vegetable sauces and vegetarian dishes. Using the ingredient list above, first fry the prepared onion, carrots, leek, celery and mushrooms in 2 tablespoons of sunflower or corn oil until golden brown, stirring regularly to prevent the vegetables from burning. Add 1 teaspoon of tomato purée to add colour and cover the ingredients with cold water. Bring to a simmer and poach for 30 minutes, regularly removing oil and scum from the surface. Strain the stock and use as required.

SOUPS

Soup is justifiably popular across the world. It is made with an endless variety of ingredients and can be thin or thick, smooth or chunky. In general, most recipes are suitable – or are easily adapted – for dairy-, egg-, gluten-, soya- and nut-free diets (see box page 68).

GENERAL RULES FOR MAKING SOUP

- Cut ingredients to the same size so they cook evenly and look uniform in chunky soups. Make sure the ingredients are no smaller than 5 mm/ ¼ inch so they can be recognized and do not over-cook and fall apart during cooking.
- When softening vegetables by gently frying them in butter or oil, stir frequently to prevent them sticking and burning. Remove any burnt vegetables before adding liquid to the pan or they will taint the flavour of the soup.
- Simmer, do not boil, soups. If soup is allowed to boil the ingredients are likely to over-cook and lose their fresh flavour; thin, clear soups may become cloudy.
- Regularly skim the surface of the soup to remove any fat and scum – this will improve the appearance and flavour of the soup.
- Add green vegetables to soup towards the end of the cooking period so they do not over-cook and lose their vivid colour and fresh flavour.
- Blend potatoes until just smooth. If potatoes are over-blended the soup will become thick and gluey.
- To control the thickness of smooth puréed soup, strain the cooked ingredients and most of the liquid into a clean container. Purée the ingredients with one-third of the liquid until smooth then gradually add the strained liquid to the purée until it reaches the required consistency.

SMOOTH SOUPS

Smooth soups that are served as a starter to a meal tend to be perfectly smooth, with the thickness of double cream. When smooth soups are eaten as a warming, hearty meal, they should be thicker so they are more substantial and satisfying to eat.

Smooth soups are thickened by two main methods:

1 By puréeing the cooked ingredients in a liquidizer or using a hand-held blender until smooth (food processors tend to produce a coarse purée). This method is ideal for soups made with vegetables that naturally thicken soup when softened and puréed, such as root vegetables, potatoes, squashes and pulses. This method does not require flour to thicken the soup and is ideal for gluten-free diets (see Peppery Watercress and Spinach Soup page 70).

2 By thickening the soup with wheat flour (and for gluten-free diets with cornflour). This method is used when the flavouring ingredients are unsuitable for puréeing or do not purée to a smooth, creamy consistency. Flour is mixed with fat to form a paste called a roux (see Flour-thickened Sauces page 72). The liquid base of the soup is then gradually stirred into the roux and brought to a simmer. As the soup simmers it thickens to a fine, smooth consistency.

CHUNKY SOUPS

Chunky soups tend to be heartier and more satisfying than smooth soups as they usually contain ingredients rich in starch and protein, as well as vegetables that add flavour, colour and texture.

Thin clear soups, eaten all over the world, are made by gently simmering the soup ingredients in stock or broth. They are delicately flavoured, low in fat and are made more substantial with ingredients rich in carbohydrate, including pasta, noodles, rice, pearl barley and potatoes.

Chunky soups made with a thicker base are made by simmering evenly diced or sliced ingredients together in stock until tender. The soup base is thickened by puréeing a proportion of the ingredients in the cooking liquid, or by thickening the strained cooking liquid with flour. The remaining cooked ingredients are then returned to the pan to add texture and enhance the appearance of the soup.

NOTES FOR FOOD ALLERGY SUFFERERS

DAIRY-FREE DIET: Soup ingredients are often gently fried in butter. Use olive oil, a neutral flavoured oil or dairy-free margarine instead.

Soup is sometimes thickened with a roux, a mixture of flour and butter. In place of butter use an equal quantity of dairy-free margarine or 1 tablespoon of oil per 30 g/1 oz of butter used in the recipe.

Milk and cream are often added to smooth soup towards the end of cooking to enrich its flavour. Use soya milk, oat milk or rice milk instead. When soup is garnished with a swirl of cream, use a small quantity of pouring soya cream in strongly flavoured soups, where its mild beany taste will not be evident. Alternatively, drizzle soup with a small quantity of extra virgin olive oil to add richness.

GLUTEN-FREE DIET: Smooth soups thickened with puréed ingredients are ideal for gluten-free diets. Many soups are traditionally thickened with a roux made with wheat flour and butter. Replace the wheat flour with an equal quantity of cornflour to make the roux. For soups that contain wheat noodles, pasta or bread, replace these with gluten-free rice or buckwheat noodles, rice and millet pasta and gluten-free bread. You can also make croutons for garnishing soup with gluten-free bread (see page 70).

EGG-FREE DIET: Egg is often included in Asian soups as it provides protein and texture. Simply omit the egg and use more protein-rich ingredients, such as fish, meat, poultry, beans or pulses.

NUT-FREE DIET: Some Asian and Middle Eastern soups use ground almonds and other nut varieties to enrich and thicken soup. As nuts are integral to the consistency and flavour of these soups it is best to choose an alternative recipe that does not use nuts. When frying or browning ingredients in oil, make sure the oil is free of nut oils.

SOYA-FREE DIET: Soya bean curd, more commonly known as tofu, and soy sauce are often used in Asian soups. Replace tofu with another protein-rich food such as meat, fish, poultry or egg. Replace soy sauce by adding $1/2$ teaspoon of salt and 1 teaspoon dark brown sugar per 1 tablespoon of soy sauce and a little richly flavoured stock.

CHUNKY WINTER VEGETABLE SOUP

This hearty soup is ideal for lunch on cold winter days. Half of the ingredients in the soup are puréed to form a thick, creamy base for the remaining vegetables. **Serves 4**

INGREDIENTS

30 g/1 oz butter or 2 tbsp sunflower or corn oil

● DAIRY   dairy-free margarine or oil

1 onion, sliced thinly

1 leek, sliced thinly

3 large carrots, cut into 2 cm/³/₄ in dice

2 celery sticks, sliced thinly

2 large potatoes, peeled and cut into 2 cm/³/₄ in dice

1 bay leaf

1 sprig thyme

570 ml/1 pint white chicken or vegetable stock

290 ml/10 fl oz milk

● DAIRY   soya milk

TO GARNISH

extra virgin olive oil for drizzling

1 tbsp finely chopped chives

1 Place the butter or oil in a medium-sized heavy-bottomed saucepan, add the onion, leek, carrots, celery and a little seasoning, cover with a lid and fry gently until very soft. This will take at least 20 minutes. Stir occasionally to prevent the vegetables sticking to the pan. Do not allow the vegetables to brown.

2 Add the potatoes, bay leaf, thyme and stock to the pan. Season the soup with a pinch of salt and grind of pepper and simmer for 20 minutes, or until the potatoes are tender. Do not allow the potatoes to over-cook or they will break up, affecting the appearance and consistency of the soup.

3 Using a slotted spoon, lift out one-third of the cooked vegetables and reserve. Remove the bay leaf and thyme and liquidize the remaining soup until smooth. To remove any remaining lumps, pass the soup through a fine-meshed sieve, into a clean pan, gently pressing it through with a wooden spoon.

4 Reheat the soup, taste and season as necessary.

5 Tip in the reserved vegetables, add the milk and bring the soup back to a simmer to warm the vegetables through. To serve, ladle the soup into warmed soup bowls, lightly drizzle the soup with olive oil and sprinkle with the finely chopped chives.

PEPPERY WATERCRESS AND SPINACH SOUP WITH GARLIC CROUTONS

This is a vibrant soup in both taste and colour. To retain the wonderful bright green colour and zingy flavour of the leaves, the watercress and spinach is wilted in the hot soup for the briefest moment before it is puréed. **Serves 4**

FOR THE SOUP

30 g/1 oz butter

● **DAIRY**

1 tbsp sunflower or corn oil

1 onion, finely sliced

1 large potato, peeled and diced

860 ml/1½ pints White Chicken or Vegetable Stock (see pages 64 and 66)

110 g/4 oz watercress

110 g/4 oz baby spinach leaves, washed and drained

salt and freshly ground black pepper

FOR THE GARLIC CROUTONS

4 slices white bread, crusts removed and cut into 5 mm/¼ in dice

● **GLUTEN**

gluten-free white bread

4 tbsp vegetable or olive oil

2 garlic cloves, cut in half lengthways

salt

TO GARNISH

4 sprigs watercress

1 Preheat the oven to 180°C/350°F/ gas mark 4.

2 In a small pan, gently warm the oil and garlic cloves for the croutons until the garlic begins to sizzle. Remove from the heat and allow the oil to cool. Do not remove the garlic until the oil is cold.

3 Place the butter or oil for the soup in a medium-sized heavy-bottomed pan, add the onion, season with the salt and pepper, cover with a lid and fry gently until very soft and sweet.

4 Meanwhile, make the croutons. Spread the cubes of bread on a baking tray in one layer and drizzle with the garlic-flavoured oil, turning the bread over in the oil until the cubes are evenly covered. Lightly sprinkle with salt and bake for 5–10 minutes, or until the croutons are golden brown. Leave to cool on a wire rack, covered in absorbent paper to absorb excess oil.

5 Add the potato and stock to the softened onions. Bring the stock to simmering point and simmer for about 10 minutes, or until the potato is soft.

6 Add the watercress and spinach leaves to the pan and simmer for 30 seconds, or until wilted.

7 Liquidize the soup to a smooth purée. Bring the soup back to a simmer, taste and season as necessary. Serve immediately in warmed soup bowls, garnished with a sprig of watercress and a sprinkling of croutons.

DAIRY-FREE DIET: The roux in flour-thickened sauces is made with butter, the oil used for browning and frying or the fat that collects in the base of a roasting tray as meat or poultry roast. Using oil or fat from a roast is suitable for a dairy-free diet but sauces thickened with a flour and butter roux should be made with an equal quantity of dairy-free margarine or 1 tablespoon of oil per 30 g/1 oz butter.

Flour-thickened sauces made with stock or cooking liquids used to poach or stew ingredients are safe for dairy-free diets, provided butter is not used to fry the ingredients beforehand. White sauce is traditionally made with cows' milk but can be made just as well with sweetened soya milk. For a very rich white dairy-free sauce, substitute half the soya milk with soya cream.

GLUTEN-FREE DIET: Flour-thickened sauces are traditionally thickened with a plain wheat flour and fat roux. Use an equal quantity of cornflour in place of wheat flour. It produces perfectly smooth textured, glossy sauces.

EGG-FREE DIET: Egg is not used in flour-thickened sauces.

NUT-FREE DIET: Provided the flour is milled in a nut-free factory and the fat used does not contain nut oils, flour-thickened sauces are suitable for nut-free diets.

SOYA-FREE DIET: Provided soya milk is not used as the liquid base for the sauce and the roux is made with soya-free fat then flour-thickened sauces are suitable for soya-free diets.

SAUCES

Sauces are integral to the food we eat. They add endless variety, flavour, colour and moisture and improve the consistency and appearance of food. Sauces are extremely versatile and ingredients unsuitable for your dietary requirements can be easily avoided or substituted to dramatically increase the repertoire of dishes available to you.

Sauces can be classified by the way they are thickened to coat or bind food: flour-thickened sauces are based on a wheat flour and fat paste, or roux (see White Sauce opposite); reduction sauces are thickened by boiling down to a syrupy consistency (see Red Wine Sauce page 78); puréed sauces are based on softened vegetables (see Rich Italian Tomato Sauce page 80); emulsified sauces are thickened by whisking melted butter, oil, cream or yogurt into water-based ingredients (see Mayonnaise page 83).

FLOUR-THICKENED SAUCES

Flour-thickened sauces have a number of roles in cooking. Lightly thickened sauces are used to thinly coat the ingredients they accompany or to add moisture and thickness to baked dishes; thicker sauces, made with a higher proportion of roux, are generally used to bind ingredients together, for example in a pie or tart.

WHITE SAUCE

This very simple flour-thickened sauce has a smooth, creamy consistency that is perfect for lightly coating or binding delicately flavoured ingredients. Due to its bland flavour, white sauce is usually flavoured with herbs and vegetables or cheese (see overleaf).
Makes 570 ml/1 pint

INGREDIENTS

40 g/1½ oz butter
● **DAIRY** dairy-free margarine or 2 tbsp vegetable oil

40 g/1½ oz plain flour
● **GLUTEN** 30 g/1 oz cornflour

570 ml/1 pint milk
● **DAIRY** sweetened soya milk or rice milk

salt and freshly ground black pepper

1 Melt the butter or oil in a medium-sized heavy-bottomed pan, over a medium heat.

2 Stir in the flour, using a wooden spoon, to form a thick, smooth roux.

3 Cook for 30 seconds, stirring continuously. Remove from the heat.

4 Add a splash of the milk and stir vigorously until the roux has absorbed all the liquid evenly. Add another splash of milk and stir vigorously until the roux has again absorbed all the liquid and is an even texture. As more liquid is incorporated, you can add it in progressively greater 'splashes'.

5 Repeat this process until all the milk has been incorporated and the roux becomes a smooth sauce. Do not add the liquid too quickly or the sauce will become lumpy.

6 Place the pan back on a medium heat. Stirring continuously, bring the sauce to the boil.

7 Reduce the heat and simmer gently for 1 minute to cook the flour. The white sauce should be smooth, glossy and the consistency of double cream. Add seasoning to taste.

VARIATIONS ON WHITE SAUCE

BÉCHAMEL SAUCE

A slightly more upmarket version of white sauce, béchamel sauce is used to add creaminess to dishes such as lasagne and vegetable gratins. Before making the sauce, flavour 570 ml/1 pint of milk by gently bringing it to a simmer with 4 slices of onion, 2 bay leaves, 6 whole black peppercorns and 3 parsley stalks, then remove from the heat and set aside until cold to extract the flavour of the added ingredients. Strain the flavoured milk through a sieve and then use as normal in the main recipe for white sauce.

CHEESE SAUCE

As well as its common use in dishes such as cauliflower cheese and macaroni cheese, this sauce is good with baked, poached or steamed fish. Simply add 110 g/4 oz grated mature Cheddar or Parmesan to the finished sauce and stir well. Don't reheat the sauce after adding the cheese or it will lose its flavour and become greasy.

PARSLEY SAUCE

Add 2 tablespoons of finely chopped parsley to white sauce in the last few minutes of cooking. Parsley sauce is a good accompaniment to white fish, poached chicken or boiled gammon.

SAGE AND ONION SAUCE

Gently fry 1 finely sliced onion until soft but not coloured and 1 tablespoon of finely chopped fresh sage in 1 tablespoon of butter or oil. Stir into the cooked white sauce and gently simmer for a further 2 minutes. This sauce is particularly good with roast pork.

RICH WHITE SAUCE

This egg-free sauce is a good alternative to egg custard fillings in savoury tarts. To make it, simply use half milk, half double cream in the basic white sauce recipe.

THICKENING SAUCES WITH CORNFLOUR

Do not simmer sauces thickened with cornflour for more than a minute or keep them warm for more than 15 minutes or the cornflour will break down and the sauce will become thin.

STOCK-BASED FLOUR-THICKENED SAUCES

Stock and poaching or stewing liquid flavoured with meat, chicken, fish and vegetables are also thickened with a roux to produce mild flavoured sauces. Due to their delicate flavour these sauces benefit from the addition of herbs, aromatic vegetables including onions, celery and mushrooms, a little wine or a squeeze of lemon juice.

CHICKEN SAUCE

This delicate, velvety sauce is ideal for binding chicken or game pie fillings or, with added flavouring ingredients such as herbs, wine and lemon, for serving with pan-fried poultry, game and pork. **Serves 4**

INGREDIENTS

40 g/1½ oz butter or 2 tbsp sunflower or corn oil

dairy-free margarine or oil

40 g/1½ oz plain flour

30 g/1 oz cornflour

570 ml/1 pint White Chicken Stock (page 64) or liquid from poaching a chicken

1 bay leaf

salt and freshly ground black pepper

1 Melt the butter or heat the oil in a heavy saucepan over a medium heat.

2 Stir in the flour, using a wooden spoon, to form a thick, smooth roux. Cook for 30 seconds, stirring continuously. Remove from the heat.

3 Add a splash of the stock and stir vigorously until the roux is smooth. Add another splash of stock and stir vigorously until the roux is smooth again. Repeat this process until all the stock has been incorporated. Do not add the liquid too quickly or the sauce will become lumpy.

4 Place the pan back on a medium heat and add the bay leaf. Stirring continuously, to prevent the sauce sticking to the base of the pan, bring the sauce to the boil.

5 Reduce the heat and simmer the sauce for 1 minute to cook the flour. It should be smooth and lightly coat the back of a spoon. Add seasoning to taste.

VARIATIONS

These variations can also be made with vegetable stock or white fish stock (see page 64), in place of chicken stock, to serve with pan-fried fish or shellfish.

CHICKEN AND WHITE WINE SAUCE
Off the heat, add 4 tablespoons of wine to the roux (before the stock) and stir continuously until it is incorporated. Gradually add the stock to the mixture. When all the liquid is incorporated and the sauce is smooth, add a bay leaf and bring to the boil. Simmer for 1 minute, stirring continuously, to cook the flour and to boil off the alcohol in the wine. Serve with pan-fried or poached chicken, game birds, pork or veal.

CHICKEN AND HERB SAUCE
Add a handful of chopped tarragon and parsley to Chicken and White Wine Sauce, just before serving. Serve with pan-fried or poached chicken, game birds, pork or veal.

CHICKEN AND MUSHROOM SAUCE
Slice half an onion and a handful of button mushrooms and fry gently in 1 tablespoon of oil or butter until very soft, then add to Chicken and White Wine Sauce above. Serve with pan-fried or poached chicken, game birds, pork or veal.

CHICKEN AND LEMON SAUCE
Make as for basic chicken sauce and add 2 tablespoons of lemon juice just before serving. Season as necessary. Serve with pan-fried or poached chicken, game birds, pork or veal.

REDUCTION SAUCES

These sauces, characterized by their richly coloured, glossy appearance and syrupy consistency, are generally made in a wide, uncovered pan used to pan fry or roast meat, poultry or fish beforehand. Also referred to as pan sauces, they are served with pan-fried, roasted, baked and stewed dishes.

Much of the colour and flavour of these sauces derives from the browned juices of pan-fried and roasted food on the base of the pan. The browned juices are loosened by adding water, wine, stock or liquid used for poaching or stewing, to the pan. The liquid, coloured and flavoured by the juices, is then reduced in volume by boiling to concentrate it to a syrupy liquid that boils with large, slow-moving bubbles. As the sauce boils, fat and other impurities rise to the surface, where they can be skimmed off, clarifying and purifying the flavour of the sauce. Boiling is also an effective method for removing raw tasting alcohol in wine and spirits used to flavour pan sauces. Cream, added to pan sauces to enrich and soften their flavour, also thickens pan sauces when boiled and concentrated.

This reducing method, an ideal thickening method for dairy- and gluten-free diets, is used to improve the flavour, consistency and appearance of simple sauces such as Rich Italian Tomato Sauce (page 80), sauces that accompany stews and rich, pure concentrated pan sauces served with pan-fried meat, fish or poultry (see Red Wine Sauce with Shallots and Mushrooms page 78).

GENERAL RULES
FOR REDUCING
SAUCES

Reducing liquids takes time and to save time, pan sauces are often thickened with a flour and fat roux. Flour-thickened sauces, as a result, are often not as richly flavoured or coloured and are not as clear and pure in flavour.

- Use a wide shallow pan placed over a medium heat.
- Seasoning a liquid before reducing its volume is likely to result in over-salted, peppery sauces. Boiling off water, to thicken sauces, concentrates the remaining ingredients and any seasoning present.
- Always boil acidic and alcoholic ingredients to remove their sharp, raw flavour as this will affect the flavour of the sauce.
- Recipes may call for the sauce to be reduced by half. This means that the sauce must be boiled until only half of the original volume of liquid remains, to double its viscosity, flavour and colour.
- A recipe may specify a sauce be reduced to a syrupy consistency. This means the liquid is sufficiently viscous to cling to the back of a spoon without immediately running off. As the sauce boils and thickens the bubbles become larger and move more slowly.
- If a pan sauce becomes too thick or too strongly flavoured, add a tablespoon or two of water or stock.
- Once the sauce has reached the required consistency season it with a small quantity of salt and freshly ground black pepper.

NOTES FOR FOOD ALLERGY SUFFERERS

DAIRY-FREE DIET: Provided meat, fish, poultry and vegetables are browned, fried or roasted in oil only and cream is not added to the sauce, pan sauces are perfectly suitable for dairy-free diets.

GLUTEN-FREE DIET: Pan sauces are ideal for gluten-free diets as they are generally flour free. Flour is sometimes added to thicken pan sauces that are already richly flavoured and coloured, and when a large volume of sauce is required to cover the ingredients in stews. When a pan sauce calls for flour simply use cornflour instead. As cornflour loses it thickening properties with prolonged boiling, mix 2 teaspoons of cornflour with a tablespoon of water, per 290 ml/10 fl oz of sauce, and add to the sauce once its flavour is concentrated and rounded and the dish is ready to be served. Bring the liquid back to the boil for 1 minute, to cook the flour, and serve immediately.

Adding a small quantity of double or whipping cream to a pan sauce and boiling it until the sauce reaches thin coating consistency provides an alternative method for enriching the flavour and thickening the consistency of pan sauces.

EGG-FREE DIET: Pan sauces rarely contain egg.

NUT-FREE DIET: Pan sauces are safe for nut-free diets provided the oil used to cook the ingredients to make the sauce is nut-free.

SOYA-FREE DIET: Pan sauces are safe for soya-free diets provided the oil used to cook the ingredients is soya-free.

Making cream sauces

- Use whipping cream, double cream or full fat crème fraiche for thickening pan sauces. Half-fat cream products and single cream curdle when boiled as they do not contain enough fat to emulsify with the sauce.
- Add cream to a sauce once it has reached the required concentration of flavour.
- Cream is likely to curdle when added to sauces that contain raw alcohol, vinegar or lemon juice. Always boil them well before adding cream.
- Once cream is added to a sauce and boiled, it will thicken very quickly. If the sauce becomes too thick and oily around the edge of the pan, stir in two or three tablespoons of water.
- Once the sauce has reached the required consistency, season with a small quantity of salt and freshly ground black pepper. Taste and season again as necessary.

RED WINE SAUCE WITH SHALLOTS AND MUSHROOMS

This deliciously rich sauce is suitable for gluten-, dairy-, egg-, nut- and soya-free diets. It improves in both flavour and colour when it is added to the browned cooking juices on the base of a pan used for frying meat. **Serves 4**

INGREDIENTS

2 tbsp sunflower or corn oil

1 tsp butter

● **DAIRY** omit for dairy-free diet

2 shallots, thinly sliced

110 g/4 oz button mushrooms, finely sliced

salt and freshly ground black pepper

200 ml/7 fl oz red wine

290 ml/10 fl oz chicken or beef stock

1 sprig fresh thyme

1 Heat the oil and butter in a heavy saucepan, add the shallots and mushrooms, season with a pinch of salt and a grind of pepper, cover with a lid, and fry gently until the shallots are soft and lightly browned.

2 Add the red wine to the pan and boil for 1 minute to remove the alcohol. Then add the stock and thyme.

3 Boil the sauce over a moderate heat until it is thick and syrupy and boils with large, slow-moving bubbles. Carefully spoon off any fat and scum that collects on the surface.

4 Once the sauce has reached a syrupy consistency and lightly coats the back of a spoon, taste and season the sauce with more salt and pepper as necessary. Remove the sprig of thyme and serve as required.

VARIATIONS

PEPPERCORN SAUCE

Add 1 teaspoon of black peppercorns to the sauce with the stock and thyme at step 2. Pass the finished sauce through a sieve into a clean pan. Bring back to the boil and serve with grilled or fried steak.

REDCURRANT AND MINT SAUCE

Add 1 tablespoon of redcurrant jelly, 1 tablespoon of balsamic vinegar and one sprig of mint with the stock and thyme at step 2. Pass the finished sauce through a sieve into a clean pan. Bring back to the boil and serve with fried, grilled or roast lamb.

WHITE WINE SAUCE

Serve this light coloured, delicately flavoured sauce with poultry, fish, veal and pork. White wine sauce to accompany fish should be made with 290 ml/10 fl oz fish stock instead of 2 tablespoons of jellied stock stated in the recipe. Cream thickens and enriches the flavour of this sauce. **Serves 4**

INGREDIENTS

2 large or 4 small shallots, finely sliced

1 handful button mushrooms, finely sliced

2 tbsp sunflower or corn oil

1 tsp butter

● DAIRY   omit for dairy-free diet

150 ml/5 fl oz dry white wine

290 ml/10 fl oz water

2 tbsp jellied White Chicken Stock (page 63)

1 sprig thyme

2 tbsp whipping cream, optional

● DAIRY   omit for dairy-free diet

a squeeze of lemon juice

salt and freshly ground black pepper

1 In a small pan, covered with a lid, gently fry the shallots and mushrooms in the oil and butter (if using) until very soft. Do not allow them to brown.

2 Transfer the vegetables to a frying pan, stir in the wine and half the water and boil for 2 minutes.

3 Add the jellied stock, the remaining water and thyme. Reduce the sauce over a moderate heat until it thickens to a syrupy consistency. Carefully spoon off any fat that collects on the surface.

4 Add the cream (if using), boil for 1 minute and add the lemon juice. Taste and season as necessary. Remove the sprig of thyme and serve as required.

VARIATIONS

WHITE WINE AND TARRAGON SAUCE

Add a tablespoon of finely chopped tarragon to the finished sauce. Heat the tarragon through and serve before it loses its fresh colour.

LEMON SAUCE

For a rich, creamy lemon sauce to serve with fish, whisk in 3 tablespoons of whipping cream into White Wine Sauce made with 290 ml/10 fl oz fish stock. Boil the sauce for 1 minute to return it to a syrupy consistency and add another squeeze of lemon juice. Taste and season as necessary and serve immediately.

LEEK AND MUSTARD SAUCE

Gently fry 2 finely sliced leeks in the place of the shallots and mushrooms and continue as for the recipe above. For a sauce enriched with cream, whisk 1 heaped teaspoon of Dijon mustard into the finished sauce, taste and season as necessary. For a sauce made without cream, use a level teaspoon of Dijon mustard so the sauce is not too sharp. Serve with poultry, pork and firm white fish.

PURÉED VEGETABLE SAUCES

Puréed sauces are made by cooking vegetables until soft and puréeing them until smooth. Such sauces are often richly flavoured and coloured and are served with pasta, meat, fish and vegetables.

RICH ITALIAN TOMATO SAUCE

This rich tomato sauce is great on pasta and pizza bases and served with fish, poultry and vegetables. **Serves 4**

INGREDIENTS

1 large onion, finely diced

3 tbsp olive oil

salt and freshly ground black pepper

1 garlic clove, finely chopped

2 x 400 g cans chopped tomatoes

1 bay leaf

1 sprig thyme

2–3 parsley stalks

1 large pinch caster sugar

1 Place the onion in a heavy saucepan with the olive oil. Season with salt and pepper, cover with the lid and fry gently, over a low heat, until the onion is very soft but not coloured.

2 Add the garlic and stir over a medium heat for 1 minute.

3 Add the tomatoes, herbs and sugar and bring to a simmer. Simmer the sauce with the lid off for 20 minutes.

4 Remove the herbs and liquidize until smooth. Pass the sauce through a sieve back into the pan and bring back to a simmer. Taste and add more seasoning as necessary. Use as required.

VARIATIONS

TOMATO AND HERB SAUCE
Add 1 tablespoon of chopped fresh herbs such as basil, oregano or parsley to the sauce just before serving to conserve their fresh flavour and colour. Serve with pasta, poultry, fish and vegetables such as pan-fried courgettes and aubergines.

TOMATO SAUCE WITH CAPERS AND BLACK OLIVES
Add 2 teaspoons of rinsed and drained capers (preferably capers preserved in salt) and 1 tablespoon stoned, roughly chopped black olives in the last 5 minutes of cooking. Serve with grilled fish and pasta.

TOMATO SAUCE WITH BACON
Gently fry 110 g/4 oz finely chopped, smoked streaky bacon with the onion. When the onion is soft, remove the lid and stir over a moderate heat until the onions and bacon are lightly browned. Continue as from step 2 of Rich Italian Tomato Sauce. Serve with pasta.

DAIRY-FREE DIET: Puréed vegetable sauces are suitable for dairy-free diets provided olive oil or a neutral flavoured oil, and not butter, is used to soften onions, carrots and any other aromatic vegetables flavouring the sauce.

GLUTEN-FREE DIET: Puréed sauces are made with vegetables that soften when cooked and have the ability to thicken liquids when puréed. As a result, flour is not required in puréed sauces.

EGG-FREE DIET: Egg is not used in puréed vegetables sauces.

SOYA-FREE DIET: Use butter, olive oil or a neutral flavoured oil that does not contain soya bean oil to soften the vegetables.

NUT-FREE DIET: Use butter, olive oil or a neutral flavoured oil that does not contain nut oils to soften the vegetables.

EMULSION SAUCES

Emulsion sauces include piquant French Salad Dressing and rich creamy Mayonnaise. Both sauces are thickened by forming an emulsion between oil and vinegar or lemon juice. Salad dressings quickly separate back into vinegar and oil when left to stand. Mayonnaise contains egg yolk which acts as an emulsifier, holding the oil droplets and water-based ingredients in a stable emulsion that remains thick and creamy.

FRENCH SALAD DRESSING

This is the perfect light dressing for prepared salads. **Serves 4**

INGREDIENTS

1 tbsp white or red wine vinegar

salt and freshly ground black pepper

2 tbsp neutral flavoured oil such as sunflower, corn or grapeseed oil

2 tbsp extra virgin olive oil

1 Spoon the vinegar into a bowl and add a teaspoon of salt and four grinds of pepper.

2 Whisk the vinegar until the salt has dissolved and whisk in the vegetable and olive oil a tablespoon at a time to emulsify and thicken the dressing.

3 Taste and add more seasoning as necessary. Serve immediately.

VARIATION
MUSTARD DRESSING

Add 1 teaspoon of Dijon mustard to the vinegar at step 1 and continue making the dressing as above. This dressing is thicker than simple French Dressing as the mustard is a good emulsifier.

DAIRY-FREE DIET: Basic French Salad Dressing (page 81) and Mayonnaise (opposite) are dairy free. Avoid salad dressings that are enriched and thickened with cream. Mayonnaise provides a good rich, creamy dairy-free base for cold sauces and dips (see page 84).

GLUTEN-FREE DIET: Although bought salad dressings and mayonnaise often contain wheat flour to thicken and stabilize them, their homemade equivalents are suitable for gluten-free diets.

EGG-FREE DIET: Although French Salad Dressing (page 81) is suitable for egg-free diets, mayonnaise is not, as egg yolk is a core ingredient. Egg-free alternatives to mayonnaise include rich and creamy

Horseradish Cream and Mustard Cream Dressing (see page 85) or ready-made egg-free mayonnaise, available from health food shops.

NUT-FREE DIET: Avoid salad dressings made with nut oils and use olive oil or nut-free neutral flavoured oils to make homemade French dressing. Mayonnaise is made with neutral flavoured oil or a half and half mixture of neutral oil and olive oil. Olive oil used alone prevents the mayonnaise from emulsifying properly.

SOYA-FREE DIET: Avoid using neutral flavoured oils that contain soya bean oil when making salad dressings and mayonnaise.

MAKING MAYONNAISE

Homemade mayonnaise is thick, yellow, glossy and bears little resemblance to manufactured mayonnaise. It is greatly superior in flavour and is not hard to make, provided a few basic rules are followed.

Homemade mayonnaise is free of gluten, dairy products and nut oils but cannot be made without egg yolk, which forms a stable emulsion between the oil, vinegar and lemon juice. The egg yolk also helps to form the creamy consistency and rich flavour. However, mayonnaise can be substituted successfully with egg-free thick natural yogurt, soured cream or dairy-free natural soya yogurt in dips and sauces.

- Mayonnaise is made with raw egg yolks that could contain salmonella bacteria. To reduce the risk of food poisoning, use very fresh eggs and store homemade mayonnaise in the fridge for no more than 2 days. It is also best to avoid serving homemade mayonnaise to pregnant women, small children or the very old, as they are most at risk of contracting salmonella poisoning.
- Make mayonnaise with ingredients that are at room temperature.
- As mayonnaise is delicately flavoured it is easy to over-flavour with lemon juice, vinegar and seasoning. As the mayonnaise is being made, taste it before adding the full quantity of these ingredients. If the mayonnaise tastes too acidic use water instead of more vinegar and lemon juice. Add half a pinch of salt and a grind of pepper at a time to avoid over-seasoning.

MAYONNAISE

The delicate flavour of mayonnaise is delicious as it is, or flavoured with other ingredients (see Mayonnaise-based Dips and Sauces page 84). Serve with chips, cold seafood or chicken or poached salmon, with salads and spread in sandwiches. Mayonnaise is not suitable for egg-free diets. **Makes 290 ml/10 fl oz, to serve 4–6**

INGREDIENTS

2 large egg yolks, at room temperature

½ tsp salt and freshly ground black pepper

½ tsp Dijon mustard

1 tbsp white wine vinegar

290 ml/10 fl oz sunflower or corn oil or half olive oil, half vegetable oil

a squeeze of lemon juice

1 Put the egg yolks, a pinch of salt, two grinds of pepper, the mustard and half the vinegar into the bowl and beat with a wooden spoon.

2 To incorporate oil into the egg mixture, without it curdling, add the oil very slowly at first, drop by drop, from the prongs of a fork. Stir vigorously after each addition of oil until it can no longer be seen on the surface or around the sides of the bowl. Continue in this way until the mayonnaise mixture begins to thicken. This stage should take about 5 minutes. (Do not add the oil too quickly or the mayonnaise will curdle.)

3 As the mayonnaise begins to thicken, start to add the oil a teaspoon at a time, beating the mixture continuously.

4 When half of the oil is incorporated add a teaspoon of the remaining vinegar to prevent the mayonnaise curdling or becoming too oily.

5 Continue adding the oil a tablespoon at a time, beating well in between. If the mayonnaise starts to look greasy, taste it and depending on its flavour add the remaining vinegar or a teaspoon of water.

6 Once all the oil is incorporated, the mayonnaise should be glossy and thick enough to hold its own shape. Taste. If the mayonnaise is bland, stir in a squeeze of lemon and a little more seasoning. Use as required or cover and store in the fridge for up to two days.

MAYONNAISE-BASED DIPS AND SAUCES

The recipe for mayonnaise provides a gluten-, dairy-, nut- and soya-free rich and creamy base for a wide variety of sauces and dips. For egg-free diets, substitute mayonnaise with soured cream, plain Greek yogurt or soya yogurt. As the following sauces and dips contain mayonnaise they must be eaten fresh or kept for no longer than 2 days in the fridge to reduce the risk of salmonella poisoning.

GARLIC MAYONNAISE
Follow the main recipe for Mayonnaise, stirring 2 finely crushed garlic cloves into the finished recipe. Serve as a dipping sauce with crudités, cold cooked prawns, deep-fried battered or breaded vegetables, chicken or fish.

TARTARE SAUCE
Stir 1 teaspoon of Dijon mustard, 2 teaspoons of finely chopped onion, 2 finely chopped pickled gherkins, 2 teaspoons of rinsed and drained capers and 1 teaspoon each of finely chopped parsley and finely chopped tarragon into 290 ml/10 fl oz of mayonnaise. Taste, and season as necessary with salt and black pepper. Serve with fish.

ANCHOVY MAYONNAISE
Stir 2 finely crushed garlic cloves, 6 anchovy fillets, mashed with a fork, and 1 tablespoon of lemon juice into 290 ml/10 fl oz of mayonnaise. Serve with steamed asparagus spears, warm or cold poached or grilled fish, shellfish and chicken.

CURRIED MAYONNAISE
Stir 1 finely crushed garlic clove, 1 teaspoon Madras curry powder (for gluten-free diets check for wheat flour in the curry powder), 1 tablespoon lemon juice, 2 teaspoons mango chutney (check label for nuts), salt and pepper into 290 ml/10 fl oz mayonnaise. Serve with cold chicken, sliced raw vegetables, new potatoes, crisps or bread sticks.

AVOCADO AND WATERCRESS DIP

This light green, creamy and slightly peppery sauce is wonderful served with cold poached salmon and new potatoes or as a dip for sliced raw vegetables, slices of toasted pitta bread or tortilla chips. **Serves 4 as a sauce and 6 as a dip**

INGREDIENTS

1 large handful watercress

flesh of 1 avocado

1 tbsp lemon juice

1 garlic clove, crushed

salt and freshly ground black pepper

150 ml/5 fl oz mayonnaise

● EGG ▶ soured cream

1 Boil some water in a small pan, add the watercress and boil for 30 seconds, then place immediately under cold running water until cold.

2 Blend the cooked watercress, avocado, lemon juice, crushed garlic and seasoning together until smooth.

3 Stir in the mayonnaise (or soured cream) and taste. If necessary, season with a little more salt, pepper and lemon juice.

4 Serve or store covered in the fridge for up to 4 hours. If kept for longer the avocado in the sauce will discolour.

HORSERADISH CREAM

This is not suitable for dairy-free diets. Sweet but sharp horseradish cream is an interesting and delicious egg-free alternative to mayonnaise to accompany cold fish and meat. **Serves 4**

INGREDIENTS

150 ml/5 fl oz fresh whipping cream

2 tsp prepared or freshly grated horseradish

2 tsp white wine vinegar

1 tsp Dijon mustard

1 tsp caster sugar

salt and freshly ground black pepper

1 Place all the ingredients in a bowl and whisk together until the cream just holds its shape. Do not over-whip or the sauce will curdle.

2 To thin the sauce down to double-cream consistency for salad dressing, add 2 tablespoons of cold water and whisk.

MUSTARD CREAM DRESSING

This is not suitable for dairy-free diets. This sauce can either be served thick, as an egg-free alternative to mayonnaise, or thinned with water to the consistency of double cream and used as a creamy salad dressing. **Serves 4 as a sauce and 6 as dressing**

INGREDIENTS

290 ml/10 fl oz whipping cream

4 tsp Dijon mustard

2 tsp caster sugar

salt and freshly ground black pepper

Place all the ingredients in the bowl and whisk together until the cream just holds its shape. Do not over-whip or the sauce will curdle. If the sauce becomes too thick, stir in a tablespoon of water at a time, to thin it to the required consistency.

Chapter 10 | FRYING

Frying – cooking food in hot oil – is a method mainly used to cook delicate or tender foods quickly before they become tough and dry. There are three main methods of frying: pan-frying, stir-frying and deep-frying.

PAN-FRYING

Pan-frying is a method used to cook thin portions, slices, strips and diced tender meat, poultry, fish, vegetables and fruit in a small quantity of hot oil. Pan-frying is also used to cook, brown and crisp the surface of minced and shaped foods such as sausages, burgers and fish cakes. Larger or tougher cuts of meat, whole fish and whole or jointed birds are also pan-fried over a high heat to brown them before stewing, braising, poaching, roasting or baking, to add colour and a rich flavour to the finished dish.

OILS AND FATS USED FOR PAN-FRYING

Both neutral flavoured oils, which tend to be stable at high temperatures, and more flavoursome but less heat-stable fats and oils, are used for pan-frying. Neutral flavoured oils are used where the flavour of oil is unwanted. The best neutral flavoured oils for frying are sunflower oil, safflower oil, rapeseed oil, corn oil and vegetable oil (note: this may contain soya bean oil or groundnut oil).

Fats and oils with flavour are used to add depth and complexity to a dish. Flavourful fats and oils used for pan-frying include butter, beef dripping, bacon fat, olive oil, sesame oil and nut oils. Because flavourful oils and fats tend to burn at temperatures too low to fry effectively, they are usually mixed with an equal quantity of a neutral flavoured oil to increase their stability at high temperatures. Pure beef dripping is an exception – it can be used alone for frying and is ideal for browning beef for stewing. Butter and olive oil can be used on their own, but only to fry delicate foods that require very gentle frying or very little browning.

GENERAL RULES FOR PAN-FRYING AND BROWNING

- Use a wide, shallow, heavy-bottomed pan.
- The oil should be hot enough to make the food sizzle as it is added to the pan. If the oil is too cool the food is liable to boil in its own juices and over-cook before it is browned properly.
- When butter is added to oil, the oil is hot enough for frying and browning when the butter starts to foam.
- Season food with salt and pepper just before frying. Salting food too early will draw the juices out of it, making the surface wet and difficult to brown.
- Do not overcrowd the pan as the oil will cool down causing the food to boil in its own juices and not brown.
- Meat, poultry and fish tend to stick to the base of the pan in the initial stages of pan-frying. Providing the oil is sufficiently hot the food will release itself when it is fully browned after 2–5 minutes. Do not attempt to prise the meat, fish or poultry off

the base of the pan as you will break the surface of the food. Turn the food once it has released itself.

- Do not cover frying food with a lid or the resulting steam will cause it to boil, toughen and fail to brown.
- Once the food is evenly browned on all sides and cooked to your requirements remove from the pan to prevent it cooking further. Keep it warm in a low oven while any remaining food is fried or a pan sauce is prepared.
- When you are frying a large volume of food, fry the food in batches. Loosen the browned cooking juices after frying each batch to prevent a build-up of juices on the base of the pan, as they are likely to burn with prolonged cooking and affect the flavour of your food.
- Tender strips or dice of meat, poultry or fish should be no less than 2.5 cm/1 inch thick and uniform in size so that they brown and cook at the same rate and remain moist in the centre. Smaller pieces will over-cook and toughen.

NOTES FOR FOOD ALLERGY SUFFERERS

DAIRY-FREE DIET: Butter used in fried savoury dishes can be replaced with olive oil or neutral flavoured oil. However, when butter is used to flavour sweet dishes it is not so easily substituted, as the dish tastes oily made with oil or dairy-free margarine.

Be aware that ghee is often used to fry food in Indian dishes. Ghee, or clarified butter, is made by removing the milk proteins in melted butter to leave pure butter fat, which has a rich, buttery flavour and is stable at high temperatures. Although the flavour of the dish will not be so rich, replace ghee with an equal quantity of a suitable frying oil such as vegetable or sunflower oil.

GLUTEN-FREE DIET: Although all oils and fats are suitable for gluten-free diets, meat, fish, poultry and vegetables are sometimes coated in seasoned flour or egg and breadcrumbs before pan-frying. Meat and poultry are also often coated in flour and browned before stewing, to add colour, flavour and to thicken the stew. In place of wheat flour, use cornflour.

NUT-FREE DIET: Groundnut or peanut oil is often used in Asian cooking for frying at high temperatures. Replace with a suitable neutral oil such as sunflower or corn oil. Read the label before using vegetable oil as it sometimes contains groundnut oil (peanut oil). Also be aware that seed oils such as sunflower, safflower and sesame oil sometimes do not suit people with nut allergies.

Nut oils such as walnut and hazelnut are sometimes added to neutral oils to add their characteristic flavour to pan-fried dishes. Instead, use a neutral flavoured oil only or flavour the oil with butter or olive oil instead. The shortfall in flavour can be made up using more strongly flavoured ingredients such as garlic, ginger and coriander.

SOYA-FREE DIET: Vegetable oil usually consists of a blend of soya bean oil and other vegetable oils. Current regulations do not require manufacturers to list soya bean oil on the ingredients list as it is believed to be totally safe for people with soya allergies. This is because the protein that causes soya allergy is filtered out of the oil during processing. You may still choose to use alternative neutral flavoured oils instead such as sunflower oil, rapeseed oil or corn oil

CRISPY FILLET OF SEA BASS

A simple and delicious way to cook sea bass, this method is also suitable for other firm-fleshed white fish such as cod, haddock, turbot and halibut, and oily fish such as salmon and mackerel. Serve with boiled new potatoes tossed in olive oil and sea salt or Oven Baked Chips (page 136) and steamed fine green beans. **Serves 4**

INGREDIENTS

2 tbsp olive oil

4 sea bass fillets, with skin intact and scaled

salt and freshly ground black pepper

4 lemon wedges

1 Heat the olive oil in a heavy-bottomed frying pan. Season the skin of each fillet and place skin side down in the pan. The oil should sizzle when the fish is added to the pan. If it is not hot enough wait for a few moments before trying again.

2 As the fish starts to fry, the skin will stick to the base of the pan. Do not attempt to loosen it as this will damage the skin or break up the fillet. Fry the fish over a moderate heat. As the skin becomes crisp and brown it will free itself from the bottom of the pan.

3 Turn the fish and fry for 1 minute on the flesh side. The fish is cooked when the flesh feels firm, but remains slightly translucent in the thickest part of the fillet.

4 Serve the fish immediately, skin side up, and garnished with a lemon wedge.

SALMON FISH CAKES WITH TARTARE SAUCE AND LEMON

Fish cakes are great for a starter or an informal meal. They are also easily adapted to suit egg-free, gluten-free and dairy-free diets. If eggs are off limits, serve these fish cakes with Parsley Sauce (page 74). **Serves 4**

INGREDIENTS

400 g/14 oz peeled potatoes, diced

450 g/1 lb salmon fillet with the skin left on

570 ml/1 pint milk

● **DAIRY** soya milk

1 bay leaf

2 slices onion

salt and freshly ground black pepper

30 g/1 oz butter

● **DAIRY** 2 tbsp olive oil

1 egg, beaten

● **EGG** 1 tbsp poaching milk and 1 tbsp breadcrumbs

2 finely sliced spring onions

½ tbsp each chopped dill, parsley and tarragon

140 g/5 oz dried white breadcrumbs

● **GLUTEN** gluten-free breadcrumbs

4 tbsp sunflower or corn oil for frying

TO SERVE

Tartare Sauce (page 84)

4 lemon wedges

1 Simmer the potatoes in boiling salted water for 20 minutes, or until tender.

2 Place the salmon skin side down in a frying pan. Pour the milk over the fillets. If the fillets are exposed, add extra milk or water to cover. Add the bay leaf, sliced onion and seasoning. Bring the milk slowly to a simmer and gently poach the fish for about 10 minutes, or until it is just cooked. Reserve the poaching liquid, and allow the fish to cool.

3 Meanwhile, mash the potatoes with 100 ml/3½ fl oz of the poaching milk and the butter or olive oil.

4 Separate the flakes of salmon and mix with the mashed potatoes, the egg (or for egg-free fishcakes, the milk and breadcrumbs), spring onions and herbs. The consistency should be soft but firm enough to hold its shape. Add one or two tablespoons of poaching milk if the mixture is too stiff. Taste and add more seasoning if necessary.

5 Wet your hands to prevent the mixture sticking to them and shape the mixture into 8 round, flat cakes no more than 2.5 cm/1 inch thick.

6 Press the fish cakes into the bread-crumbs and brush off any loose crumbs.

7 Heat the oil in the frying pan over a moderate heat. When the oil is hot, place 4 fish cakes at a time into the pan and fry until golden brown on both sides. Remove from the pan and keep warm in a low oven while the remaining fish cakes are cooked.

8 Place two fish cakes in the centre of each plate with a lemon wedge. Serve the Tartare sauce separately in a bowl.

DUCK BREASTS WITH BRAISED LENTILS

These richly flavoured braised lentils are an interesting hearty accompaniment to duck, other game, chicken, pork and pan-fried white fish. Duck breasts have a thick layer of fat below the skin and do not require any additional cooking oil or fat for pan-frying. This dish is delicious served with Mashed Potatoes (page 136) and steamed green vegetables. **Serves 4**

INGREDIENTS

4 duck breasts, skin on

FOR THE SAUCE

3 tsp plain flour

cornflour

● GLUTEN

100 ml/3½ fl oz red wine

290 ml/10 fl oz chicken stock

1 sprig thyme

salt and freshly ground black pepper

FOR THE LENTILS

1 tbsp sunflower or corn oil

4 rashers smoked streaky bacon, rind removed and cut across into thin strips

1 onion, cut into small dice

1 carrot, finely diced

1 celery stick, finely diced

2 sprigs thyme

salt and freshly ground black pepper

1 large garlic clove, finely chopped

200 g/7 oz Puy lentils

2 bay leaves

100 ml/3½ fl oz red wine

570 ml/1 pint rich stock, made with 290 ml/10 fl oz jellied White Chicken Stock (page 64) and 290 ml/10 fl oz water

1 Heat the oil in a medium-sized saucepan, add the bacon, onion, carrot, celery, thyme and a little seasoning, cover with a lid, and fry gently until very soft and sweet, about 20–30 minutes.

2 Add the garlic and cook for another 30 seconds, stirring continuously. Add the lentils, bay leaves, red wine and stock. The lentils should be covered by an inch of liquid, so top up with a little water if necessary. Bring to a simmer over a moderate heat and simmer, uncovered, for approximately 30–45 minutes until tender. Spoon off any fat or scum that collects on the surface and, if necessary, top up with water so the lentils remain covered.

3 Meanwhile, prepare the duck breasts. With a small sharp knife, score through the fatty skin, with diagonal cuts 1.25 cm/½ inch apart and then again in the opposite direction to form a diamond pattern. Take care not to cut into the meat below.

4 Sprinkle the skin with salt and rub into the scored fat. This helps to draw the water out of the duck fat and encourages the skin to become crisp and golden brown.

5 Place a dry heavy-bottomed frying pan over a medium heat. When the pan is hot enough to make the duck breasts sizzle, place them well apart, skin side down, on the base of the pan. Fry the breasts gently until the fat under the skin

has melted into the pan and the skin is brown and crisp.

6 After approximately 10 minutes the duck skin should be crisp and golden brown. Lightly season the skin with salt and pepper before turning the duck breasts over.

7 Gently brown the lean side for 8 minutes, by which time the duck breasts should be cooked medium rare (moist and rosy pink in the centre). If the duck breasts are well browned but still very rare in the centre, fry very gently for another minute or so on both sides. Place the duck breasts in a low oven while you repeat the process with the remaining two.

8 Once all the duck breasts are cooked, tip out the fat and place the pan back on a moderate heat. Stir in the flour and slowly add the wine to form a smooth sauce. Pour in the chicken stock, add the thyme and loosen the browned cooking juices on the bottom of the pan with a wooden spoon. Boil the sauce until it is reduced by half or evenly coats the back of a spoon. Remove the sprig of thyme, taste and season as necessary. Keep warm over a low heat.

9 Once the lentils are cooked, taste and season as necessary.

10 To serve, place a spoonful of lentils in the centre of the plate, cut the duck breast in thick slices, on the diagonal, and arrange on top. Spoon over the sauce and serve immediately.

BEEF BURGERS WITH TOMATO AND CORN SALSA

Homemade beef burgers make a delicious, nutritious and popular lunch for children or the whole family. Place the cooked burgers in soft, warmed buns (see gluten-free rolls page 186) with the salsa, bought or homemade Mayonnaise (page 83) and cos lettuce. **Makes about 8 burgers**

FOR THE BURGERS

675 g/1½ lb good quality lean, minced beef

½ an onion, finely diced

2 tsp dried mixed herbs

3 tsp Worcestershire sauce

● GLUTEN   omit as it contains gluten

1 tsp salt and freshly ground black pepper

sunflower or corn oil for frying

FOR THE TOMATO AND CORN SALSA

2 tbsp cooked or canned sweetcorn

4 ripe tomatoes, seeded and diced

½ small red onion, finely diced

1 tbsp freshly chopped coriander leaves

1 tbsp freshly squeezed lime juice

½ tsp salt and 3 grinds black pepper

1 Stir all the salsa ingredients together in a bowl until thoroughly mixed. Cover with clingfilm and store in the fridge. The salsa has a better flavour if made a few hours or a day before serving. Remove from the fridge 30 minutes before serving as it tastes best at room temperature.

2 Preheat the oven to 120°C/250°F/ gas mark ½.

3 Combine all the burger ingredients together in a bowl until well mixed. To test the burgers for flavour, fry a spoonful of the mixture in a little oil until cooked through, then taste. Add more seasoning and Worcestershire sauce as necessary.

4 With wet hands, shape the mixture into 8 flat rounds 2 cm/¾ inch thick, with a circumference roughly the same as the buns.

5 Heat 3 tablespoons of oil in a large frying pan over a medium heat. When the oil is hot enough to make a spoonful of the mixture sizzle, place the burgers in the pan. Do not overcrowd the pan – cook in two batches if necessary.

6 Brown for approximately 2–2½ minutes each side for rare to medium-rare burgers and 3–4 minutes for medium to well done.

7 As the burgers are cooking, warm the buns in the preheated oven on a baking tray.

8 To serve, split the warmed rolls in half, spread generously with mayonnaise (if using), arrange some lettuce on top, place the burgers on the lettuce, spoon some corn and tomato salsa over each burger and cover with the top half of the buns.

FILLET STEAK WITH RED WINE SAUCE

This recipe uses fillet steak but sirloin or rump are just as suitable. Ask the butcher to cut fillet steak into 4-cm/1½-inch-thick portions so that they can be fried to a deep brown on the outside and remain pink, moist and tender in the centre. **Serves 4**

FOR THE SAUCE

1 quantity Red Wine Sauce with Shallots and Mushrooms (page 78)

FOR THE STEAK

4 x 4-cm/1½-inch-thick fillet steaks, at room temperature

2 tbsp sunflower or corn oil

30 g/1 oz butter or 1 extra tbsp oil

salt and freshly ground black pepper

1 Lightly season the steaks on both sides.

2 Heat the oil and butter in a heavy-bottomed frying pan over a high heat. When the butter starts to foam, add the steak to the pan. (For rare, or blue, steak use oil only as it can be heated to a higher temperature for rapid browning.) Do not overcrowd the pan.

3 As the steak starts to fry it sticks to the bottom of the pan. Do not attempt to loosen the steak as this will prevent it browning. As the steak browns it will gradually free itself. When it does, turn it and brown the other side. Fillet steak should ideally be served rare to medium-rare, to take full advantage of its meltingly tender qualities. If you prefer it 'medium' or 'well done' see box below. Keep the steaks warm in an oven set at its lowest temperature, while the sauce is finished.

4 Pour any remaining oil out of the pan, pour in the sauce and bring to the boil, scraping the base of the pan to loosen the browned steak juices. Spoon the sauce over the steaks and serve immediately.

COOKING FILLET STEAK

BLUE
• Fry for 1½–2 minutes per side. The meat will be hot but feel soft and slightly flabby.

RARE
• Fry for 2–3 minutes per side. Rare steak feels soft and gives easily when pressed.

MEDIUM
• Fry for 3–3½ minutes per side. Medium rare steak feels firmer and gives a little under the fingers when pressed.

WELL DONE
• Fry for 4–5 minutes per side. Well-done steak is firm and does not give when pressed.

Sirloin and rump steak
These steaks are slightly tougher than fillet steak so are usually eaten in thinner slices; reduce the cooking times given above by 30 seconds on each side.

HOMEMADE PORK AND APPLE SAUSAGES WITH RICH ONION GRAVY

Unlike many bought varieties, these sausages are egg-, dairy-, nut- and soya-free. They can also be easily adaped for gluten-free diets. **Makes 8 sausages**

FOR THE SAUSAGES

450 g/1 lb minced pork belly

½ an onion, very finely diced

½ Granny Smith apple, peeled, quartered, cored and coarsely grated

2 tbsp fine white breadcrumbs

● GLUTEN gluten-free breadcrumbs

1 tbsp finely chopped leaves of fresh thyme, sage and curly parsley

½ garlic clove, crushed

1 tsp salt and 5 grinds freshly ground black pepper

sunflower or corn oil for frying

FOR THE ONION GRAVY

1 tbsp sunflower or corn oil

½ an onion, finely sliced

salt and freshly ground black pepper

2 tsp plain flour

● GLUTEN cornflour

290 ml/10 fl oz Brown Chicken Stock (page 64)

1 tbsp red wine

1 sprig fresh thyme

1 Preheat the oven to its lowest setting.

2 Place all the sausagemeat ingredients, except for the oil, in a bowl and mix together thoroughly with your hands.

3 Divide the sausagemeat into four and, with wet hands, shape the quartered

mixture into 8 even-sized sausages no thicker than 2.5 cm/1 inch. (If the sausages are thicker they may start to dry out and crumble before the centre is properly cooked.)

4 Gently fry the sausages in hot oil, turning them frequently until they are cooked through and golden brown all over, about 15 minutes. Do not overcrowd the pan as the sausages will be hard to turn and may fall apart. If the sausages stick to the base of the pan, allow them to release themselves or they may break as you try to loosen them.

5 Transfer the cooked sausages to a baking tray and keep warm in the oven while you make the sauce.

6 Tip out all except 1 tablespoon of hot fat from the frying pan, add the sliced onion and some seasoning, cover and fry gently, until very soft. Remove the lid and continue to fry the onion, stirring continuously, until golden brown.

7 Stir the flour into the onion and gently cook for another 30 seconds.

8 Remove the pan from the heat and gradually stir in the stock and wine, to make a smooth sauce. Add the thyme and simmer over a moderate heat until the sauce is thick enough to thinly coat the back of a spoon. Taste and season as necessary.

9 To serve, place the sausages on warm plates and spoon over the onion gravy.

STIR-FRYING

This frying method is commonly used in Asian cookery. Shellfish, crisp vegetables, firm fish, tender poultry and meat, noodles or rice are quickly fried in a few tablespoons of oil over a very high heat until just cooked through. To prevent food from sticking or cooking unevenly it is stirred continuously with a wooden spoon. Although a large frying pan is perfectly suitable for stir-frying, a wok is traditionally used as its narrow base and high, rounded sides allow the flames to hug the sides of the pan. This allows the food to cook on the sides and base as it is stirred. The high sides also help to prevent food escaping as it is stirred.

Stir-frying is not suitable for food that easily falls apart when cooked such as potatoes and many varieties of fish. Prawns are ideal for stir-frying and the most suitable fish include firm-fleshed fish such as tuna and monkfish. The best poultry and meats for stir-frying include chicken or turkey breast, and pork or beef fillet.

GENERAL RULES FOR STIR-FRYING

- Use a wok or large frying pan so that the frying food can be stirred and tossed around.
- Make sure the oil is almost smoking before adding your ingredients. The ingredients should sizzle noisily when they are added to the pan.
- Ingredients must be added to the wok in a particular order so they are just cooked through when served. First add the ingredients that require longer or thorough cooking, such as hard vegetables and meat, poultry and fish. Once the first batch of ingredients is heated through, add more delicate ingredients such as garlic, ginger and vegetables that are more likely to wilt or burn in the hot oil if cooked for too long. Cooked noodles and rice are added last to briefly warm them through, as they break up when over-cooked.
- When the ingredients are almost cooked, water, stock, soy sauce and other flavouring ingredients are added to the pan to make a sauce. Cornflour is often added to a stir-fry sauce to thicken it to a syrupy consistency just before serving.

NOTES FOR FOOD ALLERGY SUFFERERS

DAIRY-FREE DIET: Stir-fries rarely contain dairy products.

GLUTEN-FREE DIET: Soy sauce and wheat noodles contain gluten. Replace soy sauce with Tamari sauce which is wheat free and wheat noodles with rice noodles.

EGG-FREE DIET: Egg is sometimes added to stir-fried dishes but can be easily omitted from a recipe.

NUT-FREE DIET: Groundnut or peanut oil is often used for stir-frying. Vegetable oil may also contain groundnut oil so always read the label. Seed oils including sunflower, safflower and sesame oil are also sometimes not suitable for people with nut allergies. Replace these oils with another suitable neutral oil such as rapeseed or corn oil.

SOYA-FREE DIET: Vegetable oil either comprises 100 per cent soya bean oil or a blend of vegetable oils. Other suitable oils include sunflower oil or rapeseed oil.

Soy sauce or Tamari sauce, often used to add a salty sweet flavour to stir-fries, can be replaced to a certain degree with salt, dark brown sugar, stock and thorough browning (see page 58).

SINGAPORE STIR-FRIED NOODLES

Once the ingredients are prepared this dish does not take long to cook. It is delicious served on its own or with stir-fried greens. **Serves 4**

INGREDIENTS

320 g/11 oz fine egg and wheat noodles

● EGG rice noodles

● GLUTEN rice noodles

4 tbsp sunflower or corn oil

110 g/4 oz smoked streaky bacon rashers, cut across into thin strips

110 g/4 oz shiitake mushrooms, finely sliced

110 g/4 oz cooked chicken or pork, sliced into thin strips

110 g/4 oz peeled prawns

2 large garlic cloves, finely chopped

1 tbsp finely chopped ginger

1 tbsp Madras curry powder

● GLUTEN check label for wheat

1 tbsp caster sugar

1 or 2 fresh red chillies, seeded and finely sliced lengthways into strips

1 celery stick, finely chopped

110 g/4 oz beansprouts (soya sprouts)

● SOYA mung beansprouts or omit and use 1 more celery stick for crunch

2 tbsp soy sauce

● GLUTEN Tamari sauce

● SOYA 1 tsp salt, 2 tsp dark brown sugar and 2 tbsp Brown Chicken Stock (page 58)

2 tbsp sherry

250 ml/8 fl oz Chicken Stock (page 58)

6 spring onions, finely sliced on the diagonal

2 tbsp roughly chopped coriander leaves

1 Cook the noodles as advised on the packet. Cool under running water and toss in 2 tablespoons of the oil.

2 Heat a large frying pan or wok over a high heat and pour in the remaining 2 tablespoons of oil. When the oil is hot, add the bacon to the pan and fry until lightly browned. Add the mushrooms and chicken or pork and fry, stirring continuously, until lightly browned.

3 Add the prawns, garlic, ginger, curry powder, sugar and chilli and stir-fry for 1 minute.

4 Turn the heat down to moderate and add the celery, beansprouts, soy sauce (Tamari or salt, dark brown sugar and stock), sherry and stock. Bring the liquid ingredients to a simmer and warm the celery and beansprouts through for 30 seconds, stirring continuously.

5 Add the drained noodles and toss all the ingredients until thoroughly mixed and the noodles are heated through. Do not over-cook the noodles or they will break up.

6 Taste a little of the sauce and add salt and pepper as necessary.

7 Heap the noodles onto four plates, sprinkle with the spring onions and coriander leaves and serve immediately.

STIR-FRIED KING PRAWNS WITH GARLIC, BLACK PEPPER AND LIME

It is essential to use shell-on prawns for this wonderful recipe, as the shells provide much of the flavour. As you peel the cooked prawns the juices come off on your fingers and it is almost a sin not to lick them. However, you may want to accompany each plate of prawns with a finger bowl filled with warm water and a slice of lemon. Serves 4

INGREDIENTS

2 tbsp sunflower or corn oil

400 g/14 oz fresh, uncooked, shell-on king prawns (approximately 8 per person)

salt and finely ground black pepper

3 garlic cloves, finely chopped

juice of 2 limes

1 tsp sugar

4 wedges of lime

1 Heat the oil in a wok or large frying pan over a high heat.

2 When the oil is hot, tip the prawns into the pan and season with salt and four grinds of black pepper. Fry the prawns, stirring continuously until they are pink all over. Cook the prawns in batches and keep warm in a low oven as you cook the rest. Do not overcrowd the pan as the prawns will boil in their own juices rather than fry.

3 When all the prawns are cooked, return them to the pan and turn the heat down to moderate. Add the garlic, lime juice and sugar. Continue to fry gently, stirring continuously, for another minute.

4 Taste the cooking juices to check the seasoning and add more as necessary.

5 To serve, pile the prawns and a wedge of lime on the plates, spoon over any juices and serve immediately.

STIR-FRIED LEAFY GREENS

Stir-fried leafy greens are delicious eaten with Thai curries and other stir-fried dishes. They are also a great source of calcium, particularly for those on a dairy-free diet. As this dish is cooked extremely quickly, and it needs to be served immediately from the wok to the table, it is ideal for cooking in front of your guests. **Serves 4**

INGREDIENTS

2 tbsp sunflower or corn oil

1 garlic clove, finely sliced

2.5 cm/1 in piece root ginger, sliced into matchsticks

110 g/4 oz spinach leaves, washed and drained thoroughly

200 g/7 oz bok choy, washed and drained thoroughly

110 g/4 oz watercress, washed and drained thoroughly

4 Chinese cabbage leaves, sliced across into finger-sized strips

4 small spring onions, finely sliced on the diagonal

2 tbsp light soy sauce

Tamari sauce

½ tsp salt, 1 tsp dark brown sugar and 2 tbsp Brown Chicken Stock (page 58)

● **GLUTEN**

● **SOYA**

1 Gather, weigh and prepare all the ingredients for this recipe before you start cooking. Once you start, it is cooked in less than 2 minutes.

2 Heat the oil in the wok or frying pan over a moderate heat.

3 Gently fry the garlic and ginger for about 1 minute or until lightly browned. Garlic tastes bitter if it is allowed to brown too deeply.

4 Add the prepared leaves and toss in the pan until they are just beginning to wilt.

5 Add the spring onions and soy sauce (or Tamari, or salt, sugar and stock). Warm the onions through for 30 seconds and serve immediately. Taste and season as necessary.

VARIATION

STIR-FRIED VEGETABLES
Substitute the spinach leaves with 110 g/4 oz of one or a mixture of thinly sliced shiitake mushrooms or green pepper, trimmed fine green beans, purple sprouting broccoli, baby corn or beansprouts.

DEEP-FRYING

Deep-frying in hot oil is a speedy method for cooking small pieces or portions of tender meat, poultry, delicate white fish and vegetables. The food is cooked in neutral flavoured oil that can be heated to the high temperatures required for frying food quickly.

Deep-frying is an ideal method for delicate foods that become dry and tough with prolonged cooking, as the food is usually first coated in batter or egg and breadcrumbs, which protects it from the intense heat of the oil. The batter or breadcrumb coating forms a barrier between the hot oil and the delicate food and seals in the cooking juices, keeping the food moist and tender. The coating also becomes crisp and golden brown, providing contrast in flavour, texture and colour to the moist, uncoloured food inside.

BATTERS

Batters are made from seasoned flour mixed with liquids such as water, milk, lager or beaten egg. The lightest batters are made with self-raising flour mixed with sparkling water or lager. The water or beer lightly binds the flour grains together and activates the raising agents in the flour to produce bubbles. The bubbles produced by the raising agents and present in the liquid aerate and lighten the mixture. As the batter cooks in the hot oil, the liquid boils away, leaving a crisp golden shell around the food.

BREADCRUMB COATINGS

Breadcrumbs are used to form a crisp, deep golden crust around delicate foods such as poultry and white fish. The food is first dipped in seasoned flour, then into beaten egg and then into fresh or dried breadcrumbs. The flour prevents the egg running off the food. Egg binds the breadcrumbs to the food and sets as the food is cooked to seal in the cooking juices. The breadcrumbs become crisp and golden in the hot oil, adding texture, flavour and colour to the food.

GENERAL RULES FOR DEEP-FRYING

- Use vegetable, sunflower or corn oil for deep-frying as they can be heated to 180°C/350°F without smoking, the ideal temperature for deep-frying.
- Oil expands when it is heated so do not overfill the pan. The pan should be no more than a third full when cold.
- Heat the oil over a moderate heat to 180°C/350°F. If you do not have a thermometer, carefully lower a small piece of bread into the oil and time how long it takes to turn crisp and golden brown. If the oil has reached 180°C/350°F, the bread will turn golden brown in 40 seconds. If the bread takes longer to colour then the oil is not hot enough; if it takes less time the oil is becoming dangerously hot. To reduce the temperature of hot oil, turn off the heat source and carefully add a handful of torn bread. Remove when browned then, after a few minutes, test the temperature of the oil with another piece of bread.
- Food for deep-frying should be dry. Wet food will cause the oil to spit, which could cause burns.
- Coat food in batter or breadcrumbs just before frying or the coating will be soggy and greasy.
- Deep-fry food in small batches to prevent it sticking together and reducing the temperature of the oil. If the oil is not hot enough the food will be greasy and pale.

Safety note

Never leave a pan of hot oil unattended. If the oil becomes too hot, it will start to smoke before bursting into flames. If this happens turn off the heat and smother the flames with a fire blanket or a close-fitting pan lid. Do not pour water onto the oil as this is likely to spread the fire.

- Deep-fried food is cooked when it is crisp, golden and floats on the surface. Uncooked food contains a high proportion of water and sinks to the bottom of the pan. As it cooks, the food loses moisture and rises to the surface.
- Once the food is cooked, lift it out of the pan with a slotted metal spoon. Place on absorbent kitchen paper to remove excess oil. Lightly sprinkle the food with fine salt to improve its flavour and to draw out the oil.
- To keep fried food warm while other batches are cooking, arrange in a single layer on a baking tray, and place in a warm oven with the door ajar to allow air to circulate.

NOTES FOR FOOD ALLERGY SUFFERERS

DAIRY-FREE DIET: Cows' milk is sometimes used to make soft tender batters. Use soya milk or use water or beer instead, for a lighter, crisper batter. Breadcrumb coatings are ideal for dairy-free diets provided the breadcrumbs do not contain traces of milk. Always read the label on bread before using.

GLUTEN-FREE DIET: Batters made with wheat flour can be substituted with a specific blend of rice flour, cornflour, tapioca flour and baking powder given in the recipes in this section. Rice flour provides body, cornflour provides lightness and tapioca flour – mixed with liquid – provides the binding power to adhere the batter to the food. Avoid using beer or lager in batter as both are made with barley malt, which contains gluten. Japanese tempura batter, which provides a delicate, crisp shell, is ideal for gluten-free diets as it is made with cornflour and sparkling water. For a breadcrumb coating, use gluten-free rice flour and gluten-free breadcrumbs in place of wheat flour and breadcrumbs.

EGG-FREE DIET: Egg is often used in batter as it binds and sets the batter around the food. Opt for a light batter made from flour and water or beer. Foods are often dipped in egg before being crumbed but this is unnecessary if you use very fresh fish and poultry. Simply dip it directly into very fine fresh breadcrumbs. The crumb coating will not be as even or as dense but will stick sufficiently to the food to form a light, crisp coating.

NUT-FREE DIET: Groundnut, or peanut, oil is commonly used for deep-frying in Asian cookery but can be replaced with other neutral flavoured oils including sunflower, rapeseed and corn oil. Avoid Arachis oil as this is also made from peanuts. Homemade batter is suitable provided it is made with nut-free flour. Breadcrumb coatings are ideal for nut-free diets, provided the breadcrumbs do not contain traces of nuts. Always read the label on bread before using.

SOYA-FREE DIET: Vegetable oil is ideal for deep-frying but is usually 100 per cent soya bean oil or a blend of oils including soya bean oil and sometimes groundnut oil. Replace it with other neutral flavoured oils such as sunflower or corn oil. Homemade batter is suitable for soya-free diets, provided it is made with soya-free flour. Breadcrumb coatings are ideal provided the breadcrumbs do not contain traces of soya. Always read the label on bread before using.

BATTERED COD

White fish such as cod or haddock taste their best in crisp, golden batter and make a great treat for a family supper. Serve with Oven-Baked Chips (page 136), Tartare Sauce (page 84) and a wedge of lemon. **Serves 4**

INGREDIENTS

sunflower or corn oil for deep-frying

4 x 170 g/6 oz boned and skinned cod or haddock fillets

4 lemon wedges

FOR THE BATTER

150 ml/5 fl oz sparkling water or lager (for a robust beery flavour)

● GLUTEN

1 egg white, made up to 150 ml/5 fl oz with sparkling water and whisked

110 g/4 oz self-raising flour, seasoned with salt and pepper

● GLUTEN

55 g/2 oz potato flour, 55 g/2 oz cornflour, 1 tsp gluten-free baking powder, salt and pepper, sifted together

1 Fill a deep-fat fryer or large, heavy-bottomed pan no more than one-third full of oil. Gently heat the oil over a low to moderate heat until it reaches 180°C/350°F (at which point, a cube of bread will fry to golden brown in 40 seconds). Maintain the oil at this temperature over a low heat.

2 While the oil is heating, pour the water or lager (or egg white and water) into a wide, shallow dish. Sift the seasoned flour onto the liquid, whisking continuously with a fork. The batter should have the consistency of thick double cream. If it is too thin, add a little more flour; if it is too thick add a little more water.

3 Turn the fish over in the batter until completely coated. Lift the battered fish above the bowl to allow excess batter to run off.

4 Lower the fish into the hot oil and fry until it floats to the surface and the batter is golden brown, for about 6–8 minutes. Fry only one or two pieces of fish at a time. Do not overcrowd the pan.

5 Lift the fish out of the oil with a slotted spoon and place on a baking tray covered with two layers of absorbent kitchen paper. Sprinkle lightly with salt. While you fry the remaining fish, keep the cooked fish warm in a low oven with the door ajar, to allow air to circulate around it so that it remains crisp. Don't cover deep-fried food or it becomes soggy.

6 To serve, place the battered fish on warm plates with a generous helping of chips, a lemon wedge and Tartare sauce served separately.

FRITTO MISTO DI MARE

Fried mixed seafood (shown above) is great as finger food for a party – with garlic mayonnaise, chilli dipping sauce or soy sauce – or as a starter or informal lunch piled on plates with lemon wedges and lightly dressed green salad.

To serve 4, dip 110 g/4 oz each of king prawns, thickly sliced squid rings, whitebait, finger-sized strips of sole and monkfish fillets into 1 quantity of batter (see opposite) and deep-fry until the fish floats to the surface. Drain on absorbent paper, lightly sprinkle with salt and serve immediately.

VEGETABLE FRITTO MISTO

To make a delicious vegetable fritto misto use a selection of the following: courgette, sliced on the diagonal; small florets of broccoli and cauliflower; wide strips of red and green pepper; top and tailed green beans; thin slices of aubergine, cut in half; trimmed spears of asparagus; onion wedges; and whole, small or thickly sliced large mushrooms. Serve with lemon wedges and Garlic Mayonnaise (page 84).

CRISPY FISH RIBBONS

Crunchy on the outside and tender and moist on the inside, Crispy Fish Ribbons make a delicious starter or finger food served with lemon wedges, Tartare Sauce (page 84) or Garlic Mayonnaise (page 84). In this recipe the fish is coated in flour, egg and breadcrumbs. For an egg-free version, simply omit the flour and egg and roll the fish in fine fresh breadcrumbs only. A thin layer of breadcrumbs will stick to the moist surface of the fish to form a light, crisp coating when deep-fried. Served with tomato sauce, they're also a great homemade alternative to fish fingers for children's parties. **Serves 4**

INGREDIENTS

sunflower or corn oil for deep-frying

450 g/1 lb skinned sole or plaice fillets, sliced across into finger-sized strips

2 tbsp plain flour, seasoned with salt and pepper

● GLUTEN → rice flour, seasoned with salt and pepper omit

2 eggs, beaten and poured into a wide, shallow dish

● EGG → omit

225 g/8 oz fine fresh or dried breadcrumbs

● GLUTEN → gluten-free breadcrumbs

TO SERVE

4 lemon wedges

1 Fill a deep-fat fryer or large heavy-bottomed pan no more than one-third full of oil. Heat the oil over a low to moderate heat until it reaches 180°C/350°F (at which point, a cube of bread will fry to golden brown in 40 seconds). Maintain the oil at this temperature over a low heat.

2 Place the flour and breadcrumbs on large plates and pour the eggs into a wide, shallow dish. Roll the pieces of fish in the seasoned flour. This will help the egg to stick to the fish.

3 Dip the floured fish into the beaten egg and then roll in the breadcrumbs until evenly coated. Gently shake the breaded fish to remove any loose crumbs. For egg-free Crispy Fish Ribbons, roll the fish in breadcrumbs only.

4 Gently slip a handful of crumbed fish into the hot oil and fry until the coating is crisp and golden brown, gently turning the pieces of fish over in the oil so they cook evenly. The fish ribbons are cooked when they float to the surface and are crisp and golden brown. Do not allow the ribbons to become too dark or the fish will over-cook and become dry and tough.

5 Lift out of the oil with a slotted spoon onto a baking tray covered with absorbent kitchen paper. Sprinkle with salt. Keep warm in a low oven with the door ajar so air can circulate around the fish. If the oven door is shut the crispy coating will become soggy.

6 Fry the remaining fish in the same way. Serve immediately, piled high on the plate with lemon wedges and one of the suggested sauces.

VARIATION
CRISPY CHICKEN RIBBONS
Slice skinned chicken breasts into thin strips, coat in breadcrumbs and fry as above. Serve with lemon wedges and Garlic Mayonnaise (page 84).

Chapter 11 | GRILLING

Although grilling takes a little longer than frying – because the food is not in direct contact with the heat source – it provides a simple, tasty cooking method for a wide variety of foods. Food is first brushed with oil, melted butter or a marinade before being placed under the intense, dry heat of the grill. Although neutral flavoured oils are suitable for grilling, butter and olive oil are more commonly used to moisten, baste and enrich the flavour of grilled food.

Ideally, food for grilling should be no thicker than 4 cm/1¾ inches thick: any thicker and the surface of the food will be over-browned before the centre is cooked. Steak, pork and lamb chops and sausages are delicious grilled. Flattened small birds, jointed portions of poultry and breast fillets also grill beautifully, as do fish steaks, fish fillets, small whole fish and shellfish. Whole fish are often slashed to allow the heat to reach the centre of the fish before the skin blackens. Firm oily fish, such as tuna and salmon, are especially good for grilling, as they are slow to dry out under the hot grill. White fish is more delicate and benefits from regular basting during cooking, to prevent it from becoming dry. Some vegetables, particularly aubergine, courgette and tomato, grill very well when brushed with oil or butter.

Recipes using the grilling method are also perfect for char-grilling and barbecuing.

MARINADES

Delicate white fish, lean poultry and tender cuts of meat that tend to dry out and toughen quickly when cooked are often marinated overnight in an oil-based marinade before grilling. Marinades made with olive oil or neutral flavoured oils help to retain moisture in the food, as they are absorbed by the meat or fish, and are often used to baste the food while it grills.

GENERAL RULES
FOR GRILLING

- Heat the grill to its highest setting 10 minutes before grilling.
- Grilling time depends on the temperature of the heated grill, the distance of the food from the grill, the thickness of the food and its temperature before it is cooked. To reduce the grilling time, remove chilled food from the fridge 30 minutes before grilling. The colder the food the longer it takes for the heat to reach its centre and the greater the likelihood of it over-browning before it is cooked through.

NOTES
FOR FOOD
ALLERGY
SUFFERERS

Grilled food is prepared with very few added ingredients – butter or oil, or a marinade made from oil, wine, herbs, spices or seasoning – and served simply in its cooking juices. Provided olive oil is used instead of butter for dairy-free diets and oils containing nuts or soya are avoided for nut-free and soya-free diets, grilled food is largely safe for the allergies covered in this book.

- To moisten the food while it cooks and to help it brown, brush with oil or melted butter before grilling.
- Unless the skin on a chicken breast or fish is intact, season with salt after it is grilled, as salt draws out the juices and prevents food from becoming crisp and well browned.
- Depending on the power of the grill, position the food 2.5–5 cm/1–2 inches away from it to allow the food time to cook through before it over-browns.
- Brush both sides of the food with oil or butter halfway through cooking to moisten it and to encourage browning and crisp edges.
- If the food is browning too fast, move it further away from the heat. Conversely move the food closer to the grill if it is grilling too slowly.
- A 2.5-cm/1-inch-thick fish steak should take between 5 and 8 minutes to cook through. A steak twice as thick will take around 10 minutes. If the surfaces are beginning to burn and the centre is not cooked sufficiently, place in a hot oven until cooked.
- Meat is denser than fish and should be cut no thicker than 4 cm/1½ inches for grilling. A 2.5-cm/1-inch-thick portion of meat, brought to room temperature before cooking, will take will take 2–2½ minutes on each side to grill to medium rare: a 4-cm/1½-inch-thick portion will take 3–4 minutes on each side.
- Halfway through cooking time, the grilled surface of the food should be lightly browned and crisp around the edges. To ensure the food is cooked evenly on both sides, turn it over, brush with oil or butter and grill the other side for the same length of time or until it is evenly browned, crisp and cooked to the required 'doneness'. See the Pressure Test (page 112) and Knowing when Fish is Cooked (page 119).

LEBANESE CHICKEN KEBABS

Start this recipe a day in advance, to allow the marinade to flavour and moisten the meat. Children and adults alike love these delicious kebabs. Serve them with Tabbouleh (page 140) or Rice Salad with Pistachio Nuts (page 144). **Serves 4**

FOR THE MARINADE

3 tsp paprika

1 tsp ground cumin

freshly ground black pepper

3 garlic cloves, crushed

3 tbsp lemon juice

4 tbsp extra virgin olive oil

FOR THE KEBABS

600 g/1 lb 5 oz skinned chicken breasts, cut into 5 cm/2 in cubes

1 large onion, cut into eighths from root to shoot

2 large green peppers cored, seeded and cut into 5 cm/2 in squares

salt

4 lemon wedges

alternating the ingredients. Lightly sprinkle with salt and season with black pepper.

5 Place the kebabs on a rack in a roasting tray or on a clean grill pan to catch the cooking juices. Brush the kebabs with marinade and grill them about 2.5 cm/1 inch away from the heat.

6 Grill the kebabs for 10–12 minutes, basting them with marinade and turning them every 2–3 minutes to brown and lightly char (for extra flavour) evenly on all sides. If the kebabs are browning too quickly, move the kebabs another inch or so from the grill.

7 To check the chicken is cooked through, gently press the chicken pieces with the thumb and forefinger. The chicken should feel firm.

8 To serve, place a kebab on a warm dish, spoon over some of the cooking juices and serve with a wedge of lemon.

VARIATIONS

LAMB KEBABS
Slice meat cut from the leg or fillet into 2.5 cm/1 inch cubes, thread onto skewers and marinade in the same way as above. Grill for 10–12 minutes so that they are lightly charred on the outside (see picture above) and still slightly pink and moist in the centre.

SEAFOOD KEBABS
Marinate 225 g/8 oz prawns; 450 g/1 lb firm white fish, cut into 3 cm/1½ inch dice; and 225 g/8 oz scallops in place of the chicken. Grill for approximately 2 minutes each side, occasionally basting the seafood with marinade, to keep it moist under the grill.

1 A day in advance, make the marinade. Place the paprika, cumin, three grinds of black pepper, crushed garlic and lemon juice in a bowl. Whisk together well. Drizzle in the olive oil, whisking continuously until the marinade is emulsified and thick. Do not add salt at this stage as it draws the moisture out of the chicken.

2 Place the cubes of chicken, onion and green pepper in a storage container, pour in the marinade and turn the pieces of chicken over to ensure they are evenly coated. Cover and refrigerate for at least 4 hours or, ideally, overnight.

3 To cook, preheat the grill for 10 minutes until it is really hot. If it is not hot enough the chicken will take longer to brown and may dry out in the process.

4 While the grill is heating up, assemble the chicken kebabs. Thread the pepper, onion and chicken onto the skewers,

LAMB STEAKS MARINATED IN RED WINE, OLIVE OIL, ROSEMARY AND GARLIC

This recipe makes the most of lamb's perfect match with rosemary and garlic. The marinade gives the meat a lovely rich flavour and helps to keep it moist as it cooks. Make sure the grill is really hot so that the surface of the lamb becomes brown and crisp while the meat is still pink and rosy inside. Serve with Crushed New Potatoes (page 137) or couscous, and steamed green beans or a lightly dressed green salad. **Serves 4**

INGREDIENTS

4 x 2-cm/1-in-thick lamb steaks, cut from the upper leg (or use lamb chops)

4 lemon wedges

FOR THE MARINADE

2 tbsp red wine

2 garlic cloves, crushed

6 grinds black pepper

4 tbsp olive oil

4 sprigs rosemary

salt

1 A day in advance, mix the red wine, garlic cloves and black pepper together. Do not add salt at this stage as it will draw the moisture out of the lamb. Drizzle in the olive oil, whisking continuously until the marinade is emulsified and thick.

2 Arrange the lamb steaks in a single layer in a shallow dish. Pour the marinade over the lamb. Turn the lamb steaks over to cover them evenly in the marinade and place the sprigs of rosemary on the lamb.

3 Cover the dish with clingfilm and refrigerate for at least 8 hours, but ideally 24 hours, for the flavours to develop. Occasionally turn the steaks to ensure they are marinating evenly.

4 Remove from the fridge 30 minutes before cooking to bring them up to room temperature. This helps the heat from the grill to penetrate and cook the centre of the lamb before the surface is overly browned.

5 Preheat the grill to the hottest setting for 10 minutes.

6 Set the marinade aside and place the steaks on a rack, standing in a roasting tray, to catch the juices. Sprinkle the lamb with salt and place on an oven shelf positioned so the lamb is 4 cm/1¾ inches away from the grill.

7 Grill the lamb for 4 minutes and turn over, baste with some of the marinade, sprinkle with salt, season with freshly ground black pepper and grill the second side for another 3 minutes. Take the steaks from under the grill and press the meat with the tips of your second and third finger to check its progress (see the Pressure Test page 112). If the lamb is still too rare cook for another minute on the same side or until the lamb is brown and crisp on the outside and pink in the centre. When the lamb is cooked, place on four warmed plates with a lemon wedge, spoon over any cooking juices and serve immediately.

Chapter 12 | ROASTING AND OVEN-BAKING

ROASTING

Roasting involves cooking large joints of meat and whole birds at high temperatures, in the dry heat of the oven. A small quantity of fat or oil is spooned over the food as it cooks to prevent it from drying out and to help it brown and crisp up. Using fat in this way is known as basting. Once meat or poultry is cooked, richly flavoured gravy is made by loosening the browned juices on the base of the roasting pan with stock, wine and the water which has been used to boil accompanying vegetables.

Vegetables are also roasted, often in the same roasting tray as the meat.

OILS AND FATS USED FOR ROASTING

Neutral flavoured oils such as sunflower, vegetable or corn oil or pure beef dripping are the most suitable basting fats for meat roasted at high temperatures, as they will not burn in the bottom of the roasting pan. Burnt fat affects the flavour of the meat and the cooking juices used to make gravy. As poultry and fish are roasted at slightly lower temperatures, olive oil and butter (both of which burn at very high temperatures) are often used to enrich their flavour and the cooking juices that form the basis for an accompanying sauce.

ROASTING MEAT

Lean and tender cuts of beef, lamb or pork are initially cooked in a very hot oven (200°C/400°F/gas mark 6 plus) to brown the meat and to melt the fat on the surface of the meat. If there is no fat around the meat, it is either rubbed with oil or beef dripping or covered with bacon rashers to moisten the surface as it roasts. Once the meat begins to brown, the temperature is reduced to prevent the meat from cooking too quickly.

HOW TO ROAST MEAT

- Preheat the oven while the meat is being prepared for roasting.
- Trim any excess fat so that the top surface is evenly covered with a thin layer of fat.
- If fat is lacking, cover the top surface of the meat with streaky bacon or rub butter, beef dripping or oil over the meat. Alternatively, the meat can be browned

---

NOTES FOR FOOD ALLERGY SUFFERERS

DAIRY-FREE DIET: Butter is only used for roasting because it enriches the flavour of poultry, fish and their cooking juices. Olive oil is a great dairy-free alternative, as it also adds flavour.

GLUTEN-FREE DIET: Gravy made with the cooking juices is often thickened with wheat flour. An equal quantity of cornflour can be used instead to thicken gravy.

Alternatively, boil the cooking juices, some stock and any water used for boiling accompanying vegetables in the roasting pan until the liquid is reduced to delicious, syrupy gravy.

NUT- AND SOYA-FREE DIETS: Avoid using groundnut oil for nut-free diets and soya bean oil or vegetable oil (made with soya bean oil) for soya-free diets.

beforehand in hot oil, on the hob, then roasted at a temperature below 200°C/400°F/gas mark 6.

- Season with salt and pepper (out of the roasting pan or your gravy will be salty).
- Weigh the prepared joint to calculate how long it will take to cook using the roasting times given in the recipe. A solid piece of meat will take longer to cook than a joint of the same weight, containing bones (bones carry heat to the centre of the meat). The shape of the joint is also important. A long, thin joint will take less time to cook than a shorter, thicker piece of meat of the same weight.
- Every 20 to 30 minutes remove the meat from the oven, shut the oven door and spoon the hot fat over the meat. Return the meat immediately to the oven.
- Check the meat halfway through the cooking time. It may be cooking faster than calculated (see Knowing When Meat Is Cooked page 112).
- When the meat is cooked, remove from the oven, cover in foil and rest for at least 10 minutes. This allows the free-flowing juices inside the meat to be reabsorbed by the meat fibres. This makes the meat more succulent and easier to carve.

ROASTING
POULTRY

Poultry is ideal for roasting as its flesh is tender and partially protected from drying out by the skin and the layer of fat beneath it. To add extra protection from the dry heat of the oven and to brown and crisp the skin, lean birds such as chicken, guinea fowl and game birds are smeared with softened butter or drizzled with oil or covered with streaky bacon, particularly over the breasts and legs. Turkeys are also lean and because of their size and the length of time they require in the oven, they are wrapped in greaseproof paper and foil, in addition to oil or butter and rashers of streaky bacon, to ensure the meat remains moist. An hour before the turkey has finished cooking, the paper, foil and streaky bacon are removed to allow the skin to brown evenly.

Duck and goose do not require butter or oil while they roast due to the thick layer of fat below the skin, which slowly renders down, moistening the meat, until only the browned, crisp skin remains.

HOW TO ROAST
POULTRY

- Preheat the oven to the required roasting temperature.
- Place the bird on a board and remove any excess fat from inside the bird.
- If required, stuff the bird (see opposite).
- Weigh the bird to calculate its cooking time once it is prepared or stuffed. As a general rule, poultry requires 40 minutes per kg or 20 minutes per lb.
- Spread softened butter or drizzle and rub oil over the bird, particularly the breasts, legs and wings, as they are most prone to drying out.
- Lightly season the bird with salt and pepper before placing it in the roasting pan.
- Place lean birds on the base of the roasting tray. Place fatty birds such as duck and goose on a wire rack (to hold it above the fat that will melt off).
- Once the bird starts to brown, baste it in the hot fat every 20–30 minutes.
- Once the bird is cooked, remove from the oven, cover in foil and leave to rest for 10 minutes. This makes the bird more succulent and easier to carve.

STUFFING FOR
ROASTED BIRDS

The Christmas turkey, roast chicken and other birds, such as pheasant, guinea fowl and poussin, are made infinitely more special if stuffed with a fruity or herby flavoured stuffing. Stuffing absorbs the rich flavoured cooking juices produced by the roasting bird and helps to keep the bird moist as it cooks.

Birds may be stuffed with:
- Oranges, lemons or apples, onions, garlic and herbs, placed into the body cavity of medium-sized birds to keep the bird moist and flavour the meat and gravy (see Mediterranean Roast Chicken page 114).
- A stuffing based on minced meat or starchy ingredients such as breadcrumbs or rice, which will soak up the cooking juices.

HOW TO STUFF BIRDS

Medium-sized and small birds: Because of their small size, chickens and guinea fowl are often stuffed in the neck and body cavity (to provide enough stuffing). Spoon the stuffing into the bird until the cavity is loosely filled, as stuffing swells as it cooks. Tightly packed stuffing is liable to burst out of the bird or not cook through. Once the neck end of the bird is stuffed, secure the flap of neck skin over the stuffing with skewers.
Large birds: Because turkeys are so large, stuff the neck cavity only. If the body cavity is stuffed, the turkey must be cooked for a longer period to ensure the stuffing is cooked properly, resulting in over-cooked, dry meat. Do not over-stuff the neck cavity as the stuffing swells as it cooks and will push its way out of the bird. Secure the neck skin firmly over the stuffing with skewers. Any extra stuffing can be shaped into balls and placed into an ovenproof dish to bake separately.

ROASTING A STUFFED BIRD

Stuffed birds require 40 minutes per kg or 20 minutes per lb to cook. To prevent the bird from overcooking, roast at 180°C/350°F/gas mark 4 for the first half of the cooking time, to brown the skin, and then at 160°C/325°F/gas mark 3 for the second half to cook it through.

NOTES FOR FOOD ALLERGY SUFFERERS

DAIRY-FREE DIET: Butter is often used to soften diced vegetables for stuffing mixtures. Replace it with olive oil or a neutral flavoured oil.

EGG-FREE DIET: Beaten egg is often used to bind stuffing. Stuffing made without egg will be more crumbly but just as delicious. Alternatively, in place of each egg used, add 1 tablespoon of breadcrumbs and, if the stuffing mixture is dry, 1 tablespoon of water.

GLUTEN-FREE DIET: Breadcrumbs are used as the base of meat-free stuffings and to bind and add bulk to meat-based stuffing. Sausagemeat used as the base of meat-based stuffing may also contain 'rusk', or toasted breadcrumbs, but you can use the sausagemeat recipe on page 94. Gluten-free breadcrumbs or cooked brown rice are just as suitable for stuffing.

NUT-FREE DIET: Nuts are often added to stuffing to add texture and flavour. Although the flavour will not be the same, nuts can be replaced with lightly cooked celery for crunch and chopped dried fruit for added texture and flavour.

SOYA-FREE DIET: Check the label of bought sausagemeat for added soya products. To be sure, make your own sausagemeat (see page 94).

KNOWING WHEN MEAT IS COOKED

THE PRESSURE TEST

Generally used to measure how well small cuts of roasted meat and individual portions of meat are cooked, the pressure test is also very useful used in conjunction with the skewer test for larger pieces of roasted meat and whole birds. To test how well meat is cooked, press it firmly with a fore and middle finger: raw meat feels soft and flabby; rare meat is not flabby but feels soft and gives easily under the fingers when pressed; medium-rare meat is firmer but still soft enough to give under the fingers when pressed but springs back as the fingers are removed; well-done meat feels firm and does not give when pressed.

USING A MEAT THERMOMETER

Insert the thermometer into the centre of the deepest part of the meat. Leave it in place for at least 30 seconds before taking your reading: 60°C/140°F is rare and still deep red; 70°C/160°F is medium-rare and pink; 80°C/175°F is well done and brown. Before testing the temperature of poaching meat, remove it from the poaching liquid.

THE SKEWER TEST

If you do not have a meat thermometer, insert a skewer into the middle of the deepest part of the joint, leave for a few seconds then remove. If there are no juices the meat is raw; if the juices are dark pink and tricking from the hole, the meat is rare; if light pink juices are flowing freely from the hole the meat is medium-rare; if the juices are colourless and flow freely, the meat is well done.

KNOWING WHEN WHOLE BIRDS ARE COOKED

Twenty minutes before the end of the estimated roasting time, remove the bird from the oven to check its progress. The skin of the bird may be crisp and golden brown but use one of the following tests to confirm whether the bird is ready to eat or requires more cooking. White-fleshed birds, including turkey, chicken and guinea fowl, must be well cooked to kill any salmonella bacteria present in the meat. Duck and goose meat present a far lower risk of salmonella poisoning and are traditionally eaten pink (despite the fatty skin, duck and goose meat is very lean and eating it when pink ensures the meat is moist and tender).

CHECKING THE COOKING JUICES

Insert a sharp, pointed knife into the deepest part of the breast and thigh: very little juice means that the meat is still raw in the centre; deep pink, bloody juices trickling from the cut mean the meat is rare; slow-flowing, light pink juices mean that the meat is almost cooked or medium-rare, ideal for dark-fleshed birds such as duck, goose and game birds such as pigeon; free-flowing colourless juices signify that the flesh is cooked through, ideal for white-fleshed poultry such as turkey, chicken and guinea fowl.

USING A MEAT THERMOMETER

White-fleshed poultry and meat-based stuffing must reach 80°C/175°F (well done) before they are safe to eat. Dark-fleshed birds such as goose and duck are best eaten pink at 70°C/165°F (medium-rare). For this reason, use meat-free stuffing for dark-fleshed birds as it is safe to eat cooked to 70°C/165°F.

THE PRESSURE TEST

The breast meat of birds is often pan-fried in hot oil until well browned and finished off in a roasting oven. To avoid cutting into the breast meat to check the progress of the cooking meat, use the pressure test (above).

TRADITIONAL ROAST RIB OF BEEF

There is nothing to beat the taste of rare beef with rich gravy. Serve with Roast Potatoes (page 135), steamed or boiled green vegetables and mustard or horseradish sauce. The beef is delicious cold so even if there are only two of you it's worth cooking a large joint and enjoying the leftovers. **Serves 6**

INGREDIENTS

FOR THE BEEF

2–2.5 kg/4½–5½ lb rib of beef

2 tsp dry English mustard

● GLUTEN
check label for wheat

salt and freshly ground black pepper

FOR THE GRAVY

1 tbsp flour

● GLUTEN
cornflour

150 ml/5 fl oz red wine

290 ml/10 fl oz White or Brown Chicken Stock (page 64)

salt and freshly ground black pepper

1 Preheat the oven to 220°C/425°F/gas mark 7.

2 Place the meat on a board and rub salt, pepper and mustard powder over the fat. Place the beef in a roasting pan and cook on the middle shelf of the oven to brown for 20 minutes. Reduce the heat to 180°C/350°F/gas mark 4 and roast the beef for another 15 minutes per 450 g/1 lb for medium-rare meat; 20 minutes per 450 g/1 lb for well done meat. To ensure the beef is cooked perfectly and does not over-cook, test the meat (see opposite) 30 minutes before you estimate it will be ready. If the meat requires more cooking, return it to the oven for 15 minutes and test again.

3 When the meat is ready, transfer it to a carving board, cover with foil and leave to rest for 20–30 minutes.

4 To make the gravy, pour the juices in the base of the roasting pan into a transparent jug and leave for 1 minute to allow the fat and cooking juices to separate. Spoon 2 tablespoons of the fat back into the roasting pan and carefully remove the remaining fat from the surface of the cooking juices.

5 Add the flour to the fat in the pan, stir to a smooth paste and cook over a moderate heat for 1 minute, stirring continuously with a wooden spoon. Gradually stir in the red wine and stock, loosening the browned cooking juices on the base of the pan, to form a lump-free sauce. Add any cooking juices collecting around the resting beef to the gravy and bring to the boil, stirring constantly. Simmer for 2 minutes to cook the flour, taste and season with salt and pepper and keep warm over a low heat. As the beef is carved more juices will collect under the meat and these should be poured into the gravy, as they add lots of flavour.

6 Thinly slice the beef and arrange on warmed plates with the gravy served separately from a sauce jug.

MEDITERRANEAN ROAST CHICKEN WITH POTATOES, RED PEPPERS AND GARLIC

This recipe is truly delicious, simple to prepare and gives you time to do other things while it cooks. It is free from dairy, egg, gluten, nuts and soya and is a fantastic dish to serve to family and guests for Sunday lunch or an informal dinner. **Serves 4–6**

FOR THE CHICKEN

2 kg/4½ lb roasting chicken

½ onion, cut into two

2 garlic cloves

½ lemon, cut in half

2 sprigs thyme

1 tbsp olive oil

salt and pepper

FOR THE VEGETABLES

1.2 kg/2¾ lb large floury potatoes, each cut into 6 long wedges

2 red peppers, each cut into 8 strips

2 onions, each cut into 6 from shoot to root (ensure a little of the root is left to hold the pieces together as they cook)

4 ripe tomatoes, quartered

6 garlic cloves, in their skin

2 large pinches of sea salt

freshly ground black pepper

4 sprigs rosemary or thyme

FOR THE GRAVY

290 ml/10 fl oz White Chicken Stock (page 64)

1 Preheat the oven to 180°C/350°F/gas mark 4.

2 Place the bird on a chopping board. Remove any excess fat from the body cavity and place the onion, garlic cloves, lemon and thyme in the body cavity.

3 Place the prepared chicken in the centre of a roasting pan large enough to hold the vegetables not more than two vegetables deep (so they cook and brown evenly).

4 Spread the vegetables and garlic around the chicken. Drizzle 4 tablespoons of olive oil over the chicken (taking care to include the legs, to help prevent them drying out) and the vegetables. Sprinkle over the sea salt and season well with pepper.

5 Toss the vegetables around in the pan then spread out around the chicken to cover them evenly in oil and seasoning. Tuck the herb sprigs under the potatoes to prevent them from scorching. Also make sure the red peppers, onion wedges and garlic cloves are well down in the pan to prevent them burning.

6 Place the pan in the middle of the preheated oven and cook for 30 minutes.

7 Remove the pan from the oven and baste the chicken in the oil and juices collecting in the bottom of the pan, and turn the potatoes and vegetables over carefully using a fish slice. Place the pan back in the oven and roast for another 20 minutes.

8 Baste the chicken again and turn the vegetables over once more. If the potatoes are golden brown on the outside and soft inside, transfer the vegetables to a serving dish and keep warm. The chicken will require at least another 15 minutes in the oven.

9 After this time, test to see if the chicken is done by inserting a small knife into the deepest part of the leg and breast. If the juices run clear then it is cooked. Also, the cooking juices collected in the body cavity should be caramel in colour. If the juices are dark red the chicken requires at least another 15 minutes in the oven.

10 Once the chicken is cooked, place a wooden spoon in the body cavity and with the help of a fish slice or slotted spoon, tip the chicken to allow the cooking juices in the body cavity to run into the roasting pan. Spoon off most of the fat.

11 Add the chicken stock to the roasting pan and boil the gravy until it thinly coats the back of a spoon. Taste and season as necessary.

12 To serve, carve the chicken and arrange on warm plates. Spoon over some of the gravy in the roasting pan. Hand the roast vegetables round separately making sure everyone has a roasted garlic clove on their plates to squeeze and spread over their chicken.

VARIATION

Carrots, parsnips, butternut squash, new potatoes, courgettes, shallots and fennel also roast extremely well around a chicken.

BROWN RICE, MUSHROOM, PARSLEY AND LEMON STUFFING

The brown rice, flavoured with mushrooms, herbs, garlic and lemon, absorbs the cooking juices to make a wonderfully rich, crumbly stuffing suitable for white- and dark-fleshed birds. This stuffing is also delicious made with cooked bulgur wheat in place of rice. **Makes enough stuffing for a 2 kg/4½ lb roasting chicken**

INGREDIENTS

140 g/5 oz brown rice

30 g/1 oz butter or 2 tbsp olive oil

1 onion, finely diced

110 g/4 oz fresh mushrooms (button, flat or wild), finely sliced

2 garlic cloves, finely chopped

2 tbsp finely chopped parsley

finely grated rind of 1 lemon

juice of ½ lemon

salt and freshly ground black pepper

1 Place the rice and a teaspoon of salt in a saucepan. Cover with twice the volume of cold water and cover with a lid. Bring to the boil then gently simmer for 20–30 minutes, or until the rice is tender.

2 Meanwhile, heat the butter or oil in the frying pan, add the onion, mushrooms, a pinch of salt and two grinds of pepper, cover and fry, stirring occasionally, until the onions are very soft and sweet. Add the garlic and continue to fry for another 30 seconds. Remove the pan from the heat.

3 Once the rice, onions and mushrooms are cooked, mix together with the parsley, lemon rind and juice. Mix thoroughly, taste and add seasoning or more lemon juice as necessary. The stuffing should taste delicately lemony. Use as required (see How to Stuff Birds page 111).

VARIATION

BROWN RICE, MUSHROOM, OREGANO AND ORANGE STUFFING
Replace the lemon with the zest of 1 orange and the juice of ½ orange and replace 1 tablespoon of the parsley with finely chopped oregano.

APPLE AND CHORIZO STUFFING

A really punchy, colourful stuffing that complements chicken, guinea fowl and poussin beautifully. Serve the stuffed bird with brown rice or Crushed New Potatoes (page 137) **Makes enough for a 2 kg/4½ lb roasting chicken**

INGREDIENTS

1 small onion, finely diced

1 celery stick, finely diced

olive oil for frying

3 garlic cloves, finely chopped

1 tsp ground paprika

½ quantity sausage mixture for Homemade Pork and Apple Sausages (page 94)

200 g/7 oz peeled, cored and coarsely grated Granny Smith apples

110 g/4 oz Spanish chorizo sausage, cut into thin slices and then across into thin strips

● **GLUTEN** check label for wheat

● **DAIRY** check label for dairy

● **SOYA** check label for soya

1 tbsp oregano or thyme leaves, roughly chopped

1 tbsp finely chopped flat-leaf parsley

juice of ½ lemon

salt and pepper

1 Gently fry the onion and celery in 2 tablespoons of olive oil, in a covered frying pan, until the onion is soft and sweet. Add the garlic and paprika and continue to fry, stirring continuously, for another 30 seconds. Remove from the heat.

2 Place all the ingredients in a large bowl, season with ½ teaspoon of salt and black pepper and thoroughly mix everything together with your hands.

3 To check the seasoning fry a flattened spoonful of the stuffing in a little oil until cooked through. Taste and add more seasoning if necessary. Use as required.

VARIATION

APPLE, APRICOT AND SMOKED HAM STUFFING

For a milder flavoured stuffing, replace chorizo sausage with 110 g/4 oz smoked ham, thily sliced and cut into short strips, and replace 110 g/4 oz of the grated apple with roughly chopped, ready-to-eat apricots; omit the ground paprika.

OVEN-BAKING

The term oven-baking refers to small pieces or individual portions of meat and poultry, small to medium-sized whole fish or thickly sliced vegetables arranged in a roasting tray, drizzled with oil and cooked at high temperatures in the oven. Assembled dishes of food such as lasagne are also 'baked' in the oven until browned.

BAKING POULTRY AND MEAT

Oven-baking is a good method for cooking small portions of meat and jointed poultry. These can either be baked alone or with other ingredients – see Sticky Finger Chicken Drumsticks (page 123) or Baked Moroccan Chicken (page 121).

KNOWING WHEN THE MEAT IS COOKED

To check if small portions of meat or poultry are cooked use the pressure test (page 112) and look at the colour of the juices when the meat is pricked with a skewer. Beef, lamb and duck are best served pink with light pink juices. Pork and poultry should feel firm when pressed. Make a small cut down to the bone on the underside of jointed chicken portions to check the meat is no longer pink and the juices run clear.

BAKING FISH

Baking is mainly used to cook small fish such as sardines, medium-sized whole fish, including sea bass and trout, or portions of fish that are too thick to cook through by pan-frying. As oven-baked fish cooks quickly and has little time to brown and crisp up in the oven, whole fish and portions of fish are often browned in the frying pan first. Although the skin of fish offers some protection from the heat of the oven, both oily and white-fleshed fish are drizzled with oil or sealed in a parcel of foil or greaseproof paper with butter or olive oil, herbs and lemon and effectively steamed.

To reduce the length of time thick fish take to bake in a hot oven they are sometimes slashed through the skin at 5 cm/2 inch intervals, halfway to the bone, so that heat can quickly penetrate to the centre. Marinating the fish in an oil-based marinade beforehand adds flavour and helps to keep the slashed fish moist as it cooks.

BAKING TIMES FOR FISH

In an oven preheated to 200°C/400°F/gas mark 6, fish will take the following amount of time to cook.

Portions of fish

- a 2.5-cm/1-inch-thick portion will take 10–12 minutes (less if it has been browned in a pan first)
- a 5-cm/2-inch-thick portion will take 20–30 minutes, depending on the density of the flesh (less if it has been browned in a pan first).

NOTES FOR FOOD ALLERGY SUFFERERS

Meat, poultry, fish and vegetables, simply baked with a small quantity of fat or with other flavouring ingredients and served with their cooking juices are usually safe for dairy-, gluten-, egg-, soya- and nut-free diets. However, recipes where food is baked in a richly flavoured sauce are often not so suitable, though they can usually be adapted to suit your particular dietary requirements.

Many oven-baked dishes, for instance lasagne, traditionally contain dairy products, wheat or eggs. Nuts are included in some baked dishes but soya products are rarely used.

Whole fish

The time it takes for whole fish to cook partly depends on their shape. Long, narrow fish will take less time to cook than rounder fish. In an oven preheated to 200°C/400°F/gas mark 6...

- a small fish will take approximately 15–20 minutes
- a medium-sized fish will take approximately 25–30 minutes.

KNOWING WHEN FISH IS COOKED

Fish cooks at a lower temperature and more quickly than meat and is therefore easier to over-cook. Cooked fish is best eaten when the flesh is still moist and tender and is just opaque. Fish that is fully opaque is over-cooked and likely to taste coarse and dry, so look for these signs:

- Whole fish are cooked through when the eyes turn white and the dorsal fin comes away from the body cleanly and easily when pulled.
- When portions of fish are cooked through the flesh is almost opaque and starts to separate into large flakes when pressed with the fore and middle fingers.

BAKING VEGETABLES

One of the simplest foods is the baked jacket potato, turned in a little oil and salt and baked until soft and fluffy inside and crisp on the outside. Root vegetables, onions, squashes, courgettes, marrow, aubergine, tomatoes and fennel are also delicious sprinkled with oil and herbs and seasoning and baked until soft inside and brown and crisp around the edges.

HONEY BAKED SAUSAGES

Children love sausages cooked in this way. For a meal, serve 2 to 3 large sausages per child and for parties allow 4 chipolatas each. Sausages often contain 'rusk' or toasted breadcrumbs and are not suitable for a gluten-free diet – see the gluten-free recipe for Homemade Pork and Apple Sausages on page 94. **Serves 4**

INGREDIENTS

12 good quality pork sausages
check label for gluten
check label for dairy
check label for egg

- GLUTEN
- DAIRY
- EGG

2 tbsp runny honey

1 tbsp sunflower or corn oil

1 Preheat the oven to 180°C/350°F/gas mark 4.

2 Place the sausages in a single layer in a roasting pan and drizzle with oil. Bake for 15 minutes, or until they start to brown.

3 Remove from the oven and drizzle over the honey. Turn the sausages over in the honey until evenly coated then return to the oven for another 10 minutes or until the sausages are golden brown. Serve immediately or the sausages will stick firmly to the base of the roasting pan.

BAKED FILLET OF SALMON WITH SHALLOTS, TARRAGON AND LEMON

This recipe features a quick and simple method for cooking salmon. It is delicious served with brown rice or boiled new potatoes, and steamed green vegetables. Alternatively, serve cold with Mayonnaise (page 83) and lemon wedges. **Serves 4**

INGREDIENTS

4 x 180 g/6½ oz thick salmon fillets, with skin

2 shallots, thinly sliced across

salt and freshly ground black pepper

4 sprigs fresh tarragon

½ lemon, sliced across into 4 rounds

1 tbsp extra virgin olive oil

1 tbsp white wine

1 Preheat the oven to 180°C/350°F/ gas mark 4.

2 Place the salmon fillets skin down in an ovenproof dish. Sprinkle the shallots over each fillet, and season with salt and pepper. Arrange one sprig of tarragon and one slice of lemon on each salmon fillet. Drizzle the olive oil and white wine over the salmon.

3 Cover the dish with baking foil and bake on the middle shelf of the preheated oven for 25–30 minutes, or until the salmon is cooked and firm in the thickest part of the fillet.

4 To serve, lift the salmon fillets onto warmed plates using a fish slice and spoon over the cooking juices. Add a lemon wedge to the plate and serve.

BAKED MOROCCAN CHICKEN WITH FENNEL, OLIVES AND APRICOTS

A simply made, very attractive and tasty dish, this is particularly good served hot or cold with couscous or cold with Rice Salad with Pistachio Nuts and Pomegranate Seeds (page 144). **Serves 4**

INGREDIENTS

4 skinned chicken breasts, cut across into 2 cm/³/₄ in slices

1 garlic clove, finely chopped

1 fennel bulb, outer leaves discarded, sliced lengthways into 8 wedges

1 handful ready-to-eat dried apricots, cut in half

1 handful good quality black olives

juice and finely grated zest of 1 orange

juice and finely grated zest of 1 lemon

2 tbsp olive oil

1 tbsp soft brown sugar

salt and freshly ground black pepper

1 The night before the chicken is to be eaten, mix all the ingredients, except the sugar and salt, in a bowl. Cover and leave to marinate overnight in the fridge.

2 Preheat the oven to 200°C/400°C/ gas mark 6.

3 Spread the chicken mixture over the bottom of the roasting tray in one layer. Sprinkle the sugar over the chicken and season with salt and pepper.

4 Bake on the middle shelf of the preheated oven for 20–30 minutes, or until the chicken is firm when pressed between thumb and forefinger and the ingredients have turned an even golden brown. Turn the ingredients over halfway through cooking so that they brown evenly.

5 To serve, spoon onto warm plates or serve cold with salads.

LASAGNE AL FORNO

Lasagne is a well-loved dish for family meals and informal suppers and one that can be adapted for gluten-, egg- and dairy-free diets. Serve with a lightly dressed green salad or tomato salad. **Serves 4–6**

INGREDIENTS

2 quantities Béchamel sauce made with flour or cornflour (page 74)

225 g/8 oz fresh or dried lasagne pasta

● **GLUTEN** — gluten-free lasagne

● **EGG** — fresh pasta usually contains eggs

● **NUTS** — check label for traces of nuts

1 tbsp chopped fresh oregano or thyme

BOLOGNAISE SAUCE

sunflower oil or olive oil

500 g/1lb 2 oz good quality lean minced beef or lamb mince

salt and freshly ground black pepper

2 large carrots, diced

1 large onion, diced

1 garlic clove, finely chopped

2 x 400 g cans chopped tomatoes

290 ml/10 fl oz White Chicken Stock (page 64)

290 ml/10 fl oz water

1 bay leaf

1 sprig thyme

FOR THE TOPPING

3 tbsp freshly grated Parmesan di Reggiano cheese

● **DAIRY** — 3 tbsp dried breadcrumbs mixed with 1 tsp dried mixed herbs, ½ tsp salt and 3 grinds black pepper

2 tbsp olive oil

1 First, make the bolognaise sauce. Heat 2 tablespoons of oil in a large pan. When the oil is hot enough to make the meat sizzle, add half the meat, season it with ½ tsp salt and several generous grinds of pepper. Break up any lumps as the meat fries. Once the meat is well browned, remove it and loosen the browned juices on the base of the pan with a large splash of water. Add the loosened juices to the browned meat. Add another 2 tablespoons of oil to the pan and when it is hot, cook and season the next batch of meat. Remove the meat and loosen the browned juices from the pan again.

2 Turn the heat down, then tip the chopped carrots and onions into the pan, adding a little more oil if necessary. Season, cover with a lid and allow to fry gently until soft. Remove the lid and continue to fry, stirring regularly, until the vegetables are lightly browned. Add the chopped garlic and gently fry for another minute, stirring continuously.

3 Tip the meat back into the pan, add the tomatoes, stock, water and herbs and stir well. If necessary, add more stock or cold water to cover the ingredients by 5 mm/¼ inch and bring to a gentle simmer. Cook, uncovered, for 1½ hours, or until the meat is tender, on the hob. As the sauce cooks, skim the fat from the surface. Keep the liquid topped up with water to at least 5 mm/¼ inch above the ingredients. For the last 30 minutes of cooking, allow the liquid to reduce in volume so that it is level with the meat in the sauce. Taste and season.

4 Meanwhile, make the béchamel sauce and preheat the oven to 180°C/350°F/ gas mark 4.

5 To assemble the lasagne, cover the bottom of a 24 x 30 x 8 cm/9 x 12 x 3 inch ovenproof greased dish with one layer of pasta. Spread a generous layer of bolognaise sauce over the pasta, sprinkle over a large pinch of oregano or thyme then spoon béchamel sauce over the meat. Add another layer of lasagne

sheets and continue to layer the sauces and herbs as before. Continue to layer the lasagne in this way until the lasagne is 2 cm/³⁄₄ inch below the rim of the dish. Pour over the remaining sauce.

6 Sprinkle the grated Parmesan over the lasagne (or the herby breadcrumbs) and lightly drizzle with olive oil.

7 Bake for 30–35 minutes, or until it is bubbling and golden brown.

STICKY FINGER CHICKEN DRUMSTICKS

A very popular dish for informal meals and children's parties, this is great served with brown rice and salad. **Serves 4**

INGREDIENTS

8 chicken drumsticks, trimmed of excess skin

FOR THE MARINADE

2 tbsp sunflower or corn oil

2 tbsp soft brown sugar

1 garlic clove, finely chopped

1 heaped tsp ground paprika

1 tbsp white wine vinegar

2 tbsp tomato ketchup

● GLUTEN check label for wheat
● NUTS check label for traces of nuts
● SOYA check label for soya
● DAIRY check label for milk products

pinch of cayenne pepper or chilli flakes, optional

salt and freshly ground black pepper

1 The night before the chicken is to be eaten, place the chicken drumsticks in a large bowl. Mix the marinade ingredients together and pour over the chicken. Turn

the chicken drumsticks to ensure they are thoroughly coated in marinade. Cover and marinate overnight in the fridge.

2 Preheat the oven to 180°C/350°F/ gas mark 4.

3 Spread the chicken in its marinade over the base of a roasting pan and bake for about 30–40 minutes, basting and turning the chicken in the marinade two or three times.

4 Remove the chicken from the oven when it is golden brown and the marinade is reduced and sticky. Check that the meat is firm and is no longer pink in the centre. If it requires longer in the oven, add 2 or 3 tablespoons of water to the pan and cover the chicken with foil. Cook for another 10 minutes or until the chicken is cooked through.

5 Remove from the oven, turn the chicken over in the sauce and serve either hot or cold.

| # POACHING AND STEWING

POACHING

Poaching is a method for cooking meat, poultry, fish and eggs slowly and gently in barely simmering liquid. It is mainly used to cook delicate foods, including tender cuts of meat, fish and poultry, which have a tendency to dry out and toughen when cooked at high temperatures. The cooking method referred to as 'boiling' is in fact prolonged poaching and is mainly used for tenderizing large joints of meat, such as gammon and beef, in water or stock flavoured with vegetables, herbs and seasoning. As the cooking liquid is enriched with the nutrients and flavour from the ingredients cooked in it, it is used as the base for an accompanying sauce or for richly flavoured soup.

HOW TO POACH

- Food is poached in a large pan on the hob, where the temperature of the poaching liquid can be closely watched and controlled, or in a low oven.
- To poach small portions of food on the hob, choose a wide shallow pan with a heavy base – such as a frying pan – so that the portions can lie side by side. Don't pile them on top of one another as they will be difficult to remove and may break up.
- Check food regularly as it poaches, ensuring that it remains covered with liquid and is maintained at a slow simmer. Do not allow the poaching liquid to boil or the meat or fish will toughen and dry out.
- To poach small pieces of tender meat, fish or poultry cut into strips or dice, add them to barely simmering poaching liquid to gently cook through. Lift them out with a slotted spoon when they feel firm between thumb and forefinger.

POACHING FISH

Fresh fish is either poached in fish stock, in milk mixed with an equal quantity of water or a strongly flavoured liquid called court bouillon. Smoked fish is always poached in milk as water-based poaching liquid darkens and toughens the flesh. In contrast, the proteins in the milk soften the flavour and texture and lighten the colour of smoked fish.

Whole fish

To poach a whole fish, submerge it in cold poaching liquid and slowly heat to a gentle simmer to prevent the flesh shrinking. If the fish is large, you'll need a long, narrow pan called a fish kettle. If the fish is to be eaten hot, cook it for 5 minutes per 450 g/1 lb of fish. If it is to be eaten cold, remove the pan from the heat when the poaching liquid starts to simmer and leave to cool. When the poaching liquid is tepid the fish is cooked and can be lifted out of the pan.

Fillets of fish

If possible, buy fish fillets with the skin intact, as it holds the flesh together while the fish cooks and when it is lifted out of the pan. When poaching fish fillets on the hob, place them skin side down in the pan, to protect them from the hot pan base. In the oven, place the fish fillets skin side up, to protect them from the dry heat of the oven.

In both cases, make sure the fillets are completely covered in poaching liquid.

The fillets are cooked when the flesh is almost opaque in the thickest part of the fillet and it parts into moist flakes when gently pressed with a finger. The fish will continue to cook in its own heat even when it is removed from the pan, so be careful not to over-cook it.

POACHING POULTRY AND MEAT

White meats, such as pork, veal and poultry, are left whole – or cut into strips, dice or individual portions – and poached in stock or water flavoured with vegetables and herbs. Asian dishes such as Thai curries often use coconut milk for the same purpose (see Thai Green Chicken Curry on page 130). To prevent pieces and individual portions of poultry and meat from drying out, they are added to gently simmering liquid and poached until just cooked through. Always ensure pork and chicken are adequately cooked – the flesh should feel firm under the fingers.

Poaching whole birds and joints of meat

Poaching is an ideal method for gently cooking tender whole birds and joints such as gammon (see Chicken and Mushroom Pie on page 128 and Boiled Gammon on page 129) or slowly breaking down and dissolving the connective tissue in sinewy game birds and tougher cuts of meat such as silverside of beef. To cook a whole bird or joint of meat, submerge it in cold water or stock and bring slowly to simmering point. This encourages fat and other impurities to collect on the surface of the liquid, where they can be skimmed off using a ladle. This way, the poaching liquid remains clear and pure in flavour – essential for the taste and appearance of a soup or sauce made with it.

Whole birds are poached until the meat is just beginning to separate from the carcass and the legs feel loose when moved from side to side. Tender meat such as gammon is cooked when the meat has reached 80°C/175°F (see Using a Meat Thermometer on page 112). Tougher meats are poached until the connective tissue holding the muscle fibres together has broken down and dissolved into the poaching liquid. The meat is ready when the coarse muscle fibres start to separate and the meat is soft and tender in the mouth.

NOTES FOR FOOD ALLERGY SUFFERERS

Poached foods are cooked in water-based or milk-based poaching liquids.

DAIRY-FREE DIET: Soya milk is a very good substitute for cows' milk when poaching fresh and smoked fish, white meat and poultry, and makes a very good base for parsley sauce, served with poached white fish and boiled gammon. Rice milk can also be used for poaching, although white sauces made with it are thinner.

GLUTEN-FREE DIET: Milk-based, water-based and stock-based poaching liquids are often thickened with flour to make an accompanying sauce, such as the sauce for Chicken and Mushroom Pie (page 128). Substitute an equal quantity of cornflour for wheat flour to give a smooth, fine-textured sauce.

EGG-, NUT- AND SOYA-FREE DIETS: Either omit egg, nuts and soya from the recipe or choose another dish.

PROVENÇAL FISH STEW WITH FENNEL, HERBS AND POTATOES

The ingredients in this dish are poached but I tend to think of it more as a stew. A hearty meal in a bowl, it is best served with a suitable crusty bread and lightly dressed salad. **Serves 4**

FOR THE STEW

450 g/1 lb new potatoes

extra virgin olive oil

1 bulb Florence fennel, tough outer leaves removed, sliced into 8 wedges

3 garlic cloves, finely chopped

2 tsp ground coriander

400 g can chopped tomatoes

250 ml/8 fl oz dry white wine

450 g/1 lb mussels, cleaned under running water, 'beards' pulled away and any shells that remain open when tapped, discarded

2 large sea bass, filleted and the 4 fillets cut diagonally into thirds (keep the bones for the stock)

1 tbsp chopped mint

1 tbsp chopped flat-leaf parsley

1 lemon, cut into 4 wedges

FOR THE STOCK

bones from the sea bass, chopped into pieces

2 bay leaves

2 garlic cloves

4 parsley stalks

2 sprigs mint

1 fresh red chilli, halved lengthways and stems removed

1 tbsp fennel seeds

150 ml/ 5 fl oz dry white wine

salt and freshly ground black pepper

1 Boil the potatoes until just tender, drain and allow to cool. Cut into thick slices lengthways.

2 Meanwhile, place all the stock ingredients in a pan, cover with water and season well. Slowly bring to the boil and turn the heat down to a simmer. Simmer for 15 minutes, removing any scum that collects on the surface. Do not simmer for longer or the stock will start to taste bitter. Strain through a sieve into a bowl and set aside.

3 Heat 2 tablespoons of olive oil in a large pan, add the fennel slices, season with salt and pepper and fry gently until tender and golden brown. Remove from the pan with a slotted spoon and set aside.

4 Add the garlic to the pan, fry for 30 seconds then stir in the ground coriander and tomatoes. Simmer gently until the tomatoes start to disintegrate. Remove the pan from the heat and whiz the tomato mixture to a smooth purée in a food processor or with a hand-held blender.

5 Pour the puréed tomato mixture back into the pan, add the stock and wine and bring to the boil. Simmer for 2 minutes to boil off the alcohol in the wine, then add the fried fennel, cleaned mussels, sea bass fillets and sliced potatoes. Cover, bring the stew to a gentle simmer and cook for 5 minutes, or until the mussel shells have opened wide. Discard any mussels that remain closed, as they are not safe to eat. Taste and add salt and pepper as necessary.

6 To serve, ladle into warm bowls, sprinkle with mint and parsley, drizzle with olive oil and top with a lemon wedge to squeeze over the stew.

CHICKEN AND MUSHROOM PIE

This may seem like a rather lengthy recipe but the chicken can poach while you do other things – and the wait is worth it. The meat will be beautifully tender and the stock full of flavour. This recipe is easy to adapt for dairy-, egg-, gluten- and soya-free diets and does not contain nuts. **Serves 4–6**

FOR THE CHICKEN

2 kg/4½ lb roasting chicken

1 onion, thickly sliced

2 carrots, thickly sliced

2 celery sticks, thickly sliced

1 handful mushroom stalks

2 bay leaves

1 sprig thyme

5 parsley stalks

3 grinds black pepper

FOR THE SAUCE

1 onion, thinly sliced

180 g/6½ oz mushrooms, thickly sliced

1 sprig thyme

85 g/3 oz butter

● DAIRY   3 tbsp vegetable oil

85 g/3 oz plain flour

● GLUTEN   cornflour

1 bay leaf

salt and pepper

FOR THE PASTRY

300 g/10 oz quantity Basic or Wholemeal Shortcrust Pastry (see box page 153)

● GLUTEN   1½ quantities Cornmeal and Potato Pastry (page 157)

1 beaten egg

● EGG   100 ml/3½ fl oz milk or soya milk

1 Remove any strings around the chicken and trim off any excess fat inside the neck. Place the chicken in a large pan and add the vegetables, herbs and pepper. Cover the ingredients to a depth of 2 cm/¾ inch with cold water. Cover with a lid and bring to the boil over a moderate heat.

2 Once the liquid starts to boil, remove the lid, reduce the heat to a simmer and skim off any scum and fat that collects on the surface. Poach the chicken in barely simmering water for about 1½ hours (20 minutes per 450 g/1 lb), skimming off any scum and fat on the surface and keeping the water level topped up so the chicken remains submerged. The chicken is cooked when the meat is beginning to separate from the bone and the legs move easily from side to side. Lift the cooked chicken out of the stock and allow to cool.

3 Strain the stock into a pan. Bring to the boil and reduce by a third to strengthen its flavour. Reserve 860 ml/1½ pints of the reduced stock for the sauce.

4 Meanwhile, make the sauce. Place the onion, mushrooms, thyme and butter or vegetable oil in a pan and season well. Cover with a lid and cook gently, over a low heat, until the onions are very soft but not coloured.

5 Stir the flour (or cornflour) into the onion mixture and cook over a low heat for 1 minute, stirring continuously. Add the bay leaf and a splash of stock to the pan and stir well until all the liquid has been absorbed. Add the remaining stock, little by little, stirring well between each addition. Bring the sauce slowly to the boil, stirring constantly. Simmer for 1 minute, taste and if necessary, season with more salt and pepper; set aside.

6 To prepare the chicken, peel off the skin, remove the meat and cut it into 3.5-cm/1½-inch dice.

7 Mix the sauce and diced chicken together then spoon into a 23 x 30

cm/9 x 12 inch ovenproof pie dish. Remove the thyme and bay leaf.

8 Preheat the oven to 180°C/350°F/gas mark 4.

9 Roll out the pastry and assemble the pie using techniques described on pages 150–54.

10 Brush the pastry lid with beaten egg (or milk) and bake the pie for about 30 minutes, or until the filling is bubbling and the pastry lid is golden brown.

BOILED GAMMON WITH PARSLEY SAUCE

'Boiled' gammon is actually gently poached in barely simmering water to keep it moist and tender. The creamy, aromatic flavour of parsley sauce complements the salty gammon perfectly. **Serves 4**

INGREDIENTS

2 kg/4½ lb joint of gammon

1 onion, thickly sliced

1 carrot, thickly sliced

1 celery stick, thickly sliced

2 bay leaves

4 parsley stalks

3 grinds of black pepper

1 quantity Parsley Sauce (page 74)

1 Place the gammon in a pan large enough to hold all the ingredients comfortably. Add the onion, carrot, celery, bay leaves, parsley stalks and pepper. Cover with cold water and place a lid on the pan.

2 Bring the gammon slowly to boiling point, remove the lid and lower the heat so that the gammon is poaching in barely simmering water. Poach for 20 minutes per 450 g/1 lb. Top up with water as necessary to ensure the gammon remains submerged (so that it cooks evenly). Do not over-cook the gammon (see Knowing when meat is cooked on page 112). While the gammon is cooking, make the sauce.

3 Once the gammon is cooked, lift it out onto a board and slice off the skin, leaving a thin layer of fat behind. Reserve the ham stock, as it good for making soup (particularly a lentil soup).

4 Slice the gammon as thinly as possible and serve with the Parsley Sauce.

THAI GREEN CHICKEN CURRY

For this vibrant curry, the chicken and vegetables are gently poached in coconut milk flavoured with green curry paste. The curry paste can be made the day before and stored, covered, in the fridge. **Serves 4**

FOR THE GREEN CURRY PASTE

4–6 fresh green chillies (depending on how spicy you like your curry), roughly chopped

1/2 an onion, roughly chopped

5 garlic cloves

5 cm/2 in piece fresh root ginger, roughly chopped

2 lemon grass stalks, outer leaves discarded, sliced into short lengths

2 tsp ground coriander

1 tsp ground cumin

stems from1 bunch fresh coriander, roughly chopped (save the leaves to garnish the curry)

2 tsp Thai shrimp paste

finely grated zest of 2 limes

1 tbsp sunflower or corn oil

1 tbsp water

6 grinds fresh black pepper

1/2 tsp salt

FOR THE CURRY

3 x 400 ml cans coconut milk

2 1/2 tbsp fish sauce

1 tbsp caster sugar

1 aubergine, cut into 2-cm/3/4-in dice

1 kg/2 1/4 lb skinned chicken breasts, sliced across into 2-cm/3/4-in strips

140 g/5 oz baby sweetcorn, cut in half lengthways

2 firm red chillies, deseeded and quartered lengthways

1 bunch coriander leaves, roughly chopped

2 tsp salt and freshly ground black pepper

1 Place all the curry paste ingredients in a food processor and whiz until they form a fine paste. Cover and chill until required.

2 Tip the curry paste into a large pan and gently fry in its own oil for 1 minute, stirring continuously. Add 225 ml/7 fl oz of the coconut milk to the pan and boil for 2 minutes. This draws out the flavours in the paste.

3 Add the remaining coconut milk, the fish sauce, caster sugar and aubergine to the pan and simmer for 5 minutes.

4 Add the chicken to the pan and poach at a gentle simmer for a further 5 minutes.

5 Add the baby sweetcorn and red chillies and cook for a further 2 minutes. Check that the chicken strips are cooked. They should feel firm when pressed between thumb and forefinger.

6 Remove the pan from the heat and stir in half of the chopped coriander leaves. Taste and balance the flavour of the curry with extra salt, sugar, fish sauce and lime juice as necessary.

7 Ladle the curry onto warmed plates and sprinkle with the remaining coriander leaves.

STEWING

Stewing involves slowly cooking jointed poultry or small pieces of meat and vegetables in simmering liquid until very tender. Some varieties of seafood such as squid and octopus also benefit from slow stewing. Before the meat, poultry or seafood and vegetables are immersed in liquid and stewed, they are usually browned in hot oil to add colour and a rich flavour to the dish. Once the meat, poultry or fish is tender and ready to eat, the richly flavoured sauce is often reduced by half by boiling, to concentrate its flavour, and thickened to a syrupy consistency with flour.

Many Asian curries and Moroccan tagines are also prepared by stewing meat, poultry or fish in a liquid, flavoured with spices, vegetables and herbs (see Lamb Rogan Josh on page 134 and Moroccan Chicken Tagine on page 132).

HOW TO STEW MEAT AND POULTRY

- Trim excess fat and cut meat into pieces measuring no less than 2.5 x 5 cm/1 x 2 inches (any smaller and the meat may break up during cooking).
- Season and brown prepared meat, poultry portions or fish and any vegetables, a handful at a time, in hot oil, loosening the browned cooking juices on the base of the pan with water or other liquid (see How to Pan-fry on pages 86–87). If the base of the pan seems burnt, loosen the burnt bits with water and throw the liquid away as it would spoil the flavour of the stew.
- Flour or cornflour may be stirred into the browned vegetables at this stage to thicken and deepen the colour of the sauce. The liquid can then gradually be added.
- Bring slowly to a gentle simmer. As the liquid warms up, fat will rise to the surface where it can be skimmed off.
- Once the stew has begun to simmer on the hob, cover with a tight-fitting lid and continue to simmer the stew on the hob or place in an oven preheated to 150°C/300°F/gas mark 2.
- Stews made with poultry are generally cooked for up to 1½ hours and are ready when the meat is just beginning to fall away from the bone. Stews made with meat, pork or lamb will take longer (2–2½ hours as the muscle fibres are coarser, contain more connective tissue and take longer to soften). Stewed meat is cooked when it can be cut in two easily with a fork. Overcooked meat falls apart into fine shreds.
- If the stewing sauce is thin or very fatty it can be strained into a clean pan, the remaining fat skimmed away and the sauce reduced to a syrupy consistency before the stew is served. Taste and season as necessary.

NOTES FOR FOOD ALLERGY SUFFERERS

Stews or casseroles are largely safe for egg-, soya- and nut-free diets but need some adjustment for those with a dairy or gluten allergy.

DAIRY-FREE DIET: Butter is often added to the oil used to brown meat before the stew is assembled, to enrich the flavour of the stew. Simply omit the butter and use a little more oil in its place.

GLUTEN-FREE DIET: Before browning, pieces of meat, poultry or seafood are often rolled in seasoned flour, as it thickens the cooking liquid. Alternatively, flour is added to vegetables as they are browned, to colour and to thicken the sauce. Replace wheat flour with cornflour or rice flour as it browns and thickens just as well.

MORROCAN CHICKEN, APRICOT, OLIVE AND SAFFRON TAGINE

A wonderfully rich and aromatic stew made with browned jointed chicken or lamb (see Variation opposite). It is free of dairy, gluten, eggs, nuts and soya. Serve with Tabbouleh (page 140), couscous, bulgur wheat or brown rice and green beans. Make the day before it is due to be eaten as its flavour improves overnight. **Serves 4**

INGREDIENTS

sunflower or corn oil

1.5 kg/3 lb roasting chicken, jointed into 8 portions or a pack of 4 drumsticks and 4 thighs

salt and freshly ground black pepper

150 ml/5 fl oz dry white wine

1 large onion, halved from shoot to root and sliced thickly

1 red pepper, cored, deseeded and cut lengthways into thick slices

4 garlic cloves, finely chopped

2.5 cm/1 in piece fresh root ginger, finely chopped

2 tsp cumin seeds

2 tsp ground coriander

2 bay leaves

1 cinnamon stick

400 g can chopped tomatoes

1 lemon, cut into thin wedges

a pinch of saffron stamens

1 bunch fresh coriander

570 ml/1 pint White Chicken Stock (page 64)

110 g/4 oz dried apricots, cut in half

400 g can chickpeas

1 heaped tbsp good quality green olives

1 heaped tbsp good quality black olives

1 Preheat the oven to 150°C/300°F/ gas mark 3.

2 Heat 2 tablespoons of oil in a large casserole dish. Season the skin side of each chicken portion and place half the portions, skin side down, in the pan. Gently fry the chicken until the skin is crisp and golden brown, then turn and brown the flesh side. Set aside. Brown the remaining chicken in the same way.

3 Using a wooden spoon, loosen any browned cooking juices on the bottom of the pan with the white wine and pour over the browned chicken.

4 Heat a tablespoon of oil in the pan and add the onions and red pepper. Fry gently, stirring frequently, until soft and golden brown then add the garlic, ginger, cumin seeds, ground coriander, bay leaves and cinnamon. Fry for another 30 seconds, stirring continuously.

5 Return the chicken portions and cooking juices to the pan and add the tomatoes, lemon wedges, saffron, fresh coriander stems, stock and enough water to cover the ingredients. Bring to simmering point, skimming off any fat and scum that floats to the surface.

6 When the tagine reaches simmering point, cover and cook in the preheated oven for 1 hour. Remove the pan from the oven and stir in the apricots, chickpeas and olives, cover and return to the oven for another 30 minutes or until the chicken meat is just beginning to fall from the bone.

7 The tomatoes will thicken the sauce. To thicken the sauce further, lift out the chicken and vegetables and boil the sauce until it coats the back of a spoon. Return the chicken and vegetables to the pan and bring back to a simmer. Taste and season as necessary.

8 Roughly chop the coriander leaves. To serve, spoon onto warmed plates and sprinkle with chopped coriander.

VARIATION
LAMB TAGINE

In place of chicken use 600 g/1 lb 5 oz of stewing lamb from the neck or shoulder, cut into 2.5-cm/1-inch cubes. Brown the pieces of lamb in a pan then cook for 2 hours in the oven or until the muscle fibres start to separate and the meat is easily cut with a fork. Add the chickpeas, apricots and olives in the last 30 minutes of cooking so they do not over-cook.

LAMB ROGAN JOSH

This rich, aromatic curry has lots of deep red sauce. Serve with boiled basmati rice to mop up the sauce and accompany with yogurt or soya yogurt, flavoured with chopped mint. Make the curry the day before serving, as its flavour improves overnight. **Serves 4**

INGREDIENTS

sunflower or corn oil

1 kg/2¼ lbs stewing lamb, trimmed of fat and cut into 2.5 x 5 cm/1 x 2 in pieces

salt and freshly ground black pepper

570 ml/1 pint White Chicken Stock (page 64) or water

2 large onions, finely diced

2 green peppers, cut into strips

6 garlic cloves, finely chopped

5 cm/2 in root ginger, finely chopped

3–5 fresh red chillies (depending on how spicy you like your curry), deseeded and finely diced

6 cardamom pods and 6 cloves

3 bay leaves

1 cinnamon stick

3 tsp ground coriander

3 tsp cumin seeds

6 tsp paprika

400 g can chopped tomatoes

stems from 1 bunch coriander, finely sliced

1 tsp sugar

2 tsp garam masala

● GLUTEN check label for wheat

1 bunch coriander leaves, chopped

1 Preheat the oven to 150°C/300°F/ gas mark 2.

2 Heat 1 tablespoon of oil in a large casserole over a moderate heat until hot.

Add a handful of the lamb to the pan, season and leave to stick to the base of the pan to brown. Turn and brown the other side only when the meat releases itself from the bottom of the pan.

3 Repeat this process until all the lamb is cooked, loosening the browned cooking juices on the base of the pan between batches with a splash of stock or water. Add this to the browned meat. Add a little oil to the pan between batches.

4 Season and fry the onions and peppers in 1 tablespoon of oil until golden brown. Add the garlic, ginger, chilli, cardamom, cloves, bay leaves, cinnamon, ground coriander, cumin and paprika and gently fry for 30 seconds. Return the meat and the cooking juices to the pan. Over a low heat, stir in the chopped tomatoes, coriander stems and sugar, top up with stock or water so the meat is covered. Cover with a lid and bring to the boil.

5 Remove the lid and skim off any fat or scum on the surface. Replace the lid and and cook the curry in the oven for 1½ hours, or until a piece of lamb can be cut easily with a fork. Remove the curry from the oven every 30 minutes to skim off any fat and add water as necessary, so that the meat is just covered.

6 When the meat is cooked, stir in the garam masala, taste the sauce and season as necessary. Spoon onto warm plates and sprinkle with chopped coriander leaves.

| # POTATOES

Potatoes are starchy tubers, valued for their versatility in cooking and as a source of carbohydrate, fibre, minerals and vitamin C. Potatoes also provide a starchy alternative in gluten-free diets in place of bread, pasta and couscous.

Potatoes are available as small, new potatoes – which have a firm, waxy texture when cooked – and older, floury potatoes, which become soft and fluffy when cooked. New potatoes, such as Jersey Royals and Charlottes, are best boiled and used in salads, simply tossed in olive oil or butter, lightly crushed with oil and seasoning (see Crushed New Potatoes on page 137) or gently fried. Older, floury potato varieties, such as King Edward, Maris Piper and Desiree, are suited to a wider variety of cooking methods including boiling, mashing, deep-frying, roasting and sautéing. The potato dishes in this section make ideal accompaniments to many of the recipes in this book.

ROAST POTATOES

Roast potatoes are normally served with a roast meal and roast very well in the top third of the oven at 180–200°C (350–400°F/gas mark 4–6), the standard temperature required to roast the meat or bird. Allow more time for them to brown and crisp up at the lower temperature. **Serves 4**

INGREDIENTS

1 kg/2¼ lb floury potatoes, peeled

sunflower or corn oil

salt

1 Cut the potatoes into 5 cm/2 inch pieces. Place in a large saucepan, cover with cold salted water, put the lid on and bring to a gentle simmer.

2 Cook until the potatoes can be pierced through with a table knife then drain them in a colander and allow them to steam dry for a few minutes.

3 Meanwhile, pour the oil into a roasting pan to a depth of 1 cm/¼ inch and place in the oven to heat up.

4 Once the oil is hot enough to gently sizzle when a potato is added, carefully arrange the potatoes in one layer in the roasting pan. Quickly rough up the surfaces of the potatoes with a fork to help them crisp up, spoon oil over them and place in the top third of the oven.

5 Roast the potatoes for 60–75 minutes, depending on the oven temperature. Turn the potatoes every 20 minutes to help them brown and crisp up evenly.

6 When the potatoes are crisp and golden, use a slotted spoon to transfer them to a serving dish.

OVEN-BAKED CHIPS

Golden and crispy, and made with very little oil, these chips are much healthier – but just as tasty – as the deep-fried variety. **Serves 4**

INGREDIENTS

1 kg/2¼ lb large floury potatoes

3 tbsp sunflower or olive oil

sea salt crystals and freshly ground black pepper

1 Preheat the oven to 200°C/400°F/gas mark 6.

2 Scrub the potatoes, cut them in half lengthways then slice each half into long wedges approximately 2 cm/¾ inch

thick. Place in a single layer on the base of a roasting pan.

3 Drizzle the potato wedges with oil, sprinkle with a large pinch of sea salt and season lightly with black pepper. Turn the wedges over a few times to coat evenly with oil and seasoning.

4 Bake the potatoes for 30 minutes, turning after 15 minutes to allow them to brown and crisp evenly on all sides. Serve immediately.

MASHED POTATO

Hot and fluffy mashed potatoes are traditionally served with sausages and stews, and as a topping on oven-baked dishes. Use floury potato varieties such as King Edward or Maris Piper. Waxy new potatoes become gluey when mashed. **Serves 4**

INGREDIENTS

900 g/2 lb floury potatoes, peeled

40 g/1½ oz butter
● **DAIRY** dairy-free spread or 1 tbsp olive oil

150 ml/5 fl oz milk
● **DAIRY** soya or rice milk

salt and freshly ground black pepper

1 Cut the potatoes into even-sized pieces, place in a pan of cold, salted water, cover with a lid and simmer gently for 25 minutes, or until the potatoes are sufficiently tender to push a table knife into them easily. Do not over-cook the potatoes or they will taste watery.

2 Drain the potatoes and leave in the colander to steam dry for a minute or so.

3 Tip the potatoes back into the pan, add the butter or olive oil (or dairy-free spread), the milk and seasoning. Mash the potatoes until lump free and fluffy. Taste and season again if necessary.

VARIATION
CHAMP
Add a handful of thinly sliced spring onions to the milk and simmer for 5 minutes. Add to the potatoes before mashing.

CRUSHED NEW POTATOES

New potatoes taste wonderful flavoured with garlic and good quality olive oil. Serve with pan-fried or grilled meat, poultry and fish. **Serves 4**

INGREDIENTS

675 g/1½ lb new potatoes

2 unpeeled garlic cloves

2 tbsp olive oil

sea salt and freshly ground black pepper

1 Place the potatoes in a pan with ½ teaspoon of salt and the garlic cloves, and cover with cold water. Cover with a lid and bring to the boil.

2 Remove the lid and cook the potatoes at a lively simmer for 15–20 minutes, or until the potatoes feel tender when a knife is inserted into them. Do not over-cook the potatoes or they will taste mushy.

3 When the potatoes are cooked, drain in a colander and leave them to dry for a few minutes.

4 Place the potatoes back in the pan. Squeeze the softened garlic out of its skin onto the potatoes and add the olive oil, 1 teaspoon sea salt and three grinds of black pepper.

5 Gently press down on the cooked potatoes with a potato masher a few times to break them into small pieces. Do not mash the potatoes or they will become sticky. Gently stir the crushed potatoes and other ingredients together. Taste and add a little more sea salt and pepper if necessary.

Chapter 15

GRAINS, RICE AND PASTA

GRAINS

In cooking, the term grain refers to the edible seeds of plants, mainly from the grass family. Wheat and its close relatives, barley and rye, produce grains rich in the protein gluten. Other plants from the grass family produce gluten-free grains such as rice, millet and corn. Quinoa grain, the seeds of a plant related to spinach, and buckwheat grain, the seeds of a plant related to rhubarb, are also ideal gluten-free substitutes for grains containing gluten.

GRAINS CONTAINING GLUTEN

BARLEY

At one time barley held a similar position to that of wheat in today's Western diet. However, it is now mainly used to add thickness and texture to winter soups and stews. It fulfils this role admirably but it can easily be substituted with lentils, beans or brown rice. Pearl barley, which is the type used in most recipes, needs to be simmered for approximately 45–60 minutes – on its own or in a soup or stew.

RYE

Rye is mainly used to make dense, richly flavoured rye bread and crackers but can also be eaten as a whole grain in stews and granary-style breads or rolled to form flakes for use in muesli.

WHEAT GRAINS

As wheat grain is very hard, it is first parboiled then crushed or cracked into varying sizes. Coarsely cracked wheat is known as bulgur wheat and finely cracked wheat is known as couscous; both are very easy and quick to prepare.

Bulgur wheat or cracked wheat: Bulgur wheat is a traditional ingredient in Middle Eastern cooking, and is usually served hot with meat and vegetables or cold in the salad tabbouleh. Its tender but chewy consistency makes it a great base for meat-free stuffing. To cook bulgur wheat, see the recipe for Tabbouleh on page 140.

Couscous: Couscous is a staple of North Africa where it is eaten with savoury dishes such as tagines. Semolina (roughly ground durum wheat) is steamed then dried to form fine, pale yellow granules. Couscous grains are much finer than bulgur wheat and cook more quickly. Simply place the couscous in a bowl, cover with boiling water to a depth of 2.5 cm/1 inch, stir in a pinch of salt and a tablespoon of olive oil, cover with clingfilm or a plate and leave to stand for 10–15 minutes.

Oats

Oats are a valuable breakfast cereal and baking ingredient but they contain a protein similar to gluten and should be avoided by those on a gluten-free diet (also, oats are often processed in factories that process wheat). Buckwheat flakes have a very similar texture to rolled oats and can be used in place of them to make muesli (see page 141). Millet and Rice Flake Porridge also stands in very well for porridge made with oatmeal (see Breakfast Cereals, page 141).

GLUTEN-FREE GRAINS

BUCKWHEAT Buckwheat produces black, triangular-shaped seeds, and is used widely in Chinese and Eastern European cooking. Buckwheat grain is either roasted to develop its characteristic flavour before being ground into flour, or is dried for a milder taste. Buckwheat flour has a strong flavour that is a particularly good foil for contrasting flavours (see Buckwheat Pancakes page 196). Steamed and rolled buckwheat flakes are mild in flavour and similar to oats in texture so they are a useful oat substitute in breakfast cereals. They can also be used to add texture to gluten-free bread.

CORN Corn, also called maize, is a cereal grass, related to wheat, rice, oats and barley. As well as being eaten fresh from the cob, it is dried and ground into coarse cornmeal, a staple in some parts of the world, or into the fine powder known as cornflour.
Cornmeal: Cornmeal, also known as polenta, is ground either to a coarse powder with a gritty texture or more finely, into a softer-textured flour used in baking. Cornmeal tastes of sweetcorn and gives a coarse, crumbly texture to baked goods such as pastry. Due to its coarse texture, it is usually blended with other flours for baking and is best used in foods where its flavour is beneficial (as in Cornmeal and Potato Pastry on page 157) or masked with the flavour of other ingredients (as in Spiced Date and Orange Muffins page 175).
Cornflour: A flavourless, fine white powder with a smooth consistency, cornflour is made by finely grinding the dried white centre of corn kernels. Cornflour is traditionally used to thicken sauces in Chinese cooking, and is a very good gluten-free thickening agent and substitute for wheat flour, for savoury and sweet flour-thickened sauces. Cornflour also adds lightness to gluten-free pastry, biscuits and cakes, which can be rather heavy. Used alone, cornflour produces light but very dry baked products so is best blended with other gluten-free flours.

MILLET This nutritious, ancient grain, originally eaten by the Egyptians, is finely ground and used to make flat bread in North Africa and India. Millet grain is tiny, round and either yellow, white or red, and is eaten as a wholegrain or hulled. Boiled millet grain has a light, delicate flavour with a firm bite and makes a great gluten-free substitute for couscous and bulgur wheat (see Millet Tabbouleh page 140). Fine-textured millet flakes are a good substitute for oatmeal in porridge (see Millet and Rice Flake Porridge page 141) and also add fibre and texture to gluten-free bread. Millet flour has a grainy texture rather like cornmeal and is best used for coating meat, poultry and fish before frying to form a crispy coating. It is also used to make gluten-free pasta (see page 147).

QUINOA Quinoa, pronounced 'keen-wa', was a staple of the Incas in South America. The grains are small and round with a subtle nutty flavour and provide one of the best sources of protein of any vegetable. It can be bought in health food shops and good supermarkets and is a valuable alternative grain to rice, bulgur wheat and couscous. It is also great used in stuffing to add bulk and texture.
When boiled, quinoa expands to four times its original size and cooks in approximately 15 minutes (see Quinoa Tabbouleh page 140).

TABBOULEH

This dish is traditionally made with bulgur wheat, but brown rice, millet and quinoa make very good gluten-free alternatives (see Variations below). Tabbouleh is full of colour and aromatic flavour and is a great accompaniment to Baked Moroccan Chicken with Fennel (page 121). **Serves 4**

INGREDIENTS

170 g/6 oz bulgur wheat

½ tsp salt

4 tbsp extra virgin olive oil

finely grated zest and juice of 2 lemons

salt and freshly ground black pepper

1 bunch flat-leaved parsley, finely chopped

1 handful mint leaves, finely chopped

1 handful coriander leaves, finely chopped

4 spring onions, finely sliced

4 ripe tomatoes, seeded and diced

½ a cucumber, seeded and diced

1 tsp caster sugar

1 Place the bulgur wheat in a medium-sized bowl and cover with boiling water to a depth of 2.5 cm/1 inch. Stir in the salt and a tablespoon of olive oil. Cover with clingfilm or a plate and leave the bulgur wheat to absorb the water for about 15–20 minutes, or until the grains are no longer hard but chewy.

2 Drain the bulgur wheat in a sieve then spread out to steam dry and cool on a baking tray lined with kitchen paper.

3 Whisk the remaining oil with the lemon juice and black pepper.

4 Place the bulgur wheat in a bowl, stir in all the remaining ingredients, taste and add more seasoning as necessary. Cover with clingfilm and chill for 30 minutes before serving.

VARIATIONS

BROWN RICE TABBOULEH

Rinse 225 g/8 oz brown rice under cold running water and add to a pan of boiling, salted water. Bring back to a simmer and cook the rice for 30–35 minutes, or until tender. Drain then hold the rice under a cold running tap to cool it down quickly, to prevent it from cooking further. Follow the recipe above from step 3.

MILLET TABBOULEH

Place 170 g/6 oz millet grain, 570 ml/1 pint of water and ½ teaspoon of salt in a pan. Cover and bring to the boil. Reduce the heat and simmer for 20–30 minutes, or until the millet is no longer gritty but tender and fluffy. Follow the main recipe for tabbouleh from step 3.

QUINOA TABBOULEH

Rinse 170 g/6 oz quinoa under cold running water and add it to twice its volume of salted boiling water. Bring back to a simmer and cook for 10 minutes, or until the circular germ begins to separate from the seed. Remove the quinoa from the heat, cover with a tight-fitting lid and leave it to absorb the remaining water. The quinoa will increase by three to four times in volume and should be light and fluffy in texture. Spread out on kitchen paper to cool then follow the main recipe for tabbouleh from step 3.

BREAKFAST CEREALS

A good breakfast is a vital part of a healthy, varied diet. Too often people automatically eat the same old cereal every morning. Here are some ideas for home-cooked or home-mixed cereals – some are suitable for those with a gluten allergy, some are not, but they are all delicious.

CREAMY OAT PORRIDGE

This recipe isn't suitable for those with a gluten allergy (for gluten-free 'porridge' try the Creamy Rice Pudding or Millet and Rice Porridge recipes below), but it is suitable for dairy-free diets if you use soya, rice or oat milk. This recipe serves 4.

Place 200 g/7 oz rolled oats, 570 ml/1 pint milk and ½ teaspoon salt in a pan. Slowly bring the porridge to a gentle simmer over a low heat, stirring the porridge slowly and continuously for 2–3 minutes, or until the oats have softened and the porridge is thick and creamy (add a little more milk if it is too stiff and thick). Stir in 1 large tablespoon of honey, maple syrup or sugar, spoon into bowls, pour over a little milk and serve immediately.

CREAMY RICE PUDDING

This gluten-free pudding is also delicious served as 'porridge' for breakfast. It takes an hour to cook so it is best made the night before. Reheat the porridge by adding a splash of milk and stirring it over a low heat until it starts to simmer. This recipe serves 4.

Slowly bring 1.2 litres/2 pints of milk (cows' or dairy-free) to the boil. Add 170 g/6 oz of Arborio risotto rice, ½ teaspoon of salt, 1 tablespoon of honey and 1 cinnamon stick or ½ teaspoon ground cinnamon, cover and simmer gently for 1 hour, or until the rice is soft. Serve immediately or allow to cool and store covered in the fridge until required.

MILLET AND RICE FLAKE PORRIDGE

This smooth, gluten-free porridge has a warming, delicate taste similar to semolina pudding. The rice flakes are included in the recipe to add a soft, chewy texture similar to porridge made with rolled oats. This recipe serves 4.

Place 150 g/5 oz millet flakes, 55 g/2 oz rice flakes, ½ teaspoon of ground cinnamon and ½ teaspoon salt in a pan. Stir in 860 ml/1½ pints of milk and slowly bring the mixture to a simmer over a low heat, stirring continuously. Simmer for 15 minutes, or until the millet flakes are no longer gritty and the rice flakes have softened but are still slightly chewy. Stir in 2 tablespoons honey, spoon into bowls, pour over a little milk and serve immediately.

GLUTEN-FREE MUESLI

This muesli is full of texture and flavour and is delicious served with natural dairy or soya yogurt, honey and fresh fruit. Experiment with different dried fruit and nuts or for a nut- and seed-free diet, substitute an equal weight of gluten-free flakes. Brown rice flakes, buckwheat flakes and millet flakes are all available from health food shops. This recipe makes 4 servings.

In a medium-sized bowl, mix 55 g/2 oz each of brown rice flakes, buckwheat flakes, millet flakes, roughly chopped brazil nuts, flaked almonds and chopped dried apricots with 2 tablespoons of rice bran, 30 g/1 oz sultanas, 30 g/1 oz dried cherries, 15 g/½ oz golden linseed, 15g/½ oz sunflower seeds and 1 tablespoon soft brown sugar (optional). Use as required.

RICE

Rice is eaten as a staple grain by half of the world's population – and is much loved the world over for its taste and versatility. Before it can be eaten, the tough outer hull is removed to produce the nutritious grain, brown rice. The husk and germ, left intact on brown rice grains, is extremely nutritious as it is high in fibre and minerals, including sodium, potassium, magnesium, iron, calcium and zinc. Brown rice is also rich in carbohydrate, vitamin E, thiamine, riboflavin, niacin and folic acid. Brown rice has a mild nutty flavour and a chewy texture and is altogether a superior grain to white rice in flavour and nutritional value.

Rice is classified into long-grain, medium-grain and short-grain varieties, all of which are available as brown rice or white rice.

LONG-GRAIN RICE

Long-grain varieties include basmati rice, jasmine rice and the long-grain American rice commonly used as a general purpose rice. Long-grain rice has a firm but delicate texture and is normally served plain boiled or fried with other ingredients to make Asian rice dishes such as pilau rice or Chinese stir-fried rice. It is also eaten cold in salads.

Cooking long-grain rice

Two cooking methods are used to cook long-grain rice – the boiling method and the absorption method. Brown rice requires more cooking than white rice and is best cooked by the boiling method. Boiling is also suitable for white rice, but the absorption method produces dry, light fluffy grains and is used widely in Asian and Middle Eastern cookery.

The boiling method

- Fill a large pan two-thirds full of water. Add salt and bring to a rolling boil.
- Allow 55–85 g/2–3 oz uncooked rice per person. Rinse the rice under cold running water to remove starch, which will stop the grains sticking to each other.

- Pour the rice into the boiling water and cook, uncovered, at a gentle simmer for approximately 15 minutes for white rice and 30 minutes for brown rice. White rice is cooked when the grains are tender and no longer chalky in the centre: brown rice is cooked when the grain is soft in the centre but still chewy.
- Drain the rice in a fine mesh sieve. Pour boiling water through it and allow the rice to steam-dry for a minute. Fluff up with a fork and use as required.

The absorption method

This method is used for plain boiled rice and for complete rice dishes cooked in the pot. Stock is often used in place of water to add extra flavour to the rice.

Rice products

Rice is used to make a wide variety of products that are common in Asian cooking. These are tasty in their own right, but are also useful gluten-free ingredients.

Rice noodles: White and translucent in appearance, rice noodles are made from ground rice and water. They are cut into wide ribbons, thick strands or very thin thread-like noodles known as 'glass noodles', as they become clear when cooked. Rice noodles are soaked in hot water for hot dishes, in cold water for use in salads, lightly cooked in stock-based soups or deep-fried and used as a crispy garnish.

Rice pasta: Rice is usually mixed with millet to make gluten-free pasta (see Gluten-Free Pasta, page 147).

Rice flour: This is made from brown or white rice ground to a fine powder. Brown rice flour is high in fibre and far more nutritious than white rice flour. They both have a mild flavour, creamy colour and are used in mainstream cooking to make short, crumbly biscuits and very light cakes. For gluten-free cooking, rice flour is invaluable and is used in cakes, bread, biscuits and pastry (see Chapter 16).

Ground rice: Ground rice has a gritty texture as it is more coarsely ground than rice flour. Its grittiness limits its uses to producing a very short, crumbly texture in some baked foods.

Rice bran: The bran lies between the husk and starchy centre of rice grain and is very high in fibre. It is brown in colour with a mild, malty flavour. It is ideal for adding fibre, colour and flavour to gluten-free baked foods such as bread (see Gluten-free Brown Bread, page 187) and pastry (see Gluten-free Wholemeal Rice and Almond Pastry, page 155).

- Allow 55–85 g/2–3 oz uncooked rice per person. Rinse the rice under cold running water to remove the starch, which will stop the grains sticking to each other.
- Place the rice in a pan, pour over double the volume of boiling water or stock and season with salt. Place a close-fitting lid on the pan and gently simmer for approximately 10–15 minutes, or until the water has almost been absorbed and little pits are appearing on the surface of the rice.
- Remove the pan from the heat and leave the rice, with the lid firmly on, to finish cooking in its own steam for another 10 minutes, or until tender. Fluff up with a fork and use as required.

MEDIUM-GRAIN RICE

Medium-grain rice includes Italian Arborio rice, Spanish paella rice and red Camargue rice.

Cooking medium-grain rice

Medium-grain rice such as Arborio and paella rice are versatile grains used to make Italian risotto and Spanish paella. Neither is suited to the cooking methods used for long-grain rice as the grains become mushy. The grains are first lightly pan-fried in butter or olive oil, to prevent them from sticking together, then hot stock is gradually stirred into the rice over a low heat, until the stock is absorbed and the rice is tender (see Seafood Risotto page 146). Constant stirring also helps to mix the starch on the surface of the rice grains with the liquid to give the creamy consistency of risottos and paellas.

SHORT-GRAIN RICE

Almost round in shape, short-grained rice varieties include Carnaroli, used to make risottos; glutinous rice, used widely in Asian cooking; and pudding rice, used to make rice pudding.

Cooking short-grain rice
Short-grain rice must be cooked very gently to prevent it from becoming mushy. Carnaroli rice is cooked in the same way as the medium-grain rice Arborio.

Glutinous rice is cooked by the absorption method (see above). As it is high in starch, the cooked grains of rice stick lightly to one another, which makes it easy to eat with chopsticks and to mould into sushi.

Pudding rice is gently simmered in milk flavoured with ingredients such as sugar, citrus zest and cinnamon (see Creamy Rice Pudding page 141). For dairy-free rice pudding, use rice milk or soya milk.

RICE SALAD WITH PISTACHIO NUTS AND POMEGRANATE SEEDS

Not your average rice salad, this recipe will surprise your guests with its interesting ingredients, colourful appearance and light, fragrant flavour. It's a great dish to serve at a summer lunch or as part of a buffet with barbequed or grilled meat and fish. **Serves 4**

INGREDIENTS

225 g/8 oz basmati rice

2 tbsp freshly squeezed lemon juice

1 tsp caster sugar

salt and freshly ground black pepper

5 tbsp extra virgin olive oil

1/2 a red onion, finely sliced

1 ripe pomegranate

finely grated zest of 1/2 lemon

55 g/2 oz shelled pistachios, roasted for 5 minutes in a hot oven

diced cucumber

● NUTS

1 bunch of flat-leaved parsley, roughly chopped

1 Rinse the rice in a sieve under cold running water. Bring a large pan of salted water to the boil then pour in the rinsed rice and simmer gently, uncovered, for approximately 15 minutes, or until the rice grains are tender. Do not allow the water to boil too hard as the surface of the grains is liable to become mushy before the centre is properly cooked.

2 Meanwhile, pour the lemon juice into a small bowl, add the sugar, 1/2 teaspoon of salt and 3 grinds of black pepper. Whisk until the sugar and salt have dissolved. Whisk in the oil a tablespoon at a time to form an emulsion. Taste and adjust the seasoning as necessary. Stir in the finely sliced red onion and leave to soften while the rice is cooking.

3 Once the rice is cooked, drain it in a large sieve or colander and place under cold running water until the rice is thoroughly cooled. Leave to drain for 10 minutes.

4 To remove the seeds from the pomegranate, cut it in half across the middle and, using a teaspoon, scrape out the seeds into a bowl and remove any white membrane. (Wear an apron as pomegranate juice stains.)

5 In a large bowl, mix the cold cooked rice with the lemon and onion dressing, the lemon zest, roasted pistachios (or diced cucumber), roughly chopped parsley and pomegranate seeds. Taste and season as necessary, with salt and freshly ground black pepper.

6 Cover and chill the salad for at least 3 hours before serving, to allow the rice to absorb the flavours of the other ingredients. Taste and season as necessary.

SEAFOOD RISOTTO

Most risottos are enriched with butter and Parmesan cheese, making them unsuitable for non-dairy diets. This recipe relies on olive oil, white wine, shellfish and fresh parsley for its rich, vibrant flavour. Serve with a lightly dressed green salad. **Serves 4**

INGREDIENTS

225 g/8 oz small clams, shells cleaned and beards removed

225 g/8 oz mussels, shells cleaned and beards removed

1 glass dry white wine

750 ml/1¼ pints Fish Stock or White Chicken Stock (page 64)

2 tbsp olive oil

1 small onion, finely diced

salt and freshly ground black pepper

3 garlic cloves, finely chopped

350 g/12 oz Arborio rice

150 g/5 oz raw shelled prawns, rinsed

150 g/5 oz cleaned squid, sliced into thick rings

2 tbsp finely chopped flat-leaved parsley

1 Clean the clams and mussels with a scrubbing brush under running water and discard any shells that remain open when handled.

2 Put the cleaned clams and mussels in a large pan, pour over the wine, cover and cook over a moderate heat until all the shells are wide open. Stir the shellfish from time to time to ensure they cook evenly.

3 Remove the mussels and clams from the pan with a slotted spoon, discarding any mussels that are not opened fully. Remove the meat from the shells and set aside in a bowl. Discard the shells.

4 Strain the cooking juices through a fine-meshed sieve into a measuring jug and make up to 860 ml/1½ pints with fish or chicken stock. Pour into a clean pan and set aside.

5 Place the oil in the large pan, add the onion and seasoning, cover the pan and gently fry until soft. Add the garlic and gently fry for another 5 minutes.

6 Stir the rice into the softened onion and garlic, making sure it is thoroughly covered in oil.

7 Bring the stock and shellfish juice to simmering point, add a ladleful to the rice and stir until the stock has been absorbed. Add a second ladleful and stir until it has been absorbed. Continue adding the liquid until the rice is almost tender, about 15 minutes, stirring continuously.

8 Stir the cooked clams, mussels and their juices, the prawns and squid into the rice. Cook the risotto for another 5 minutes, stirring continuously, or until the squid rings are white and no longer translucent and the prawns are pink all over. The risotto should be creamy and easy to stir, so add more stock if necessary.

9 Stir in the parsley, taste, season as necessary and serve immediately.

PASTA

Pasta is made from semolina (finely ground Durum wheat or other hard wheat varieties), as its high gluten content gives cooked pasta a slightly chewy texture. Semolina is mixed with water and sometimes egg to form a paste, which is rolled, stretched and cut into ribbons, extruded into strands or shaped in a whole variety of ways.

GLUTEN-FREE PASTAS

Gluten-free pastas, made from corn, rice, buckwheat and millet, are now available in many forms including spaghetti, rigatoni, lasagne sheets, macaroni and spirals. Rice and millet pasta (used in the recipe for Tomato and Garlicky Pasta with Prawns and Lemon shown below) is the closest to wheat pasta in appearance, texture and flavour and is very good served with both delicate and robust pasta sauces and in baked dishes such as lasagne. Corn pasta has a slightly gritty texture and strong corn flavour so it is best served with richly flavoured sauces and in baked dishes. The same goes for buckwheat pasta, which also has a strong flavour and slightly coarse texture.

Serve wheat or gluten-free pasta with Rich Italian Tomato Sauce (page 80) or Bolognaise Sauce (page 122).

Cooking pasta

Place a pan of salted water on the hob to boil (add 2 teaspoons of salt per litre/1¾ pints of water). When the water is boiling vigorously, add the pasta. When the pasta has softened and sunk below the surface of the water, stir it with a wooden spoon to prevent it sticking together or to the base of the pan. Cook the pasta at a rolling boil. Dried pasta will take approximately 12 minutes to cook; fresh pasta 4–5 minutes. Dried pasta is cooked when the hard, chalky centre has just disappeared. Fresh pasta is ready when it is smooth and tender in the mouth. Pasta should taste slightly chewy, known as 'al dente' to the Italians.

TOMATO AND GARLICKY PASTA WITH PRAWNS AND LEMON

This easy-to-prepare dish is so delicious it has become a firm favourite with my family. Its lively, aromatic flavours rely on good quality, fresh ingredients prepared just before cooking. The flat, ribbon shape of linguine pasta goes particularly well with seafood but gluten-free rice and millet fusilli also works well. The quantities are generous as your guests are very likely to ask for a second helping. **Serves 4**

INGREDIENTS

500 g/1 lb 2 oz linguine

● **GLUTEN**   rice and millet pasta or corn pasta

● **EGG**   most fresh and some dried pasta uses egg – check the label

extra virgin olive oil

4 large ripe tomatoes, roughly chopped

2 large garlic cloves, finely chopped

sea salt and freshly ground black pepper

250 g/9 oz cooked, shelled medium-sized prawns

finely grated zest of 1 lemon

finely chopped parsley or torn basil leaves

1 Cook the pasta in boiling, salted water (see 'Cooking pasta' page 147). Dried pasta will take approximately 12 minutes to cook; fresh pasta 4–5 minutes.

2 Meanwhile, add sufficient olive oil to a medium-sized pan to cover the base to a depth of 1 cm/¼ inch. Place the pan over a medium heat. Once the oil is hot, add the tomatoes, garlic and a generous pinch of sea salt and a grind of pepper. Bring slowly to a gentle simmer.

3 Once the tomatoes have begun to soften, stir in the prawns. Bring the sauce back to a simmer, remove from the heat and cover with a lid. Do not over-cook the prawns or they will become dry and tough.

4 Thoroughly drain the pasta in a colander and pour it back into the pan.

5 Stir the lemon zest into the sauce. Mix the sauce with the pasta so that the pasta is evenly coated. Taste and season with pure sea salt to bring out the flavours. Sprinkle with finely chopped parsley or torn basil leaves before serving.

| # HOME BAKING

PASTRY

Of the many styles of pastry, shortcrust is the most versatile. Not only does it have a neutral flavour that makes it ideal for a wide variety of sweet and savoury fillings, but it can be easily adapted – enriched with egg, sweetened with sugar, flavoured with cheese and finely ground nuts, or made with wholemeal flour. It is also the most adaptable pastry for food allergy sufferers.

Although it is traditionally made with flour, butter, water or egg, shortcrust pastry can be made just as well with gluten-free flours, dairy-free margarine and water. However,

NOTES FOR FOOD ALLERGY SUFFERERS

DAIRY-FREE DIET: Butter is used to add flavour, richness and colour, and to give a firm pastry that is easy to handle. Hard dairy-free baking margarine is a perfectly good alternative. Its flavour is not as rich and buttery but it makes pastry dough that is easy to handle, and is just as light and crumbly when cooked. Soft margarine is not suitable, as it produces a dough that is too soft to handle.

GLUTEN-FREE DIET: Most fine-textured gluten-free flours are suitable for making shortcrust pastry but they are best blended in specific proportions to closely imitate the properties of wheat. For example, rice flour, when used alone, produces a dry, gritty-textured pastry. However, when it is blended with cornflour, which adds lightness, and ground almonds, which add moisture and richness, the result is a gluten-free pastry to rival wheat flour pastry in flavour, texture and appearance. Stronger flavoured flours, such as buckwheat, cornmeal and soya flour, are also suitable for pastry making, provided they are blended with blander flavoured flours to prevent the pastry from overpowering the flavour of the overall dish.

EGG-FREE DIET: Cold beaten egg, mixed with a small quantity of water, is often used to bind pastry ingredients, as it adds colour and richness and softens the texture of pastry. For egg-free pastry use chilled water only (this simply gives a paler and crisper pastry than one bound with egg). Mashed potato can also be used instead of egg to bind savoury pastry (see Cornmeal and Potato Pastry page 157).

NUT-FREE DIET: Ground almonds, walnuts and hazelnuts are sometimes used to add flavour, richness and texture to shortcrust pastry. Instead, simply use a basic savoury or sweet shortcrust pastry or, for a 'nutty' flavour, wholemeal pastry. Many of the gluten-free pastry recipes that follow use ground almonds. Replace these with soya flour for a rich, soft crumbly pastry or cornmeal for a crisp textured pastry.

SOYA-FREE DIET: Pastry is suitable for soya-free diets provided soya flour and margarine containing soya bean oil is not used to make it.

due to the lack of gluten, which helps bind the ingredients, gluten-free shortcrust pastry is made differently to that made with wheat flour. You'll find recipes for both versions in this chapter.

<table>
<tr><td>

GUIDELINES FOR
MAKING
SHORTCRUST
PASTRY

</td><td>

The presence of gluten in wheat flour is both an advantage and disadvantage in pastry making. Gluten lightly binds dough together so that it does not fall to pieces when handled and is firm but crumbly when cooked. However, when too much water is added to the dough or it is kneaded or rolled too much, the gluten strands develop, toughening the pastry and causing it to harden and shrink as it cooks. Follow these steps to ensure perfect pastry:

</td></tr>
</table>

Preparing the dough
- Keep the ingredients cool and use very cold water or chilled beaten egg to bind. Warm ingredients produce a greasy, tough pastry.
- Measure your ingredients accurately. Too much or too little flour, fat or liquid may result in dry, greasy or tough pastry.
- To rub flour and fat together, use the fingertips of both hands, letting the rubbed mixture fall back into the bowl. Continue a bit at a time until the mixture resembles fine breadcrumbs. If your hands are warm, cut the flour and butter together using a scissor like action with two table knives. This way the fat will not melt into the flour and toughen the pastry.
- Stir the liquid into the flour and butter crumbs, tablespoon by tablespoon, until the mixture is sufficiently damp to clump together and form a ball of dough. Do not add too much liquid – wet dough is hard to handle and produces tough, shrunken pastry.

Rolling the pastry
- Sprinkle the work surface lightly with flour to stop the pastry sticking.
- Place the ball of dough on the floured work surface and, using a lightly floured rolling pin, flatten it into a rough circle, approximately 2.5-cm/1-inch thick.
- With firm strokes away from the body, roll the pastry out into a circle at least 2.5 cm/1 inch larger than the tin. Turn the pastry a quarter turn every four rolls to ensure it is rolled evenly and to prevent it sticking to the work surface. Pastry used to line a tart tin or pie dish should be no thicker than 3 mm/⅛ in. Pastry for small individual tarts and pies should be 2 mm thick.
- Before moving the pastry, run a palette knife under it to free any patches that may have stuck to the work surface.

Lining a tin
- Wrap the pastry around the rolling pin then lift it above the tin. Unwind the pastry into the tin or pie dish and gently press the pastry into place on the base, sides and corners with your fingers. If the pastry breaks, don't worry, it can be patched up with trimmings afterwards.
- Roll the rolling pin over the rim to remove the excess pastry.

Patching cracked pastry cases

Pastry cases sometimes crack as they cook and must be patched up before the filling is added, to prevent leakage. Brush fine cracks with beaten egg or patch up wider cracks or holes with a small amount of leftover pastry. Return the pastry case to a medium oven to set the egg or to lightly cook any pastry used for patching.

- Repair any holes by pressing the dough back together or using a little of the excess dough to fill large holes.
- Place the lined tart tin in the fridge for 30 minutes, to firm up the pastry before baking. This reduces the likelihood of the pastry shrinking and losing its shape in the oven.

Baking blind

To prevent pastry cases that contain moist fillings becoming heavy and soggy when baked, they are often 'baked blind' until crisp before they are filled.

- Cut out a large circle of greaseproof paper and crumple it into a ball (to soften it so that it fits tightly into the corners). Open the paper out and line the pastry then weigh it down with 2–3 tablespoons of ceramic baking beans or dried beans or rice.
- Preheat the oven to 200°C/400°F/gas mark 6. Do not put the pastry in the oven until it has reached the correct temperature (otherwise it may collapse and become very greasy).
- Bake the pastry for 15–20 minutes, or until it is dry and firm. Remove the paper and beans and bake for another 10 minutes, or until the pastry base is an even light golden colour and dry and crisp to touch. Watch sweetened pastry carefully as it burns easily. If the rim of the pastry is browning too quickly, reduce the oven temperature and cover the top edge and sides of the tart shell with foil.
- Leave the pastry to cool on a wire rack before adding the filling.

Assembling a single-crust pie

Single-crust pies consist of a pie filling covered with a pastry lid. They're a great way to turn the simplest filling into something a little more special.

- Spoon the filling into the pie dish and roll out the pastry lid to 3-mm/⅛-inch thick and 5 cm/2 inches larger than the dish.

- From the edge of the rolled pastry, cut long strips slightly thicker than the rim of the dish. Brush the rim of the dish with water and stick the strips of pastry to it, trimming away any excess pastry with a sharp knife. This forms a firm base for the pie lid to attach to.

- Brush the pastry rim with water and lay the rolled out pastry over the dish, using your rolling pin to lift and support it. Gently press the edges of the pastry lid down onto the pastry-covered rim to seal in the filling. Cut away any excess pastry. Scallop the edges with the tips of your fingers if you wish.

- Make a small hole in the centre of the pastry lid to allow steam to escape. Decorate the pie by sticking leaf-shaped pieces of pastry onto the lid with a little water.

- To glaze the pie, brush all over with beaten egg or milk and chill for 20 minutes in the fridge, to set the pastry. Bake the pie in a preheated oven.

BASIC SHORTCRUST PASTRY

Before making this pastry, read Guidelines for Making Shortcrust Pastry page 150.

This versatile pastry has a delicate flavour and crumbly texture that is perfect for pastry cases and pie shells for savoury or sweet fillings. It is egg free and easily adapted for dairy-free diets, but it contains wheat flour – for gluten-free pastry see pages 155–57. This recipe makes one 25–30 cm/10–12 inch tart. **Serves 8–10**

INGREDIENTS

225 g/8 oz plain flour

½ tsp salt

110 g/4 oz chilled butter, cut into 1 cm/ ⅓ in dice

dairy-free hard baking margarine

2–3 tbsp cold water

● DAIRY

1 Sieve the flour and salt into a mixing bowl and add the diced butter. Rub the flour and butter together with your fingertips until they resemble coarse breadcrumbs.

2 Using a table knife and then the fingertips, stir in 2 tablespoon of the water to bind. The dough should be just damp enough to form a ball. If the mixture is too dry to clump together, stir in another tablespoon of cold water.

3 Wrap the pastry dough in clingfilm and chill for 30 minutes. Preheat the oven to 200°C/400°F/gas mark 6.

4 Roll the pastry to the correct thickness and use as required. If the pastry is soft after being handled, rest it once more in the fridge until cold and firm.

VARIATIONS

SAVOURY RICH SHORTCRUST PASTRY
Egg enriches the flavour and softens the crumb of shortcrust pastry, making it perfect for rich flavoured fillings. To adapt the basic recipe above, mix 2 chilled egg yolks with 2 tablespoons of cold water and use as per the instructions for step 2.

SWEET SHORTCRUST PASTRY
With its delicate flavour and crisp texture this pastry is mainly used to make sweet tarts and fruit pies. It can also be used in place of sweet rich shortcrust pastry for an egg-free diet. To adapt the Basic Shortcrust Pastry recipe above, stir 70 g/2½ oz caster sugar into the butter and flour 'breadcrumbs' then bind the pastry with 2 tablespoons of cold water, as above.

SWEET RICH SHORTCRUST PASTRY
This recipe is ideal for making tart bases and rich pies. To adapt the Basic Shortcrust Pastry recipe above, stir 70 g/2½ oz caster sugar into the butter and flour 'breadcrumbs', then mix 2 chilled egg yolks with 2 tablespoons of cold water and mix into the flour, butter and sugar mixture, to form the dough.

WHOLEMEAL PASTRY
Wholemeal flour gives a nutty flavour, making it ideal for hearty sweet and savoury pies and tarts. For savoury pastry, substitute 110 g/4 oz plain flour with plain wholemeal flour and continue as above. To make sweet wholemeal pastry, substitute 110 g/4 oz plain flour with plain wholemeal flour and stir in 70 g/2½ oz of caster sugar at step 2.

Pastry quantities

This useful guide indicates what size tart tin or pie dish you require to feed a certain number of people and how much pastry you need for it.

Tart shells
To serve 2–4: line a 15 cm/6 inch tart tin with pastry made with 110 g/4 oz flour, 55 g/2 oz butter or dairy-free hard baking margarine, diced; 1–2 tablespoons cold water. For rich shortcrust pastry, mix 1 egg yolk with 1 tablespoon cold water. For sweet shortcrust pastry, add 2 tsp caster sugar to the flour and butter.

To serve 4–6: line an 18–20 cm/7–8 inch tart tin with pastry made with 170 g/6 oz flour, 85 g/3 oz butter or dairy-free hard baking margarine, diced; 1–2 tablespoons cold water. For rich shortcrust pastry, mix 1 egg yolk with 1–2 tablespoons cold water. For sweet shortcrust pastry, add 55 g/2 oz caster sugar to the flour and butter.

To serve 8–10: line a 25–30 cm/ 10–12 inch tart tin with pastry made with 225 g/8 oz flour, 110 g/4 oz butter or dairy-free hard baking margarine, diced; 2–3 tablespoons cold water. For rich shortcrust pastry, mix 2 egg yolks with 2 tablespoons cold water. For sweet shortcrust pastry, add 70 g/2½ oz caster sugar to the flour and butter.

To make 20 x 6 cm/2½ inch tarts: make the pastry using the quantities given in 'To serve 8–10' above.

Pie crusts
To make 12 x 6 cm/2½ inch pies with lids: make the pastry using the quantities given in 'To serve 8–10' above.

To make a single-crusted pie to serve 4–6: use 1.5 L/2½ pint pie dish and make the pastry lid with 300 g/10 oz flour, 140 g/5 oz butter and 3 tbsp cold water. For rich shortcrust pastry, mix 2 egg yolks with 2 tablespoons cold water. For sweet shortcrust pastry, add 85 g/ 3 oz caster sugar to the flour and butter.

To make a double-crusted pie to serve 4–6: use a 1.5 L/2½ pint pie dish or a 23–25 cm/9–10 inch round pie plate and make the pastry with double the quantities given in 'To serve 4–6' above.

MAKING
GLUTEN-FREE
SHORTCRUST
PASTRY

Preparing the dough
The absence of gluten means that gluten-free pastry requires more water for binding than its wheat flour counterpart. Where egg is used to bind, whole egg – rather than egg yolk – is used in order to bind the ingredients more firmly.

In addition, gluten-free dough must be kneaded lightly with the fingertips for 2–3 minutes until soft and smooth. This encourages the gluten-free flours to absorb liquid so the pastry is not overly crumbly. If the dough starts to crack while it is being kneaded it requires more liquid: crumble the dough back into the bowl, stir in more water a tablespoon at a time and knead again.

Rolling it out
Gluten-free pastry is very delicate and requires careful handling.
- To hold the pastry dough together, place it between 2 sheets of clingfilm.
- With the rolling pin, press and flatten the ball of pastry into a rough circle, approximately 2.5 cm/1 inch thick.

• With firm strokes away from the body, roll the pastry out into a large circle to the required thickness (no thicker than 3 mm/⅛ inch for lining a tart tin or pie dish and 2 mm thick for small individual tarts and pies), turning the pastry a quarter turn every four rolls to ensure it is rolled evenly.

For a single crust pie, consisting of a filling covered with a pastry lid, follow the instructions for Assembling a Single-Crust Pie on page 151 but roll the gluten-free pastry between two sheets of clingfilm (see below) and use the bottom sheet to support the pastry lid as you lift and turn it on to the pie dish.

Lining a tin

• Peel off the top sheet of clingfilm and transfer the rolled pastry to the tin with the remaining sheet of clingfilm uppermost.
• Gently press the pastry into the tin so that the pastry hugs the base, corners and sides, then carefully peel away the second layer of clingfilm.
• Roll the rolling pin over the rim of the tin to remove the excess pastry.
• Repair any holes by pressing the dough back together or using a little of the excess dough to fill large holes. Don't worry if the shell looks patchy as the pastry will even out in the oven. Reserve a little of the dough to patch any holes that appear as the pastry cooks.
• Place the tart shell in the fridge to firm up for 30 minutes before baking. Cold firm pastry is less likely to lose its shape in the oven.

Baking

Gluten-free pastry is prone to losing its shape in the oven unless it is baked blind first (see page 151). Like wheat-based pastry, gluten-free pastry requires a hot oven so that it quickly hardens and holds its shape. If the oven is too low, the pastry will melt, lose its shape and become tough and greasy.

RICE AND ALMOND SHORTCRUST PASTRY

Before making this pastry, read Making Gluten-free Shortcrust Pastry page 153.

This versatile gluten-free pastry is for those who are able to eat nuts. It is crisp, delicately flavoured and ideal for savoury tart shells. This recipe makes enough for one 25–30 cm/10–12 inch tart tin. **Serves 8–10**

INGREDIENTS

110 g/4 oz brown rice flour

55 g/2 oz cornflour

1/2 tsp salt

55 g/2 oz ground almonds

110 g/4 oz cold butter

● **DAIRY** dairy-free hard baking margarine, diced

1 whole egg, beaten with 1 tbsp water

● **EGG** 50 ml/2 fl oz water

1 Sieve the flours and salt into a large mixing bowl and stir in the ground almonds.

2 Rub the butter into the flour mixture with your fingertips until the mixture resembles breadcrumbs.

3 Using a table knife, stir in 1 tablespoon of the liquid until the flour and butter crumbs clump together. Add another tablespoon of liquid if the mixture is still too dry and crumbly.

4 Bring the dough together into a ball then place on a work surface lightly dusted with rice flour. Knead the dough lightly until it is smooth and soft. If it starts to crack it requires more water. Wrap in clingfilm and chill for 30 minutes.

5 Roll thinly between two sheets of clingfilm and use as required.

VARIATIONS

SWEET RICE AND ALMOND PASTRY
This crisp, sweet pastry is for those who can eat nuts. It is ideal for making sweet tarts such as French Apple Tart, page 164. For the sweet version of the above recipe, simply stir 70 g/2 1/2 oz caster sugar into the flour and butter crumbs in step 2.

WHOLEMEAL RICE AND ALMOND PASTRY
This light textured yet hearty pastry is great for pies and tarts. For the wholemeal version of the main recipe, simply substitute the ground almonds with the same weight of whole almonds, finely ground, and add 1 tablespoon of rice bran. Follow the recipe above, adding the rice bran to the bowl, with the almonds, in step 1.

RICE AND CORNMEAL SHORTCRUST PASTRY

Before you make the pastry read Making Gluten-free Shortcrust Pastry page 153.

This crisp yet crumbly gluten-free pastry is a great nut-free alternative to the previous recipes. It is ideal for savoury tarts. This recipe makes enough for a 25–30 cm/10–12 inch tart. **Serves 8–10**

INGREDIENTS

110 g/4 oz brown rice flour

110 g/4 oz cornmeal

½ tsp salt

110 g/4 oz cold butter, diced

● **DAIRY** dairy-free hard baking margarine

1 whole beaten egg mixed with 1 tbsp water

● **EGG** 50 ml/2 fl oz water

1 Sieve the flour, cornmeal and salt into a large mixing bowl.

2 Add the butter and rub into the flour with your fingertips until the mixture resembles fine breadcrumbs.

3 Using a table knife, stir in the liquid until the mixture clumps together. Add another tablespoon of water if the mixture is still too dry and crumbly.

4 Bring the dough together into a ball. Knead lightly, on a work surface dusted with rice flour, until smooth. Wrap in clingfilm and chill in the fridge for 30 minutes.

5 Roll thinly between two sheets of clingfilm and use as required.

VARIATION

SWEET RICE AND CORNMEAL PASTRY
In keeping with the main recipe, this sweet shortcrust pastry is free of gluten, nuts and soya, and is easily adapted for dairy-free and egg-free diets, too. It has a crisp texture and pale golden colour ideal for making sweet tarts. To adapt the recipe given above, simply stir 70 g/2½ oz caster sugar into the 'breadcrumbs' in step 2.

CORNMEAL AND POTATO PASTRY

Before making this pastry, read Making Gluten-free Shortcrust Pastry page 153.

Delicious, rich-tasting and gluten-, egg-, nut- and soya-free, this recipe is a great all-rounder. It is also easily adapted for dairy-free diets. The mashed potato binds the ingredients together, adds moisture and gives the pastry its flaky texture. This recipe makes enough for a 25–30 cm/10–12 inch tart. **Serves 8–10**

INGREDIENTS

85 g/3 oz brown rice flour

85 g/3 oz cornmeal

½ tsp salt

140 g/5 oz cold butter, diced

● **DAIRY** dairy-free hard baking margarine

110 g/4 oz cold plain mashed potato

1 Sieve the rice flour, cornmeal and salt together.

2 Rub in the butter until the mixture resembles fine breadcrumbs.

3 Stir in the mashed potato and bring the dough together with your fingers to form a ball.

4 Lightly knead the pastry until smooth and soft on a work surface lightly dusted with rice flour. Wrap the dough in clingfilm and rest for 30 minutes in the fridge.

5 Roll thinly between 2 sheets of clingfilm and use as required.

VARIATION

PARMESAN AND POTATO PASTRY
This flaky gluten-, egg-, soya- and nut-free pastry is delicious used for quiches and savoury tarts that have a cheese, bacon or roast vegetable filling. It forms the base of the Tomato, Red Onion and Basil Tart on page 159 and can also be used for the Tarte Niçoise (page 158). To adapt the recipe above, simply replace 55 g/2 oz of the butter with finely grated Parmesan and stir into the flour and butter crumbs at step 2.

TARTE NIÇOISE

This tart is full of flavour, colour and texture and is simple to make. It is also free of gluten, dairy products, egg, soya and nuts. The combination of tomato, black olives, tuna, onion and herbs on the cornmeal and potato base is truly delicious. Eat it hot or cold with new potatoes and lightly dressed salad. **Serves 6–8**

FOR THE PASTRY

2 quantities Cornmeal and Potato Pastry recipe (page 157)

FOR THE FILLING

½ quantity Rich Italian Tomato Sauce recipe (page 80)

2 x 185 g cans tuna, broken into chunks

2 handfuls good quality pitted black olives

½ red onion, thinly sliced

2 tsp fresh thyme leaves

50 g can anchovies

2 tbsp extra virgin olive oil

freshly ground black pepper

1 Preheat the oven to 200°C/400°F/gas mark 6. Roll the pastry to fit a shallow rectangular baking tray approximately 30 x 42 cm/12 x 16½ inches. Remove the top sheet of clingfilm and transfer the pastry to the baking tray, pastry side down. Press the pastry against the sides and into the corners of the baking tray then peel away the top sheet of clingfilm. Using a sharp knife, cut away any excess pastry that rises above the edges of the tray. Chill for 15 minutes.

2 Prick the base of the pastry shell with a fork and bake for 20 minutes, or until light golden.

3 Spread the tomato sauce evenly over the pastry base and evenly scatter the tuna, olives, onion and thyme leaves over the tart. Lay the anchovies over the ingredients and drizzle the tart with olive oil. Season with pepper (there should be no need for salt as there's enough in the other ingredients).

4 Bake the tart for 20 minutes, or until the edge of the pastry has turned crisp and golden brown. Remove the tart from the oven and check that the pastry has evenly browned underneath by lifting a corner with a fish slice. If not, place the tart back in the oven for another 5 minutes. Lower the temperature to 170°C/325°F/gas mark 3 if the tart filling is beginning to brown.

TOMATO, RED ONION AND BASIL TART

The rich, aromatic flavours of ripe tomatoes and basil make this the ideal summer tart. Serve as a starter or for lunch with boiled new potatoes and dressed green salad. Serves 6–8

FOR THE PASTRY

1 quantity Basic Shortcrust Pastry recipe (page 152)

● GLUTEN

Parmesan and Potato Pastry (page 157) or Rice and Cornmeal Pastry (page 156)

FOR THE FILLING

4 tbsp olive oil

3 large red onions, halved from root to shoot and sliced thinly

3 sprigs thyme

sea salt and freshly ground black pepper

3 garlic cloves, finely chopped

2 handfuls torn basil leaves

12 ripe but firm tomatoes, sliced into thin rounds

1 Make the pastry, roll to 3 mm/⅛ inch thick and use to line a 25–30 cm/ 10–12 inch tart tin. Chill the pastry for 30 minutes.

2 Preheat the oven to 200°C/400°F/ gas mark 6.

3 Blind-bake the pastry (see page 151) for 20 minutes, or until the pastry case is set and firm. Remove the paper and beans and return to the oven for another 5 minutes, or until the pastry is crisp and an even pale golden colour.

4 Heat 2 tablespoons of olive oil in a large frying pan, add the onions, thyme, ½ teaspoon salt and 4 grinds pepper, cover, and fry over a low heat for 20 minutes, or until the onion is soft but not coloured. Add the garlic and fry over a moderate heat for 1 minute.

5 Remove the sprigs of thyme and spread the softened onions and garlic over the base of the baked tart shell. Scatter a third of the basil leaves on top.

6 Starting at the edge of the pastry case, loosely overlap half of the tomato slices in one layer, spiralling towards the centre. Lightly season the tomatoes with sea salt and black pepper and scatter on half of the remaining basil leaves.

7 Arrange the remaining slices in the same way and season lightly with sea salt and black pepper.

8 Lightly drizzle 2 tablespoon of olive oil over the tart and place on the middle shelf of the preheated oven, reducing the heat to 170°C/325°F/gas mark 3. Bake for 45 minutes, or until the tomatoes have softened and are lightly browned on the top. Scatter with the remaining basil leaves before serving.

APRICOT AND ORANGE TART

This tart looks impressive and tastes wonderful. It is soya free and simple to adapt for dairy-, gluten- and nut-free diets. For an egg-free tart, see the variation below (this requires a few more substitutions but it is well worth the effort). Serve with Crème Anglaise (page 207) or cream, or on its own with tea or coffee. **Serves 8–10**

FOR THE PASTRY

1 quantity Savoury Rich Shortcrust Pastry recipe (page 152)

● GLUTEN

Rice and Almond Pastry (page 155) or Rice and Cornmeal Pastry (page 156)

FOR THE FILLING

110 g/4 oz softened butter

● DAIRY

dairy-free margarine

110 g/4 oz caster sugar

2 eggs, beaten

110 g/4 oz ground almonds

● NUTS

self-raising flour

30 g/1 oz plain flour

● GLUTEN

potato flour

finely grated zest and juice of 1 orange

750 g/1 lb 10 oz fresh ripe apricots, halved and stoned

TO GLAZE

3 tbsp apricot jam

1 Preheat the oven to 180°C/350°F/gas mark 4.

2 Make the pastry, roll thinly and use to line a 25 cm/10 inch tart tin with a loose base. Chill for 30 minutes.

3 To make the sponge filling, whisk the butter, sugar, eggs, almonds, flour, orange zest and juice in a bowl until light and fluffy (if the mixture curdles the cooked filling may be slightly denser but

just as delicious). Spread the mixture over the chilled pastry case and arrange the apricot halves, skin side up, on the top.

4 Bake the tart on the middle shelf of the oven for 15 minutes, or until the filling has puffed up and is turning light golden brown. Turn the oven down to 170°C/325°F/gas mark 3 and cook the tart for a further 30 minutes, or until the sponge filling is set in the centre.

5 Lift the tart out of the oven, remove the sides of the tart tin and leave to cool on a wire rack.

6 Meanwhile, melt the jam in a small pan, pass it through a sieve into a bowl to remove any pieces of fruit and leave to cool for 1 minute.

7 With a pastry brush, dab and brush the glaze over the surface of the tart, filling any gaps with glaze. Leave the glaze to set before serving the tart.

VARIATION
EGG-FREE TART

Use Basic Shortcrust Pastry (page 152) for the shell. For the filling, mix together 55 g/2 oz ground almonds, 85 g/3 oz self-raising flour and 1 tsp baking powder; whisk this mixture with the soft butter, sugar, orange zest and juice, and 100 ml/3½ fl oz apple purée (page 36) until light and fluffy. Spread the filling in the pastry case as in step 3 above and continue with the recipe.

LEMON TART

This tart is rich, creamy and very lemony. It is egg free and can be made with gluten-free shortcrust pastry, but it is not suitable for dairy-free diets as the filling relies on the mild, rich flavour of dairy cream. The tart needs to set in the fridge for at least 2 hours before serving. **Serves 8**

FOR THE PASTRY

1 quantity Sweet Shortcrust Pastry recipe (page 152)

● **GLUTEN**

Rice and Almond Pastry (page 155) or Rice and Cornmeal Pastry (page 156)

FOR THE FILLING

3 lemons

2½ tsp powdered gelatine

140 g/5 oz caster sugar

2 tsp custard powder

200 ml/7 fl oz whole milk

500 ml/17 fl oz double cream

icing sugar for decorating

● **GLUTEN**

check label for wheat

1 Make the pastry and use to line a 25 cm/10 inch tart tin with a loose base. Fill any holes or cracks in the pastry and chill for 15 minutes. Blind-bake the pastry (see page 151).

2 When the pastry shell is cooked, patch any cracks or holes with a little of the remaining pastry (see Patching Cracked Pastry Shells, page 150). Place the tin on a wire rack to cool.

3 Finely grate the zest of two of the lemons and set aside. Squeeze the juice from the zested lemons and the third lemon and pour into a small pan.

4 Sprinkle the gelatine over the lemon juice and leave to stand for 10 minutes.

5 Meanwhile, place the lemon zest, sugar and custard powder in a saucepan and slowly incorporate the milk to form a smooth mixture. Add the cream and stirring continuously, bring the mixture to a simmer to cook the custard powder. Remove from the heat.

6 Gently heat the gelatine and lemon juice, continuously swirling the mixture around the pan, until it starts to steam and the gelatine crystals have dissolved. Immediately remove the pan from the heat.

7 Pour the melted gelatine and lemon juice into the cream mixture and stir well. Allow the lemon cream mixture to cool for 10 minutes then pour into the pre-baked pastry case. If there are any thin cracks or small holes in the pastry base, brush some of the lemon filling over the pastry and leave to set for 5 minutes before pouring in the remaining filling.

8 Place the tart in the fridge and leave to set for 2 hours.

9 Remove from the fridge 30 minutes before the tart is due to be eaten to allow the filling to soften slightly. Sift icing sugar over the tart and serve.

JAM TARTS

These colourful tarts are fun to make with children, as a treat for tea parties. Use a variety of jams for different coloured and flavoured jam tarts. **Makes 18–20 jam tarts**

● GLUTEN

FOR THE PASTRY

1 quantity Basic Shortcrust Pastry recipe (page 152)

Rice and Cornmeal Pastry (page 156) or Rice and Almond Pastry (page 155)

FOR THE FILLING

340 g/12 oz raspberry, strawberry, blackcurrant or apricot jam

1 Preheat the oven to 180°C/350°F/ gas mark 4.

2 Make the pastry and let it chill for 20 minutes.

3 On a lightly floured surface, roll out the chilled pastry to 3 mm/⅛ inch thick. Cut out as many rounds as you can using a 7.5 cm/3 inch fluted pastry cutter. Bring the remaining pastry together, roll out again and cut out more rounds.

4 Line 2 x 12-hole patty tins with the rounds of pastry and place 1 heaped teaspoon of jam in each. Do not overfill with jam.

5 Bake the jam tarts on the middle shelf of the oven for 10–15 minutes, or until the pastry is crisp and light biscuit brown.

6 Run a knife around the hot tarts and lift them out with a palette knife onto a wire rack to cool.

FRENCH APPLE TART

This traditional French tart is easily adapted for dairy-, egg- and gluten-free diets. Serve with Banana Ice Cream (page 205), Vanilla Cream Sauce (page 208) or double cream. **Serves 8–10**

FOR THE PASTRY

1 quantity Sweet Rich Shortcrust Pastry recipe (page 152)

● **EGG**
● **GLUTEN**

Sweet Shortcrust Pastry (page 152)
Sweet Rice and Almond Pastry (page 155)
or Sweet Rice and Cornmeal Pastry (page 156)

FOR THE FILLING

900 g/2 lb Granny Smith apples, peeled, cored, quartered and thinly sliced

1½ tbsp lemon juice

1½ tbsp caster sugar

TO GLAZE

6 tbsp apricot jam

1 Preheat the oven to 180°C/350°F/gas mark 4.

2 Make the pastry, roll to 3 mm/⅛ inch thick and use it to line a 25–30 cm/10–12 inch tart tin with a loose base.

3 Chill the tart for 15 minutes then blind bake (see page 151) until light brown and crisp.

4 Toss the sliced apples in lemon juice to prevent them from discolouring.

5 To assemble the tart, pile the apple slices into the baked pastry case in even layers, sprinkling each layer with caster sugar, to just below the rim of the tart shell. Arrange the top layer of apple slices in overlapping concentric circles. Sprinkle with the remaining sugar.

6 Bake on the middle shelf of the oven for about 30 minutes, or until the apples are tender and lightly browned on top. The pastry should be golden brown and crisp. If the apple starts to brown too quickly, reduce the temperature of the oven to 150°C/300°F/gas mark 2. Place on a wire rack to cool.

7 Melt the apricot jam in a small pan, stirring regularly. Pass it through a sieve into a bowl and leave to cool until it is thick enough to evenly coat the back of a spoon.

8 Using a pastry brush, dab and brush the apricot glaze over the apples, filling the gaps between slices with glaze. The glazed tart should look smooth and shiny. Leave the glaze to set before serving.

CAKES

Everyone loves cake and not being able to indulge is an on-going source of consternation for those suffering from food allergies. However, this does not have to be the case: although bought cakes are usually unsuitable for people with food allergies, homemade cake recipes can be easily adapted to suit gluten-, egg-, dairy-, nut- and soya-free diets. Cakes can still be tender, moist, richly flavoured and crumbly when made with ingredients such as gluten-free flour, egg substitutes or dairy-free margarine. It is important to note that it is not possible to produce a light, moist cake that is both gluten and egg free, because one of these is needed to bind and lighten the mixture. Turn to the Knowing How to Substitute for… chapters for a comprehensive explanation of the purpose of wheat flour, eggs, dairy products, nuts and soya in cake making and how they can be substituted.

NOTES FOR FOOD ALLERGY SUFFERERS

DAIRY-FREE DIET: Most cakes can be made with dairy-free margarine instead of butter, and soya or rice milk instead of cows' milk. Butter cream icings for cakes are also just as good made with dairy-free margarine. All the recipes in this chapter can be made with dairy-free ingredients.

GLUTEN-FREE DIET: Perfectly delicious cakes can be made using gluten-free flours – if you use a mixture of neutral flavoured flours. The best combination is 50 per cent rice flour, 25 per cent cornflour and 25 per cent ground almonds. Rice flour provides the neutral flavoured base, ground almonds add richness and moisture and cornflour lightens the consistency. Potato flour is an ideal substitute for wheat flour in cakes with a moist, soft texture such as brownies. Eggs and extra baking powder are essential to bind, moisten and lighten cakes made with gluten-free flours. The general rule is to add 3 eggs for every 110 g/4 oz of flour used, which produces a feather-light cake with a spongy texture.
    Check the labels of powdery ingredients such as baking powder, icing sugar and spices, as they are sometimes mixed with wheat flour to prevent lumps forming.

EGG-FREE DIET: Egg helps bind the raw ingredients and produces a light, moist cake. It is possible to replace egg in cake mixtures with other ingredients that provide moisture and lightly bind the ingredients, such as fruit purées, mashed banana, custard and liquids such as milk (see Egg Substitutes, page 166). Self-raising flour plays an important role in egg-free cakes, as it contains gluten, which helps to bind cake mixture together, and raising agents that fill the mixture with bubbles. Extra baking powder is also added to ensure the cooked cake is as light as possible.

NUT-FREE DIET: While cakes based on ground nuts are obviously off limits, those which use nuts in small quantities can generally be easily adapted. When chopped nuts are used to add texture, replace them with an equal quantity of dried fruit. When ground nuts are used to enrich the flavour of cake mixture (see Rich Fruit Cake page 170), replace them with an equal quantity of the flour used in the recipe and an extra tablespoon of fat. Be wary of margarines – use butter or read the label on margarines to make sure they do not contain nut-based oils.

SOYA-FREE DIET: Although soya is prevalent in bought cakes, it is only present in homemade cakes if soya flour, soya milk or margarine made with soya oil are used. Replace soya flour with another neutral flavoured flour, use butter or soya-free margarine and rice milk or cows' milk.

EGG SUBSTITUTES

For successful egg-free cakes, it is important to select an egg substitute that enhances but does not overpower the overall flavour of the cake. Apricot purée has a strong fruity flavour and is best used in fruit cakes. Apple purée has a more delicate flavour and is perfect for cakes with a mild zesty flavour. Extra mashed banana works well as an egg replacer in cakes already flavoured with banana, and thick, cold custard successfully replaces egg in plain sponge cakes.

Some cake mixtures do not require eggs and instead contain a high proportion of self-raising flour, chemical raising agents and liquid, normally milk, to bind and lighten the mixture. The following egg substitutes are used in many of the recipes in this chapter.

APRICOT PURÉE   Place 170 g/6 oz stoned, dried apricots in a pan and add 150 ml/5 fl oz water. Cover and simmer gently for 15 minutes, or until the apricots are very soft. Using a hand-held blender or food processor, purée until smooth but still thick enough to hold its shape. Allow to cool and use as required. This purée can be covered and stored in the fridge for up to three days or frozen in an airtight container. Makes approximately 290 ml/10 fl oz

APPLE PURÉE   Peel, core and slice 340 g/12 oz dessert apples and place in a pan with 4 tablespoons water. Cover and cook over a medium heat for 15 minutes, or until soft. Using a wooden spoon, beat until smooth but still thick enough to hold its shape. Allow to cool and use as required. This purée can be covered and stored in the fridge for up to three days or frozen in an airtight container. Makes approximately 290 ml/10 fl oz

CUSTARD   Place 1 tablespoon egg-free, cornflour-based custard powder and 1 tablespoon caster sugar in a pan and mix together. Measure 290 ml/10 fl oz milk or dairy-free milk in a jug. Stir 2 tablespoon of the milk into the custard powder and sugar until smooth. Gradually stir in the remaining milk and place on a medium heat. Bring the custard to the boil, stirring constantly, until thickened and smooth. Remove from the heat, allow to cool and use as required. Custard can be stored, covered, in the fridge for up to three days.

REPLACING EGG WITH EGG SUBSTITUTES   In order to adapt your own recipes, use one of the following substitutions to replace each egg called for in a recipe:
- 50 ml/2 fl oz fruit purée, custard or liquid, plus 1 extra teaspoon baking powder per 110 g/4 oz self-raising flour
- for banana cakes, 1 extra small banana or ½ a large banana, plus 1 extra teaspoon baking powder per 110 g/4 oz self-raising flour.

BANANA, CINNAMON AND HONEY CAKE

This moist, light cake is egg-, soya- and nut-free and is easily adapted for gluten- and dairy-free diets. The gluten-free version requires an egg to help bind the ingredients. This is a good recipe to make with children and it's great for children's birthday parties.
Serves 8–12

INGREDIENTS

225 g/8 oz self-raising flour

• **GLUTEN**   110 g/4 oz rice flour, 55 g/2 oz cornflour and 55g/2 oz ground almonds

• **NUTS**   110 g/4 oz rice flour, 55 g/2 oz cornflour and 55 g/2 oz potato flour

1 tsp baking powder

• **GLUTEN**   2 tsp gluten-free baking powder

1 tsp ground cinnamon

110 g/4 oz butter

• **DAIRY**   dairy-free margarine

85 g/3 oz soft dark brown sugar

2 tbsp honey

finely grated zest of 1 orange

5 ripe bananas, mashed with a fork

• **GLUTEN**   replace 1 banana with 1 beaten egg

85 g/3 oz sultanas

1 Preheat the oven to 170°C/325°F/gas mark 3. Grease a 900 g/2 lb loaf tin and line it with oiled greaseproof paper.

2 Sift the flour, baking powder and cinnamon into a bowl.

3 Add the butter, sugar, honey, grated orange zest (and egg if using) to the dry ingredients and whisk together until the mixture is smooth.

4 Fold in the mashed banana and sultanas. The mixture should be soft enough to fall slowly from a spoon. If the mixture is too firm, stir in a tablespoon of milk.

5 Spoon into the loaf tin, level with the back of a spoon and bake for 45 minutes to 1 hour, or until springy in the centre. Insert a skewer into the centre – if it comes out clean the cake is ready.

6 Leave to set for 5 minutes in the tin then run a knife around the cake to loosen it; turn it out onto a wire rack. The cake can be stored for up to three days in an airtight container or wrapped well in clingfilm and frozen.

LEMON AND ORANGE MARMALADE CAKE

This wholesome citrus-flavoured cake is egg free, unless it is made with gluten-free flour. The lack of gluten means that egg is required to bind the cake, help it rise and prevent it crumbling. This delicious cake is also easily adapted for a dairy-free diet.
Serves 8–12

INGREDIENTS

225 g/8 oz self-raising flour

● GLUTEN 110 g/4 oz rice flour, 55 g/2 oz cornflour, 55 g/2 oz ground almonds and 2 tsp gluten-free baking powder

110 g/4 oz butter

● DAIRY dairy-free margarine

110 g/4 oz caster sugar

grated rind of 1 lemon

grated rind of 1 orange

1 tsp mixed spice

● GLUTEN check for wheat flour

55 g/2 oz raisins

55 g/2 oz mixed peel

1/2 tsp salt

1 tbsp lemon juice

2 tbsp chunky marmalade

175 ml/6 fl oz milk

● DAIRY dairy-free milk

● GLUTEN 3 beaten eggs instead of milk

1 tbsp Demerara sugar

icing sugar (optional)

1 Preheat the oven to 180°C/350°F/gas mark 4. Grease a 900 g/2 lb loaf tin, line with greaseproof paper and brush with oil.

2 In a mixing bowl, rub the butter (or margarine) into the flour, until the mixture resembles coarse breadcrumbs. Add the caster sugar, lemon and orange rind, mixed spice, raisins, mixed peel and salt and mix well.

3 In a separate bowl, mix the lemon juice with the marmalade.

4 Working quickly (to make the most of the raising agents), pour the milk (or beaten eggs) and the lemon juice and marmalade mixture into the cake ingredients and stir until all the ingredients are well mixed. The cake mixture should be soft enough to fall slowly from a spoon. Add a little more milk if necessary.

5 Spoon the cake mixture into the prepared tin. Level the surface with the back of a spoon, sprinkle with the Demerara sugar and bake for 40 minutes. Reduce the oven temperature to 160°C/310°F/gas mark 3 and bake for a further 20 minutes, or until the centre of the cake is firm and a skewer inserted into the centre comes out clean.

6 Leave the cake to cool for 10 minutes in the tin before turning it out onto a wire rack. If you wish, drizzle the cake with drizzle icing (see page 171). The cake can be stored in an airtight container for up to one week or frozen (un-iced).

RICH FRUIT CAKE

This traditional fruit cake is ideal as a Christmas or wedding cake and is easily adapted for gluten-, dairy-, egg- and nut-free diets. It improves in texture and flavour when stored in an airtight container for up to two months. 'Feed' it once a month with a tablespoon of brandy or rum to develop its flavour and keep it moist. **Serves 12–16**

INGREDIENTS

450 g/1 lb currants

170 g/6 oz sultanas

170 g/6 oz raisins

55 g/2 oz mixed peel

55 g/2 oz glacé cherries, halved

grated rind of 1 lemon

grated rind of 1 orange

4 tbsp brandy or rum

110 g/4 oz ground almonds

● NUTS 110 g/4 oz extra plain flour plus 1 extra tbsp butter

110 g/4 oz plain flour

● GLUTEN 55 g/2 oz rice flour, 30 g/1 oz cornflour and 30 g/1 oz ground almonds

2 tsp mixed spice

● GLUTEN check for wheat flour

½ tsp salt

225 g/8 oz butter

● DAIRY dairy-free margarine

225 g/8 oz soft dark brown sugar

4 eggs, beaten

● EGG 225 ml/8 fl oz apple or apricot purée (page 166)

● GLUTEN 6 eggs, beaten

2 tbsp black treacle

55 g/2 oz almonds, roughly chopped

● NUTS dried mixed fruit

1 Place the dried fruit, orange and lemon zest in a bowl. Stir in the brandy or rum, cover and soak overnight.

2 Preheat the oven to 150°C/300°F/ gas mark 2. Grease a 20 cm/8 inch round, deep cake tin and line the base and sides with greaseproof paper.

3 Mix the ground almonds and flour in a bowl with the mixed spice and salt.

4 In a separate large mixing bowl, beat the butter and sugar together with a wooden spoon until pale and fluffy. Beat the eggs (or fruit purée) into the creamed butter and sugar, a tablespoon at a time. If the mixture starts to curdle, mix in a spoonful of flour and almonds.

5 Fold the flour mixture into the butter and egg (or purée) mixture. Stir in 1 to 2 tablespoons of tepid water if the mixture is a little stiff.

6 Stir the treacle and almonds (or extra fruit) into the soaked fruit and fold this into the cake mixture. Do not beat or the air you have incorporated will be lost. Spoon the mixture into the prepared tin and level the top with the back of spoon.

7 Secure a double layer of brown paper around the outside of the tin with string, extending 5 cm/2 inches above the tin.

8 Cover the top of the cake with two pieces of greaseproof paper cut to the size of the tin and make a hole in the centre to allow steam to escape.

9 Bake for 3½–4 hours. Do not open the oven door until the cake has been cooking for 3 hours or it may collapse. Remove the greaseproof paper, cover and allow the cake to brown for the last half an hour. The cake is cooked when the cake is evenly browned on top, feels firm in the centre and a skewer, inserted into the middle of the cake, comes out clean.

10 Turn the cake out of the tin and allow to cool in its lining paper on a wire rack. Once cold, make holes 2.5 cm/1 inch apart through to the bottom of the cake and carefully drizzle 2 tablespoons of brandy or rum over the surface of the cake.

11 To store, leave the cake in its lining paper and wrap tightly in 2 or 3 layers of clingfilm, then in foil. Place in an airtight container and store somewhere cool and dry. Once a month, unwrap the cake and pour over 1–2 tablespoons of alcohol.

12 The cake can be covered with marzipan (contains nuts) and icing up to three weeks before it is to be eaten. For nut-free cakes, a few days before eating, spread the cake with apricot jam and cover with rolled fondant icing only.

Butter Cream Icings for Sponge Cakes

Butter cream icing, a rich and creamy icing traditionally used for filling and spreading over sponge cakes, is just as good made with softened dairy-free baking margarine instead of butter. Soft dairy-free spread may also be used but makes a very soft icing only suitable for filling cakes. The recipes below make sufficient icing to cover and fill a 20 cm/8 inch sponge cake. For a gluten-free diet, look for gluten-free icing sugar as it is sometimes padded out with wheat flour to prevent it forming lumps.

Lemon or orange butter cream icing
This is delicious with Orange or Lemon Sponge Cake (page 172). Beat the grated peel of 2 lemons or oranges into 225 g/8 oz softened butter or dairy-free hard baking margarine until soft and fluffy. Add 225 g/8 oz icing sugar to the bowl and beat until smooth.

Chocolate butter cream icing
Use this rich, chocolate icing for filling and covering chocolate sponge cakes. Beat 170 g/6 oz softened butter or dairy-free hard baking margarine in a mixing bowl until creamy and sift 85 g/3 oz good quality cocoa powder and 170 g/6 oz icing sugar onto it. Add 1 tablespoon water and beat the ingredients until they are thoroughly mixed and the icing is smooth and creamy.

Dark chocolate fudge icing
Make 1 quantity of Dark Chocolate Sauce (page 208) and leave to cool and set before filling and spreading over plain and chocolate sponge cakes.

Drizzle icings
Use lemon or orange drizzle icing to ice plain, orange or lemon sponge cakes and to decorate individual cup cakes for children's parties. Sift 140 g/5 oz icing sugar into a bowl and mix in 1 tablespoon of freshly squeezed lemon or orange juice to form a smooth, stiff paste. Drizzle or spread the icing over the cake and leave to harden.

VICTORIA SPONGE CAKE

This simple cake is extremely easy to adapt for dairy- and gluten-free diets. It is also nut- and soya-free. For an egg-free sponge, use apple purée or cold custard: apple purée gives the cake a delicate fruity flavour while custard gives it a moist pudding-like texture. Traditionally the two sponges are sandwiched together with jam but you can also use a butter cream icing (see page 171). **Serves 6–8**

INGREDIENTS

● GLUTEN

225 g/8 oz self-raising flour
110 g/4 oz rice flour, 55 g/2 oz ground almonds and 55 g/2 oz cornflour

● GLUTEN

2 tsp baking powder
4 tsp gluten-free baking powder

● DAIRY

225 g/8 oz soft butter
dairy-free margarine

● EGG

225 g/8 oz caster sugar
170 g/6 oz caster sugar

● EGG

5 eggs
225 ml/8 fl oz apple purée or custard (page 166)

● GLUTEN

add 1 more egg

strawberry jam

caster sugar

1 Preheat the oven to 180°C/350°F/gas mark 4. Grease two 18 cm/7 inch sandwich cake tins, line with grease-proof paper and lightly brush with oil.

2 Sieve the flour and baking powder together into a mixing bowl.

3 Add the butter, sugar and eggs (or apple purée or custard) to the bowl and whisk the ingredients together until thoroughly mixed. The mixture should be soft enough to fall slowly from a large spoon. Stir in 1–2 tablespoons of tepid water if necessary.

4 Divide the cake mixture between the two prepared tins, gently spread it over the base of the tins and level off with a knife. Place the tins on the middle shelf of the oven and bake for 30 minutes, or until firm and springy in the centre.

5 Allow the cakes to set in the tin for 30 seconds then run a sharp knife around the edges of the tins to loosen them. Turn the cakes out onto a wire rack, peel off the paper and leave to cool.

6 When cold, transfer one of the cakes, crust down, to a serving plate. Spread the base of one of the cakes thickly with jam and place the other cake on top, crust uppermost. Sprinkle with caster sugar and serve.

VARIATIONS

CHOCOLATE SPONGE CAKE

Add 2 tablespoons cocoa powder to the basic Victoria Sandwich Cake recipe. Add 3 tablespoons cocoa powder to the gluten-free sponge mixture, to ensure the chocolate flavour is not diluted by the extra egg used to bind the cake mixture. Fill the cake with Chocolate Butter Cream Icing or Dark Chocolate Fudge Icing (page 171) or with blackcurrant jam.

ORANGE OR LEMON SPONGE CAKE

Add 1 tablespoon juice and the finely grated zest of an orange or lemon to the basic recipe above. Fill with strawberry jam or Orange or Lemon Butter Cream Icing (page 171).

MOIST ALMOND CAKE WITH LEMON SYRUP

This light, lemony cake does not contain fat or flour and is perfect for dairy- and gluten-free diets. It does contain nuts, as the title suggests, and a large quantity of whisked egg whites, which are necessary for the light and moist consistency of this cake. It's delicious as a dessert, served with strawberries. **Serves 8**

FOR THE CAKE

340 g/12 oz ground almonds

300 g/10½ oz caster sugar

grated zest of 1 lemon

8 egg whites

FOR THE LEMON SYRUP

juice of 1 lemon

110 g/4 oz granulated sugar

1 Preheat the oven to180°C/350°F/ gas mark 4. Grease a 20 cm/8 inch round loose-bottomed cake tin, line with greaseproof paper and grease the paper.

2 Mix the ground almonds, sugar and grated lemon zest together in a large mixing bowl.

3 Whisk the egg whites until they no longer wobble when shaken.

4 Using a large metal spoon, thoroughly stir one-third of the whisked egg whites into the ground almond mixture. Gently fold in the remaining whisked egg whites – do not over mix. Gently tip the mixture into the prepared cake tin and level the top with a spatula.

5 Bake for 45 minutes to 1 hour, or until the cake is just set in the middle. A skewer inserted into the centre of the cake should come out clean. Do not over-cook the cake or it will become dry.

6 Meanwhile, place the lemon juice and sugar in a small saucepan and bring to the boil over a moderate heat. Boil until the syrup is thick enough to coat the back of a spoon. Remove from the heat and leave to cool.

7 Allow the cake to set for 5 minutes in the tin. Run a sharp knife around the cake to loosen it and when it is almost cold, remove the tin and place the cake on a serving plate.

8 Using a skewer, make holes 2.5 cm/1 inch apart all over the cake and drizzle over the lemon syrup. Loosely cover the cake with clingfilm and allow the cake to absorb the syrup for an hour before serving.

PLAIN SCONES

Traditionally, scones are made with self-raising flour, butter and milk but they are just as delicious made with gluten-free flours and baking powder, dairy-free margarine and dairy-free milk. To make gluten-free scones, beaten egg is used with milk to bind the mixture and to ensure the scones rise and hold together when cooked. For scones that are both gluten and nut free, replace the ground almonds with extra potato flour. Bite-sized scones, cut with a small pastry cutter and thickly spread with jam, make a colourful addition to the table for children's birthday parties. **Makes 8**

INGREDIENTS

● GLUTEN

225 g/8 oz self-raising flour

110 g/4 oz potato flour, 55 g/2 oz ground almonds, 55 g/2 oz rice flour and 2 tsp gluten-free baking powder

½ tsp salt

1 tbsp caster sugar

● DAIRY

55 g/2 oz butter, cut into small pieces

dairy-free margarine

● DAIRY

● GLUTEN

150 ml/5 fl oz milk

dairy-free milk

2 beaten eggs, made up to 150 ml/5 fl oz with milk

extra flour for shaping the scones

1 Preheat the oven to 220°C/425°F/gas mark 7.

2 Sift the flour, salt and sugar into a mixing bowl and rub the butter into the flour with your fingertips until the mixture resembles coarse breadcrumbs.

3 Pour in the milk (or beaten egg and milk) and mix quickly to a soft dough with a table knife.

4 Tip the dough out onto a floured surface, knead briefly until smooth and lightly roll to 2.5 cm/1 inch thick. Don't roll too thinly – the height of the scone comes mainly from the thickness of the mixture as they do not rise much.

5 Working quickly, dip a 5 cm/2 inch plain or fluted pastry cutter into flour and cut out as many scones as possible. Bring the remaining dough together, roll out once more and cut out a few more scones.

6 Place the scones on a floured baking tray and bake for 10 minutes, or until risen and golden brown on the top and bottom.

7 Serve straight from the oven or cool on a wire rack. Store in an airtight container for up to 24 hours, or freeze until required (before serving, defrost the scones and place in a hot oven for a few minutes to crisp up).

VARIATIONS

FRUIT SCONES

Add ½ teaspoon mixed spice (check label for wheat if making gluten-free scones), 30 g/1 oz sultanas and 30 g/1 oz raisins to the basic dough.

WHOLEMEAL SCONES

Use half wholemeal and half white self-raising flour. For gluten-free wholemeal scones, use ground whole almonds in the place of ground, blanched almonds.

SPICED DATE AND ORANGE MUFFINS

These egg-free muffins have a rich fruity flavour, thanks to the addition of marmalade and apricot purée, both of which also help to bind the ingredients together. Due to the low quantity of wheat flour used in this recipe it can easily be substituted with self-raising gluten-free flour and the addition of one egg. For children's parties, make bite-sized muffins in small paper cases. **Makes 12**

INGREDIENTS

55 g/2 oz cornmeal

55 g/2 oz ground almonds

cornmeal

● NUTS

● GLUTEN

55 g/2 oz self-raising flour

mix 30 g/1 oz rice flour, 15 g/½ oz ground almonds and 15 g/½ oz cornflour

1 tsp baking powder

● GLUTEN

2 tsp gluten-free baking powder

½ tsp salt

½ tsp mixed spice

● GLUTEN

check for wheat flour

110 g/4 oz butter, melted

● DAIRY

dairy-free margarine

55 g/2 oz soft brown sugar

50 ml/1¾ fl oz apricot purée (page 166)

1 tbsp coarse-cut marmalade

100 ml/3½ fl oz milk

dairy-free milk

● DAIRY

add 1 egg to the mixture

● GLUTEN

finely grated zest of 1 orange

110 g/4 oz stoned and roughly chopped dates

1 Preheat the oven to 170°C/325°F/gas mark 3. Thoroughly grease a 12-hole muffin tin or line with paper cases.

2 In a mixing bowl, stir the cornmeal, ground almonds, flour (or gluten-free flour mixture), baking powder, salt and mixed spice together.

3 Add the butter, sugar, apricot purée, marmalade, milk and orange zest (and egg if using) and whisk until the mixture is smooth (do not over-whisk or it will become dense when cooked). The mixture should fall slowly from a spoon – add more milk if the mixture is too firm. Stir in the chopped dates. The raising agent starts to work the moment it comes into contact with liquid. Work quickly to ensure the muffins rise properly.

4 Spoon the mixture into the prepared muffin tin and bake on the middle shelf of the oven for 15–20 minutes, or until the muffins are risen and firm in the centre.

5 Run a table knife around them and turn out onto a wire rack to cool. Store in an airtight container for up to three days or freeze in sealed plastic bags.

SQUIDGY CHOCOLATE BROWNIES

It is easy to feel that brownies as decadent as these must be out of bounds for dairy- and wheat-allergy sufferers. This recipe proves otherwise. They're great served as they are or fresh out of the oven with Dark Chocolate Sauce (page 208) and/or ice cream. Eggs are particularly important in this recipe as they bind and set the cake batter – for delicious egg-free brownies see opposite. **Makes 16**

INGREDIENTS

● **DAIRY**

110 g/4 oz butter
dairy-free margarine

● **NUTS**
● **SOYA**

85 g/3 oz good quality dark chocolate with 70% cocoa solids
check for traces of nuts
check for soya lecithin

● **GLUTEN**

55 g/2 oz plain flour
potato flour

225 g/8 oz granulated sugar

1 tsp baking powder

● **GLUTEN**

gluten-free baking powder

½ tsp salt

2 eggs

● **GLUTEN**

1 extra egg

1 Preheat the oven to 180°C/350°F/ gas mark 4. Line a 20 cm/8 inch square baking tin with baking parchment so that the paper stands 2.5 cm/1 inch above the tin (to protect the cooking brownies) and grease lightly with oil.

2 Melt the butter and chocolate together, over a gentle heat, stirring continuously.

3 Mix the flour, sugar, baking powder and salt together in a large mixing bowl.

4 Beat the eggs into the butter and chocolate mixture with a wooden spoon. Quickly stir in all the dry ingredients until the batter is smooth.

5 Pour the batter into the prepared tin and bake on the middle shelf for 20–30 minutes or until the centre just gives when pressed.

6 Remove from the oven and leave to set in the tin for 10 minutes before cutting into squares.

VARIATION

Stir 110 g/4 oz roughly chopped pecans or walnuts into the brownie mixture before spooning it into the baking tin.

EGG-FREE RICH CHOCOLATE BROWNIES

These brownies are made with self-raising wheat flour, which is essential to the recipe. Golden syrup and milk ensure the brownies are as light, moist and gooey as chocolate brownies made with egg. **Makes 16**

INGREDIENTS

110 g/4 oz dark chocolate with 70% cocoa solids, broken into small pieces
check for traces of nuts
check for soya lecithin

85 g/3 oz butter
dairy-free margarine

150 ml/5 fl oz golden syrup

110 g/4 oz self-raising flour

1 heaped tsp baking powder

50 ml/2 fl oz milk
dairy-free milk

½ tsp salt

● **NUTS**
● **SOYA**
● **DAIRY**
● **DAIRY**

1 Preheat the oven to 180°C/350°F/gas mark 4. Line a 20 cm/8 inch square baking tin with baking parchment so that the paper stands 2.5 cm/1 inch above the tin (to protect the cooking brownies).

2 Place the chocolate, butter and golden syrup in a pan. Gently melt together, stirring continuously.

3 Sift the flour, baking powder and salt together into a mixing bowl.

4 Pour the melted chocolate mixture and the milk onto the dry ingredients and quickly mix together until the batter is smooth.

5 Pour the brownie mixture into the lined tin and bake on the middle shelf of the preheated oven for 10–15 minutes, or until the mixture is just set in the middle. Be careful not to over-cook the brownies or they will lose their squidgy consistency. Allow to cool in the tin for 10 minutes then cut into squares.

BISCUITS

Although there is an increasing selection of 'allergy-free' biscuits on the market, homemade biscuits always taste much better and are often simple to make. The recipes below are great for tea parties, picnics and lunch boxes and can be adapted for gluten-, dairy-, egg-, soya- and nut-free diets.

CHEWY SYRUP SQUARES

Rice Krispies give these biscuits a light and chewy texture. For the gluten-free version, oats are replaced with buckwheat flakes and rice flakes, and the Rice Krispies with gluten-free puffed rice. Beaten egg added to the gluten-free ingredients helps to bind the mixture together. **Makes 24**

INGREDIENTS

170 g/6 oz butter

● **DAIRY** dairy-free margarine

55 g/2 oz soft brown sugar

100 ml/3½ fl oz golden syrup

110 g/4 oz rolled oats

● **GLUTEN** 55 g/2 oz rice flakes and 55 g/2 oz buckwheat flakes

110 g/4 oz Rice Krispies

● **GLUTEN** gluten-free puffed rice or rice krispie-style cereal

● **GLUTEN** 2 eggs, beaten

1 Preheat the oven to 180°C/350°F/ gas mark 4. Grease a 24 x 30 cm/9 x 12 inch baking tin.

2 Gently heat the butter, sugar and syrup together, stirring continuously until all the sugar is dissolved. If you are making gluten-free squares, allow the butter, syrup and sugar mixture to cool for 5 minutes then stir in the beaten eggs.

3 Stir in the remaining ingredients, mix thoroughly and tip into the prepared baking tin. Gently press the mixture down, and into the corners, until it is flat. Bake for 20 minutes, or until firm and golden brown. Do not over-brown or the squares will taste bitter.

4 Leave to set slightly for 1 minute, cut into squares and place them on a wire rack to cool. Serve fresh or store for up to two days in an airtight container.

SHORTBREAD ROUNDS

Shortbread has a rich buttery flavour and short, crumbly texture due to the large proportion of fat and the use of rice flour in the dough. For gluten-free shortbread, simply replace plain flour with ground almonds. For dairy-free shortbread, use hard baking margarine to ensure the dough is sufficiently firm to roll. **Makes about 16**

INGREDIENTS

● DAIRY

110 g/4 oz butter

hard dairy-free baking margarine

55 g/2 oz caster sugar

85 g/3 oz plain flour

● GLUTEN

ground almonds

85 g/3 oz rice flour

caster sugar for sprinkling

1 Preheat the oven to 150°C/300°F/ gas mark 2.

2 Beat the butter and sugar together with a wooden spoon until the mixture is soft and pale. Sieve the flours on top and stir into the creamed butter and sugar.

3 Form the dough into a ball with the minimum of handling and place on a floured surface. Flatten the dough to 2.5 cm/1 inch thick, cover with clingfilm and chill for half an hour to firm it up.

4 Place the dough on a floured surface and using a floured rolling pin, roll it to 5-mm/¼-inch thick. Cut into rounds with a 7.5 cm/3 inch plain or fluted pastry cutter and arrange on a baking sheet. Do not place the biscuits too close together as they expand as they cook.

5 With the minimum of handling, collect the dough trimmings together, roll and cut out more biscuits and place on the baking tray. Lightly sprinkle the biscuits with caster sugar.

6 Bake the biscuits on the middle shelf of the preheated oven for about 15 minutes or until the shortbread is an even light golden colour (do not allow the shortbread to brown or it will taste burnt). Leave to harden for 30 seconds then transfer each biscuit to a wire rack to cool.

VARIATIONS

ORANGE OR LEMON SHORTBREAD

For orange or lemon shortbread, add the grated zest of one orange or lemon to the butter and sugar.

FRUIT SHORTBREAD

Add 85 g/3 oz sultanas to the creamed butter before adding the flour in step 2.

CHOCOLATE CHIP COOKIES

These deliciously chewy cookies can be adapted very easily for dairy-, gluten- and egg-free diets. To adapt the recipe for egg-free diets, self-raising flour is used to add lightness and milk is added to provide the liquid necessary for binding the ingredients together. **Makes 18**

INGREDIENTS

● **DAIRY**
110 g/4 oz softened butter
dairy-free margarine

110 g/4 oz granulated sugar

110 g/4 oz soft light brown sugar

● **EGG**
1 egg, beaten
50 ml/2 fl oz milk

● **GLUTEN**
170 g/6 oz plain flour
85 g/3 oz rice flour and 85 g/3 oz cornmeal or ground almonds

● **EGG**
170 g/6 oz self-raising flour

● **GLUTEN**
1 tsp baking powder
gluten-free baking powder

½ tsp salt

● **DAIRY**
1 tbsp milk
dairy-free milk

85 g/3 oz good quality dark chocolate, roughly chopped

● **NUTS**
check for traces of nuts

● **SOYA**
check for soya lecithin

1 Preheat the oven to 180°C/350°F/gas mark 4. Line 3 baking sheets with oiled greaseproof paper and shake a spoonful of flour, cornmeal or rice flour over the baking tray until the oil is evenly covered. Tip away any excess flour.

2 Beat the butter and sugars with a wooden spoon or electric whisk until pale and fluffy. Add the egg (or milk) and beat well.

3 Sieve the flour, baking powder and salt into the bowl and whisk into the beaten butter mixture. Stir in the tablespoon of milk and the chopped chocolate.

4 Leaving a wide gap between cookies, spoon no more than 6 heaped teaspoons of the mixture onto each lined baking tray, as the dough spreads as it cooks.

5 Bake for about 15 minutes or until the cookies are lightly browned and just set in the centre. Do not over-cook the cookies or they will lose their chewiness.

6 Leave them to set on the baking tray for 30 seconds then transfer to a wire rack to cool. The cookies are best served freshly made but store well for up to two days in an airtight container. They can also be frozen, sealed in plastic bags.

GLUTEN-FREE BREAD

Making gluten-free cakes and biscuits is simple in comparison to making gluten-free bread. But it's bread that really matters. It is good ordinary, tasty bread that coeliac sufferers desperately want, yet cannot get. Bought gluten-free bread is often disappointingly heavy and dry, and lacks the neutral flavour and versatility of a simple everyday loaf. The techniques and recipes in this section aim to solve this problem. I have trailed these recipes with a number of coeliac sufferers and the response has always been the same: 'This is it – this is what I've been looking for.'

By blending specific gluten-free flours yourself and mixing them with the basic ingredients traditionally used to make bread – water, a little oil, yeast, salt and sugar – and the gluten substitute xanthum gum, it is possible to make gluten-free bread with a delicate yeasty flavour and soft chewy texture that is remarkably similar to wheat flour bread.

It is important to note that because of the lack of gluten, gluten-free bread is made differently to wheat bread (in fact, the method is simpler – there is no kneading, lengthy rising or knocking back):

- Gluten-free bread dough is beaten rather than kneaded to mix the ingredients together.
- Once the dough is made, it is risen in the oven to make the most of the bubbles produced by the yeast. Even with the addition of xanthum gum, gluten-free bread dough is not able to hold on to sufficient bubbles to rise in the tin before it is baked.

IMITATING THE PROPERTIES OF WHEAT FLOUR

Wheat flour makes light but chewy, open-textured bread because it is rich in the protein gluten. Gluten binds the ingredients, trapping and stretching around expanding bubbles of air, rather like bubble gum, lightening and enabling bread to rise and form its familiar texture. The bland flavour and fine texture of wheat flour also contributes to the soft texture and neutral flavour of wheat bread. In order to produce gluten-free bread that closely resembles wheat bread in flavour, appearance and texture, gluten-free flours must be carefully selected and blended in specific quantities to closely imitate the properties of wheat flour.

White gluten-free bread

Potato flour and cornflour, mixed with a small quantity of tapioca flour, rice flour and ground almonds (all available from health food shops) make an ideal flour blend for white gluten-free bread. The use of bland-tasting flour and careful seasoning with salt and sugar gives the bread its familiar delicate flavour and smell. The ground almonds, rich in almond oil, enrich the flavour and moisten the texture of the cooked bread. If you require a nut- and gluten-free bread, simply replace the ground almonds with an equal weight of potato flour and an extra teaspoon of oil.

Brown gluten-free bread

Good quality gluten-free brown bread is brown not because it is made with dark coloured flours or coloured with caramel – as is often the case with commercial breads – but because it contains fibre. Rice bran and finely ground whole almonds add fibre – hence texture and natural colour – to the blend of white gluten-free flours listed above.

OTHER
INGREDIENTS
USED FOR
MAKING
GLUTEN-FREE
BREAD

Yeast, salt and sugar

Bread owes its bubbly texture and much of its delicate aromatic flavour to the single-celled organism yeast. When mixed with the flour, water and a little sugar, yeast starts to reproduce, producing large bubbles of carbon dioxide that become trapped in bread dough, causing it to swell and rise.

Yeast is available in dried granular form in small foil packets or fresh, in chilled blocks. Dried yeast granules are simply mixed into the gluten-free flour before liquid is added. Use one 7 g/¼ oz sachet of yeast per 200 g/7 oz gluten-free flour. If you wish to use fresh yeast, dissolve it with 1 teaspoon of sugar in water (no warmer than blood temperature or the yeast will be killed off and fail to produce bubbles) before mixing it into the dough. Use 14 g/½ oz of fresh yeast per 200 g/7 oz flour.

Fine salt and caster sugar are added to the bread dough to improve the rising power of yeast and to give the bread a rounded, balanced flavour. Bread made without sugar and salt is bland. Add 1 teaspoon each of fine salt and caster sugar (or brown sugar for brown bread) per 200 g/7 oz of flour.

Chemical raising agents

Baking powder, bicarbonate of soda and cream of tartar create bubbles when mixed with liquid and are often included in gluten-free bread recipes to lighten the dough as much as possible. I do not recommend using them as they give the bread a crumbly, cakey texture and an unpleasant bitter flavour.

Water and oil

Tepid water is the best choice of liquid for bringing gluten-free bread dough together. Although milk is often used in recipes, it interferes with the rising process to produce slightly cakey bread with a soft crust. Water, in contrast, helps form a crisp crust. The amount of water needed varies slightly with different flours, and with dry and wet weather. Add half the water, then the remaining water in stages until the dough holds its shape but is soft enough to fall slowly from a spoon. Too little water and the dough will be too stiff to rise properly: too much water will make a soggy, dense bread. Adding a little neutral flavoured oil or olive oil with water enriches the flavour of bread and helps to keep it fresh for longer. Do not use more than 1 tablespoon of oil per 200 g/7 oz flour or the bread will be greasy and fail to rise properly.

Xanthum gum

Because of its binding qualities, gluten traps the bubbles created by yeast, enabling the dough to swell to twice its original volume and produce open, light-textured bread. To replicate this, gluten-free breads require alternative binding ingredients with the ability to trap bubbles. Egg is often used but it is not particularly effective. Xanthum gum is much more suitable, as it becomes gluey and elastic, much like gluten, when mixed with water. A natural gum, it is available in powdered form from health shops.

A level teaspoon of xanthum gum, sifted with 200 g/7 oz gluten-free flour and mixed with water, replaces the binding and stretching properties of gluten. Xanthum gum is used sparingly, as too much will make the dough tough and rubbery, preventing the yeast from leavening the dough properly.

GLUTEN-FREE WHITE BREAD

This loaf has a neutral and delicate flavour very similar to wheat bread. It is very simple and quick to make as it does not require time to rise before baking. Store and use like conventional bread. This recipe can also be used to make bread rolls, Italian focaccia and pizza bases (see overleaf). **Makes one medium loaf**

INGREDIENTS

110 g/4 oz potato flour

110 g/4 oz cornflour

55 g/2 oz tapioca flour

55 g/2 oz rice flour

2 tsp fine salt

2 tsp caster sugar

2 tsp xanthum gum powder

14 g/½ oz or 2 sachets dried yeast granules

55 g/2 oz ground almonds

● NUTS 55 g/2 oz rice flour and 2 extra tsps oil

2 tbsp sunflower or olive oil

millet flakes and buckwheat flakes, poppy seeds or sesame seeds to decorate (optional)

1 Preheat the oven to 200°C/400°F/gas mark 6. Lightly grease and flour a 900 g/2 lb loaf tin, tipping out any excess flour.

2 Sieve the flours, salt, sugar and xanthum gum powder into a mixing bowl. Stir in the yeast granules and ground almonds. Make sure the yeast is mixed in properly to avoid pockets of yeast activity and uneven rising.

3 Measure out 350 ml/12 fl oz of tepid water (it must be no hotter than blood temperature). Add the oil to the water.

4 Pour 300 ml/10 fl oz of water and oil onto the dry ingredients and beat with a wooden spoon until smooth, firm enough to hold its shape but soft enough to fall slowly from a spoon. If the mixture seems too firm or dry, stir in more water a tablespoon at a time until the bread mixture reaches the required consistency. If the bread mixture is too firm the bread will not rise. Equally if the mixture is too runny the dough will not be strong enough to trap the precious bubbles of air that cause it to rise.

5 Spoon the bread mixture into the prepared loaf tin. Dip a tablespoon in water and smooth the surface of the bread mixture with the back of the wet spoon. Sprinkle over the millet and buckwheat flakes and place on the middle shelf of the preheated oven to rise.

6 Bake for 45 minutes to 1 hour, or until the bread is crisp and golden brown on all sides. If the base and sides of the bread are pale, place the bread upside down in the tin and return to the oven for 10 minutes. The bread is cooked when all sides are brown and firm and the underside of the bread sounds hollow when tapped gently with your knuckles.

7 Remove the bread from the tin and place it on a wire rack to cool. Do not slice the loaf until it is completely cold. Eat really fresh, store for up to two days in an airtight container or slice and freeze in a sealed plastic bag.

WHITE BREAD VARIATIONS

WHITE BREAD ROLLS
Follow the recipe for Gluten-free White Bread but instead of using a loaf tin, using a wet spoon, neatly place tablespoons of bread mixture onto a greased and floured baking tray. Smooth the surface of each roll with the back of the wet spoon and sprinkle with millet flakes, buckwheat flakes, poppy seeds or sesame seeds. Bake in a preheated oven at 200°C/400°F/gas mark 6 for 15–20 minutes, or until crisp and golden brown on all sides.

ITALIAN FOCACCIA WITH ROSEMARY
Follow the recipe for Gluten-free White Bread, using olive oil, and spoon into a greased and floured 20–23 cm/8–9 inch round cake tin. With the back of a wet spoon, spread the dough out to fill the tin. Make shallow indents with your fingertips at regular intervals on the surface, drizzle 1 tablespoon of olive oil over the bread mixture and sprinkle with a large pinch of sea salt crystals and 1 tablespoon of chopped rosemary. Bake in a preheated oven at 200°C/400°F/gas mark 6 oven for 45 minutes, or until risen and golden brown.

ONION FOCACCIA
Peel and halve an onion and cut across into thin slices. Follow the recipe for Gluten-free White Bread, using olive oil, and spoon into a greased and floured 20–23 cm/8–9 inch round cake tin. With the back of a wet spoon, spread the dough out to fill the tin and make shallow indents at regular intervals on the surface. Spread the sliced onions over the top of the bread mixture, drizzle with 1 tablespoon of olive oil, sprinkle with sea salt and bake in a preheated oven at 200°C/400°F/gas mark 6 for 45 minutes, or until the bread is well risen and golden brown.

PIZZA ALLA MARINARA
Follow the recipe for Gluten-free White Bread, using olive oil. Divide the dough between two greased and floured (with rice flour or cornmeal) baking trays. Using the back of a wet spoon, spread the dough out into two circles measuring approximately 25 cm/10 inches across. The dough should be just under 1-cm/ ½-inch thick. Neaten the edges of the pizza bases by running a spoon around the edge of each. Drizzle each pizza base with 1 tablespoon of olive oil and bake in the preheated oven at 200°C/400°F/gas mark 6 for 20 minutes, or until the pizzas are golden brown on both sides. Spread each pizza with Rich Italian Tomato Sauce (page 80), arrange 8 anchovy fillets over the top and sprinkle over ½ tablespoon capers, 1 tablespoon pitted black olives, 1 teaspoon mixed dried herbs, a little salt and pepper and a drizzle of olive oil. Bake for another 15 minutes then serve immediately.

GLUTEN-FREE BROWN BREAD

This wholesome brown bread has the texture, colour and flavour that you would expect in a conventional wheat-based brown bread. It is good enough to use for sandwiches. **Makes one medium loaf**

INGREDIENTS

110 g/4 oz potato flour

110 g/4 oz cornflour

55 g/2 oz tapioca flour

55 g/2 oz rice flour

2 tsp fine salt

2 tsp soft dark brown sugar

2 tsp xanthum gum powder

14 g/½ oz or 2 sachets dried yeast granules

55 g/2 oz whole ground almonds

55 g/2 oz potato flour and 2 extra tsp oil

1 tbsp rice bran

2 tbsp sunflower or olive oil

a large pinch each millet flakes and buckwheat flakes to decorate (optional)

● NUTS

1 Preheat the oven to 200°C/400°F/gas mark 6. Lightly grease and flour a 900 g/2 lb loaf tin, tipping out any excess flour.

2 Sieve together the flours, salt, sugar and xanthum gum powder into a mixing bowl.

3 Stir in the yeast, finely ground whole almonds and rice bran.

4 Measure out 350 ml/12 fl oz tepid water. Add the oil to the water.

5 Pour 300 ml/10 fl oz of water and oil onto the dry ingredients and beat with a wooden spoon until smooth, firm enough to hold its shape but soft enough to fall slowly from a spoon. If the mixture seems too firm or dry, stir in more water a tablespoon at a time until the bread mixture reaches the required consistency. The mixture should fall slowly from a spoon in the same way as cake mixture. If the dough is too firm or too wet it will not rise.

6 Spoon the bread mixture into the greased loaf tin and level out with the back of a spoon dipped in water. Sprinkle over the millet and buckwheat flakes.

7 Place on the middle shelf of the preheated oven and bake for 45 minutes, or until the bread is crisp and golden brown on all sides. The bread is cooked when all sides are brown and firm and the underside of the bread sounds hollow when tapped gently with your knuckles.

8 Place the baked bread on a wire rack to cool. The texture of the bread improves as it cools and is best eaten cold. Store the bread for up to two days in an airtight container or sliced in the freezer in a sealed plastic bag.

Chapter 17

PUDDINGS AND SWEET SAUCES

PUDDINGS

Homemade puddings are commonly made with butter, cream, eggs, nuts and flour while bought puddings often contain soya products. The reason for this is that these ingredients add creaminess, structure, texture, flavour and colour to foods that are sweet and delicate in consistency. Sometimes their presence is essential – meringues, for example, rely on the unique properties of egg white. However, this chapter demonstrates how recipes for many popular and well-known puddings can easily be adapted for gluten-, egg-, dairy-, nut- and soya-free diets by substituting or simply omitting mainstream ingredients – and with delicious results, too.

MOUSSES

Rich tasting, airy mousses make wonderful puddings, served alone, with a rich custard sauce or as part of an assembled dessert. Mousses are made by gently folding flavouring ingredients, such as melted chocolate, into whisked eggs or whipped cream.

GENERAL RULES FOR MAKING MOUSSE

- Each time a whipped or whisked mixture is stirred it loses air and volume so use a large metal spoon that turns over a large portion of the mixture at a time.
- Mixtures with similar consistencies mix together with minimal stirring. To retain as much air as possible in the mousse, make the consistency of mousse ingredients more similar by stirring a large spoonful of whipped cream or whisked egg whites into the thinner flavouring ingredients before folding the two together.
- Whisk egg whites in a grease-free glass, china or metal bowl. Plastic bowls scratch easily and harbour grease, which prevents egg whites from foaming properly.
- Whisk egg whites until they stand in soft peaks and wobble slightly when shaken.
- Whip cream until it just holds its shape so that the mousse ingredients can be mixed easily together. Stiffly whipped cream forms a lumpy, heavy mousse.

NOTES FOR FOOD ALLERGY SUFFERERS

Mousses are gluten, nut and soya free. Due to the rich flavour and thickening properties of chocolate, chocolate mousse can also be made dairy free, by using whisked eggs; or egg free, by using whipped cream (see pages 189–90).

Beware egg-based mousses

These are made with raw eggs so ensure the eggs are as fresh as possible, and chill the finished mousse to reduce the risk of salmonella poisoning. Do not serve mousses to pregnant women, the elderly or young children.

BITTER CHOCOLATE MOUSSE

This wonderfully rich but light dairy-free mousse contains nothing but dark chocolate, eggs and sugar. It's a real treat. For an egg-free mousse see page 190. Use the best quality chocolate you can find as the flavour of the dessert relies on it. **Serves 4**

INGREDIENTS

110 g/4 oz best quality dark chocolate containing 70% cocoa solids, broken into small pieces

check label for traces of nuts

check label for soya lecithin

● **NUTS**

● **SOYA**

4 egg whites

1 tbsp caster sugar

2 egg yolks, at room temperature

1 Melt the chocolate very gently in an ovenproof bowl, placed over a pan of simmering water, stirring occasionally. Once melted, set aside.

2 Place the egg whites in a medium bowl and whisk until they form soft, wobbly peaks. Sprinkle the sugar over and continue to whisk until the egg whites stand upright but bend over at the tip.

3 Stir the egg yolks into the warm, melted chocolate.

4 Mix 2 large spoonfuls of whisked egg whites into the chocolate and egg mixture then gently fold in the remaining egg whites. Pour into four ramekins, holding the mixing bowl close to the ramekins to limit the loss of air.

5 Cover with clingfilm and chill, preferably overnight, or for at least 4 hours before serving.

RICH CHOCOLATE MOUSSE

This mousse is enriched and lightened with whipped cream rather than egg whites. It is unsuitable for a those on a dairy-free diet but is great for chocolate lovers and those avoiding eggs. It is delicious dusted with good quality cocoa powder and served with Coffee Custard Sauce (page 207) or with soft fruit and Fresh Summer Berry Sauce (page 209). To allow the mousse to set properly, make this mousse a day in advance. Serves 4

INGREDIENTS

170 g/6 oz best quality dark chocolate containing 70% cocoa solids, broken into small pieces

● **NUTS** check label for traces of nuts

● **SOYA** check label for soya lecithin

290 ml/10 fl oz whipping cream

2 tbsp good quality cocoa powder

● **GLUTEN** check label for wheat flour

1 Melt the chocolate very gently in an ovenproof bowl, placed over a pan of simmering water, stirring occasionally. Once melted, set aside.

2 In a large mixing bowl, whip the cream until it just holds its shape. Be careful not to over-whip it.

3 Stir a quarter of the whipped cream into the cooled melted chocolate then pour the chocolate mixture into the remaining whipped cream and gently fold together with a large metal spoon until just mixed.

4 Pour into four ramekin dishes, leaving 1 cm/½ inch of the rim free, cover with clingfilm and chill overnight to set. Dust with cocoa powder before serving.

VARIATION

RICH CHOCOLATE MOUSSE TORTE

This impressive egg-free dessert is great for dinner parties and special occasions. It can also be made gluten, nut and soya free by using suitable biscuits to make the base.

Preheat the oven to 180°C/350°C/gas mark 4. Finely crush 110 g/4 oz of chocolate-covered digestive biscuits (or gluten-free plain biscuits), stir the crushed biscuits into 55 g/2 oz melted butter and tip into a lightly oiled 20 cm/8 inch round flan ring. Press the biscuit mixture down firmly until the base of the cake tin is thinly and evenly covered. Bake in the oven for 10 minutes. Meanwhile, make a double quantity of the Rich Chocolate Mousse above. Spoon the mousse on top of the hardened biscuit base and level off the top by passing a palette knife across the rim of the tin. Loosely cover the dessert with clingfilm and leave to set in the fridge overnight. Run a sharp knife around the ede of the tin, lift off the ring and dust with cocoa powder before serving.

WHISKED SPONGES FOR ROULADES

Whisked sponge is often used as a base for fruity, creamy and mousse desserts. The light consistency of whisked sponge relies on the air bubbles incorporated into whisked egg, which expands and lightens the mixture as it bakes.

GENERAL RULES FOR MAKING WHISKED SPONGE

- Oil the baking tin, line with baking parchment and brush the paper with a light coating of oil. Sprinkle a tablespoon of caster sugar into the lined tin, shake from side to side until coated with sugar and tip any excess sugar out. Do the same with a tablespoon of flour. Do this before beginning the recipe as whisked sponge mixture quickly loses volume if left to stand.
- Whisk the eggs in a spotlessly clean china, glass or metal mixing bowl. Plastic bowls harbour grease, which prevents eggs from foaming to their full potential.
- Whisk egg yolks until they become pale, double in volume and are thick enough to leave a trail on the surface as the whisks are lifted out of the mixture.
- Whisk egg whites until they quadruple in volume and stand in firm peaks but are not stiff.
- Gently fold the mixture together using a large metal spoon.
- Fold the thinner yolks into the thicker egg white foam. The two are easier to fold together if a third of the whites are stirred into the yolks beforehand to make both foams closer in consistency. This way the mixture will require less folding, which means less chance of precious air being lost.
- Fold melted butter and flour into the mixture until just blended. Over-folding will cause the mixture to lose volume.

NOTES FOR FOOD ALLERGY SUFFERERS

DAIRY-FREE DIET: Melted butter is sometimes added to sponges to moisten and enrich the cake. If butter is included in a recipe for whisked sponge, replace it with melted dairy-free margarine.

GLUTEN-FREE DIET: Although flour is not necessary for the success of whisked sponge it is sometimes added to give the cake a more substantial texture. In place of wheat flour use an equal quantity of gluten-free flour made with 50 per cent rice flour, 25 per cent ground almonds and 25 per cent cornflour.

EGG-FREE DIET: The unique properties of whisked egg are essential in whisked sponges and cannot be replaced with any other ingredient. In place of whisked sponge use egg-free Victoria Sponge Cake (page 172).

NUT-FREE DIET: Whisked sponge is suitable for nut-free diets provided recipes using nuts are avoided and any fat used to enrich it does not contain nut oils.

SOYA-FREE DIET: Whisked sponge is suitable for soya-free diets, provided any fat used to enrich it does not contain soya bean oil.

CHOCOLATE ROULADE FILLED WITH BITTER CHOCOLATE MOUSSE AND RASPBERRIES

This pudding is dairy, gluten, nut and soya free, but very rich and wicked. The whisked sponge does not contain flour or fat and relies solely on eggs to form its airy mousse-like texture. **Serves 6**

FOR THE SPONGE

4 eggs, separated into yolks and whites

170 g/6 oz icing sugar

● **GLUTEN** check label for wheat flour

55 g/2 oz good quality cocoa powder

● **GLUTEN** check label for wheat flour

FOR THE FILLING

2 quantities Bitter Chocolate Mousse (page 189), made the day before

200 g/7 oz raspberries

1 Preheat the oven to 200°C/400°F/ gas mark 6. Oil a shallow 25 x 30 cm/10 x 12 inch baking tin and line with lightly oiled greaseproof paper, to stand an inch or so above the rim.

2 Whisk the egg yolks with half the icing sugar until thick and pale.

3 Clean the whisk and dry thoroughly then whisk the egg whites until they form peaks that do not wobble when gently shaken. Add half the remaining icing sugar and continue to whisk the egg whites until stiff.

4 Stir a large spoonful of whisked egg whites into the whisked egg yolks and mix well. Tip the remaining egg whites into the egg yolks and gently fold together.

5 Mix the cocoa powder and remaining icing sugar and sift onto the whisked egg mixture. Gently fold into the eggs until the mixture is just blended.

6 Holding the bowl just above the tin, pour the mixture into the lined baking tray, spreading it from side to side.

7 Bake for 8–10 minutes, or until the sponge is lightly set and feels springy in the centre. Do not open the door for at least 6 minutes or the sponge may collapse. Once cooked, cover with a damp tea towel to prevent it drying out.

8 Once cold, turn it out onto a large piece of greaseproof paper, dusted with icing sugar. Peel away the paper, spread the mousse over the sponge and evenly scatter the raspberries onto the mousse.

9 To roll the roulade, place one of the long ends of the rectangle square with the edge of the work surface. Tightly fold the long end of the roulade furthest from you over the first 2.5 cm/1 inch of filling then pull the greaseproof paper up and over the centre, towards you, supporting the roulade as you roll it.

10 Using the paper to support the roulade, roll the cake onto a serving plate and dust with more icing sugar. Trim away any rough ends of the roulade and serve cut into thick slices.

PANCAKES

Pancakes are traditionally made with a batter consisting of eggs, milk and flour, but they are just as good made with egg-, dairy- and gluten-free ingredients. Savoury Pancakes are delicious in baked dishes with lots of sauce, and sweet pancakes make a great dessert topped with fruit, ice cream or chocolate sauce.

GENERAL RULES
FOR MAKING
PANCAKES

- Use a large bowl to mix the batter ingredients.
- Carefully and gradually blend the dry and liquid ingredients, to make a lump-free batter. If lumps appear, pass the batter through a fine-meshed sieve.
- Once the batter is made stop stirring or gluten, contained in wheat flour, will become too developed, resulting in tough pancakes.
- Leave pancake batter to stand and thicken, covered in the fridge, for at least 30 minutes, before cooking. The flour grains swell in the liquid and burst open as the batter is cooked to make light, tender pancakes. Pancake batter for thick, risen pancakes should be cooked immediately so that the raising agents in the flour lighten the consistency of the pancakes as they rise.
- For light, tender pancakes the batter should be no thicker than the consistency of double cream. When batter is too thick, add more milk or water, a tablespoon at a time, until it reaches the required consistency.
- Cook a small sample pancake to test the consistency of the cooked pancake batter before making the pancakes. The batter may require thinning down with a little more milk or water.
- To avoid thick, soggy pancakes, pour excess batter that does not immediately set on the base of the hot pan, back into the bowl.
- To prevent pancakes sticking as they cook, apply a very thin coating of oil to the frying pan, using oiled kitchen paper.

NOTES
FOR FOOD
ALLERGY
SUFFERERS

DAIRY-FREE DIET: Cows' milk is usually used to make pancake batter because it is bland in flavour and readily available. Soya milk, rice milk and almond milk all make delicious pancakes with a mild flavour and delicate texture.

GLUTEN-FREE DIET: Light textured and tender gluten-free pancakes can be made by using finely ground rice flour, which has a suitably bland flavour, tapioca flour and arrowroot powder, which help bind the pancakes, and egg.

EGG-FREE DIET: Although eggs bind and lightly set the ingredients in cooked batter, pancakes can be made very successfully without egg. Egg-free pancakes rely on the binding properties of gluten in wheat flour and a small quantity of the binding flours arrowroot powder and tapioca flour, to hold the batter together as it cooks.

NUT- AND SOYA-FREE DIETS: Pancake batter is enriched and moistened with a small quantity of neutral flavoured oil, such as sunflower oil, corn oil or rapeseed oil stirred into the batter, and it is also fried in oil. Check that the oil you use does not contain ground nut or soya bean oil.

FRENCH CRÊPES

These pancakes are nut and soya free and are easily adapted for gluten- and diary-free diets. They are not egg free – for egg-free pancakes see page 197. Top or fill these delicious pancakes with Dark Chocolate Sauce (page 208), Fresh Summer Berry Sauce (page 209) or simply with honey, maple syrup, jam or lemon and sugar.
Makes about 12 x 25 cm/10 inch pancakes

INGREDIENTS

● **GLUTEN**

110 g/4 oz plain flour

55 g/2 oz brown rice flour, 30g /1 oz tapioca flour and 30 g/1 oz arrowroot powder

½ tsp salt

1 tbsp caster sugar

1 egg and 1 egg yolk, beaten together

350 ml/12 fl oz milk

● **DAIRY**

soya, rice or almond milk

finely grated zest of 1 orange

sunflower or corn oil

1 Sift the flour, salt and sugar into a bowl and make a wide well in the centre. Pour in the beaten egg and add a little milk. Using a wooden spoon, stir the egg and milk in small circles so that the flour is slowly drawn from the sides into the liquid.

2 As the egg and flour mixture thickens, add the milk, stirring it in little by little, until all the milk is incorporated and the batter is smooth. Stir in the orange zest and tablespoon of oil, cover with clingfilm and leave to stand for 30 minutes.

3 Pour some oil into a 20–25 cm/8–10 inch frying pan, swirl it around the pan, then pour off the excess into a bowl to re-use. Heat until the oil starts to smoke. French crêpes should be wafer thin so test your batter by swirling one tablespoon of batter in the heated pan. Once the top of the pancake starts to bubble, turn the pancake over and brown the second side. If the pancake seems a little thick, thin the batter with a tablespoon or two of milk or water.

4 Stir the batter well and pour a small ladle of batter into the hot pan. Swirl the pancake batter over the base of the pan and pour out any excess batter back into the bowl. After 30–40 seconds, when the top of the pancake starts to bubble, turn the pancake over using a palette knife and brown the second side for another 30 seconds. Repeat with the remaining batter. Cover the cooked pancakes with greaseproof paper and keep warm in a very low oven before serving.

5 To serve, spread or spoon on the filling, loosely roll up the pancakes and place on a warmed serving plate.

BUCKWHEAT PANCAKES WITH CARAMELIZED CINNAMON APPLES

These pancakes can be adapted for gluten-free diets but are not egg free. Buckwheat gives a wholesome flavour that is delicious complemented by caramelized apples and Vanilla Ice Cream (page 204). **Serves 4 (2 pancakes each)**

FOR THE PANCAKES

55 g/2 oz buckwheat flour

55g/2 oz plain flour

● GLUTEN   rice flour

½ tsp salt

1 tbsp caster sugar

1 egg and 1 egg yolk

290 ml/10 fl oz milk

● DAIRY   sweetened dairy-free milk

sunflower or corn oil

FOR THE APPLES

85 g/3 oz granulated sugar

85g/3oz unsalted butter

● DAIRY   dairy-free margarine

4 Granny Smith apples, peeled, cored and thickly sliced

1 tsp ground cinnamon

1 To make the pancake batter, sift the flours, salt and sugar into the bowl and make a wide well in the centre of the flour. Beat the egg and yolk together in a bowl and pour into the well with a little milk.

2 With a wooden spoon, stir the egg and milk in small circles so that the flour is slowly drawn from the sides of the well into the liquid.

3 As the egg and flour mixture thickens, add the milk little by little continuing to stir until all the milk is incorporated and the batter is smooth. If it contains a few lumps pass through a sieve into a clean bowl. Stir in 1 tablespoon of oil, cover with clingfilm and leave to stand for 30 minutes in the fridge.

4 Meanwhile, heat the granulated sugar in a dry frying pan over a medium heat until it and turns golden brown. Turn off the heat and stir in the butter to make the caramel sauce.

5 Stir the sliced apples and cinnamon into the caramel, cover with a lid and gently simmer over a low heat for about 20 minutes or until the apples are tender and golden brown. Remove from the heat and keep warm.

6 To cook the pancakes refer to step 3 onwards in French Crêpes page 195.

7 To serve, place a pancake flat on a warmed plate and top with a large spoonful of warm apples and caramel sauce and loosely fold or roll the pancake.

EGG-FREE PANCAKES

These pancakes have a fine, lacy texture very similar to French crêpes. Serve them with sugar and lemon, chocolate sauce and ice cream or omit the sugar and make savoury pancakes as the basis for an egg-free savoury dish. They are not suitable for those who suffer from a gluten allergy. **Makes about 12 x 25 cm/10 inch pancakes**

INGREDIENTS

55 g/2 oz plain flour

30 g/1 oz arrowroot powder

30 g/1 oz tapioca flour

½ tsp salt

3 tsp caster sugar

350 ml/12 fl oz milk
● DAIRY   sweetened dairy-free milk

1 tbsp sunflower or corn oil

zest of 1 orange

1 Sift the plain flour, arrowroot powder and tapioca flour, salt and sugar into a bowl and make a wide well in the centre.

2 Pour one third of the milk into the well. With a wooden spoon, stir the milk in small circles so that the flour is slowly drawn from the sides of the well into the liquid.

3 As the milk and flour mixture thickens, slowly add more milk, stirring it in little by little until all the milk is incorporated and the batter is smooth. If the batter contains a few lumps, pass it through a sieve into a clean bowl.

4 Stir in the oil, add the orange zest, cover with clingfilm and leave to stand for 30 minutes.

5 To cook the pancakes refer to step 3 in the method for French Crêpes (page 195).

MERINGUES

Meringue is made by folding caster sugar into whisked egg whites. As the egg whites are whisked they fill with bubbles of air, which give meringues their airy lightness. The sugar dissolves in the egg white foam to form a syrup coating around each bubble. As meringues cook, the moisture around each bubble evaporates leaving a crisp sugary shell.

GENERAL RULES FOR MAKING MERINGUES

- Egg whites should be at room temperature, as they foam better than fridge-cold eggs.
- Whisk egg whites in a clean, china, stainless steel or glass bowl. Plastic bowls tend to scratch and harbour grease. If the bowl is not spotlessly clean and dry the egg whites will not foam to their full potential.
- Do not whisk too vigorously – begin slowly and gradually increase the speed as the foam thickens with tiny bubbles.
- Sugar should not be added to whisked egg whites until they are stiff and no longer wobble when shaken.
- Only add half of the sugar or you risk the egg whites collapsing. Whisk on a fast speed until the egg whites stand in stiff peaks and have a smooth pearly appearance.
- Fold the remaining sugar into the stiff meringue as gently and as briefly as possible to avoid the meringue losing too much air and collapsing. Use a large metal spoon to reduce the number of stirs necessary for mixing in the sugar.

INDIVIDUAL MERINGUES

This recipe makes 5–6 large meringues to serve with fresh fruit steeped in Summer Berry Sauce and your favourite ice cream. It can also be used to make 20 baby meringues for children's parties. This recipe is not suitable for egg allergy sufferers.

INGREDIENTS

2 egg whites

110 g/4 oz caster sugar

TO SERVE

350 g/12 oz mixed berries, steeped overnight in 1 quantity of Fresh Summer Berry Sauce (page 209)

homemade ice cream (pages 203–5)

1 Preheat the oven to 120°C/250°F/ gas mark ½. Line a baking sheet with greaseproof paper.

2 Place the egg whites in a bowl and whisk, slowly, gradually increasing the speed as the foam thickens, until the egg whites form stiff peaks that do not wobble when gently shaken.

3 Sprinkle half of the sugar onto the whisked whites and whisk until the mixture is very stiff and has a pearly sheen. Gently fold the remaining sugar in using a large metal spoon.

4 Using 2 tablespoons, spoon 5–6 large heaped tablespoons of meringue onto the baking sheet, spacing them well apart. To make individual baby meringues, use two teaspoons to spoon heaped teaspoons of meringue onto the lined baking sheet.

5 Place the meringues on the lower shelves in the oven, to ensure they remain white. Large meringues will take 2 hours to cook; baby meringues will take 1 hour. The meringues are cooked when they are crisp and dry on the outside, mallowy in the centre and no longer stick to the greaseproof paper.

6 When they are ready, place on a wire rack and leave to cool before serving with the fruity sauce and ice cream – or, as they are for children's parties.

VARIATION

MERINGUE BASKETS

To make 5 meringue baskets, spoon the meringue mixture into a piping bag with a medium nozzle. Draw around a cup, five times, on a sheet of baking parchment, spacing the circles well apart. Place the parchment, pen side down, on a baking tray and pipe from the centre of the circles, round and round, forming a spiral until the circle is filled. To form the sides, pipe two hoops of meringue one on top of the other on the edge of the base. Pipe the four other baskets in the same way. Bake for 1½ –2 hours until the baskets are crisp and no longer sticking to the paper.

NOTES FOR FOOD ALLERGY SUFFERERS

There is no such thing as an egg-free meringue as no other ingredient has the same set of properties as egg white. However, meringues make an ideal base for dairy-, gluten-, nut- and soya-free puddings. Icing sugar is sometimes used to make meringues and can contain wheat flour to prevent it forming lumps. Check the label before using it.

FRUIT CRUMBLES

Fruit crumble is an ideal pudding to make for large family meals in the autumn, when the weather is beginning to change and robustly flavoured fruits such as cooking apples, plums and rhubarb are in plentiful supply. Crumbles can be assembled a few hours before they are to be eaten and baked in a hot oven while everyone enjoys their main course. Crumble toppings can also be made well in advance, stored in an airtight container and refrigerated for up to 2 days, or frozen. Allow frozen crumble topping to defrost before sprinkling it over freshly prepared fruit. Bake the assembled fruit crumble in a preheated, hot oven.

GENERAL RULES FOR MAKING FRUIT CRUMBLES

- Use a dish approximately 5 cm/2 inches deep. For a generous filling, the dish should be filled to three-quarters full of prepared fruit, leaving 1 cm/½ inch for the crumble topping.
- Cut fruit into bite-size pieces to retain some texture once it is baked. Fruit cut too small will become mushy.
- Taste the fruit before sweetening it with sugar. It might require more or less than the recipe suggests.
- Use chilled butter or margarine cut into dice. Soft fat is hard to rub into the dry ingredients without the mixture lumping together.
- Use your fingertips only to rub the fat into the dry ingredients to avoid the fat from warming up and softening. The cooler the ingredients the easier it is to rub them together.
- The crumble mixture is ready to use when it looks like coarse breadcrumbs.
- Bake crumble in a preheated hot oven. The crumble is ready when the topping is golden brown and lightly crunchy and the fruit below is soft, when tested with a sharp knife.

NOTES FOR FOOD ALLERGY SUFFERERS

DAIRY-FREE DIET: Hard baking margarine is an ideal alternative to butter for producing the golden brown crunchy texture of crumble topping.

GLUTEN-FREE DIET: Crumble topping is traditionally made with flour and oats but can be made just as well with a mixture of rice flour, flaked rice, millet and buckwheat.

EGG-FREE DIET: Egg is not used in crumbles.

NUT-FREE AND SOYA-FREE DIETS: Crumbles are suitable for nut- and soya-free diets provided butter or nut- and soya-free margarine is used.

APPLE AND BLACKBERRY CRUMBLE

Blackberry and apple crumble is one of the most rewarding ways to eat blackberries picked from the hedgerows. Serve with dairy or soya-free Vanilla Ice Cream (page 204), Crème Anglaise (page 207) or double cream. **Serves 4–6**

FOR THE FILLING

675 g/1½ lb cooking apples or Granny Smiths, peeled, cored, quartered and thickly sliced

225 g/8 oz blackberries, hulled and rinsed

3 tbsp soft brown sugar

FOR THE TOPPING

110 g/4 oz plain flour

● **GLUTEN**   rice flour

110 g/4 oz rolled oats

● **GLUTEN**   55 g/2 oz millet flakes, 30 g/1 oz rice flakes and 30 g/1 oz buckwheat flakes

85 g/3 oz Demerara sugar

½ tsp salt

110 g/4 oz butter, chopped into small pieces

● **DAIRY**   dairy-free hard baking margarine

1 Preheat the oven to 200°C/400°F/ gas mark 6.

2 Scatter the sliced apples and blackberries over the base of an ovenproof dish approximately 20 x 28 x 5 cm/8 x 11 x 2 inches and sprinkle over the soft brown sugar.

3 To make the topping, mix the flour, oats (or millet flakes, rice flakes and buckwheat flakes), sugar and salt together in a mixing bowl.

4 Add the butter to the dry ingredients and lightly rub together with your fingertips until the mixture resembles coarse breadcrumbs.

5 Sprinkle the crumble topping over the fruit, spreading it out so the fruit is completely covered.

6 Bake the crumble for 30–40 minutes, or until the crumble topping is crisp and golden brown.

VARIATION

RHUBARB CRUMBLE

Use 900 g/2 lb rhubarb, chopped into 5 cm/2 inch pieces, in place of the apples and blackberries. Increase the amount of Demerara sugar in the topping to 110 g/4 oz.

SORBETS

Sorbets make colourful, refreshing and delicious desserts, served with meringues or biscuits, fresh fruit and sweet fruity sauces. Sorbet is made by freezing fruit syrup or purée then beating it to a soft, smooth consistency.

RASPBERRY SORBET

Vivid and fresh in taste and colour, this sorbet is a wonderful egg- and dairy-free alternative to ice cream. It is also gluten, soya and nut free. It is delicious served simply with fresh fruit, or with Fresh Summer Berry Sauce (page 209). It also makes great ice lollies. **Serves 6**

INGREDIENTS

750 g/1lb 10 oz juicy hulled raspberries

400 ml/14 fl oz cold Sugar Syrup (page 209)

juice of 1 lemon

caster sugar to taste

1 Press the raspberries through a sieve into a bowl and mix in the sugar syrup and lemon juice. Taste and if necessary, balance the flavour with a squeeze of lemon juice or a little caster sugar.

2 Pour the raspberry mixture into a plastic container, cover with a lid and freeze for 4 hours, or until half frozen

3 Cut the freezing mixture into chunks and blend in a food processor or beat with a wooden spoon in a mixing bowl until smooth. Return the sorbet to the freezer and freeze for another 2 hours. Beat once again then return the sorbet to the freezer until firm.

4 Remove the sorbet from the freezer 15 minutes before serving, to soften.

NOTES FOR FOOD ALLERGY SUFFERERS

Sorbets consist of sugar, water and fruit and make ideal desserts for those on a dairy-, egg-, gluten-, nut- or soya-free diet.

EGG-FREE DIET: Egg white is sometimes added to sorbet to soften its texture, as it prevents large ice crystals forming in the mixture. It is not necessary to add egg white to sorbet provided sugar is used in the correct concentration and the frozen sorbet mixture is beaten until it is smooth and soft.

ICE CREAM

The richest, smoothest ice cream is made from a basic mixture of milk, cream, sugar and egg yolks. However, you can make a delicious dairy-free version with soya milk and soya cream (see Rich Chocolate Ice Cream and Vanilla Ice Cream page 204). For an egg-free ice cream that has a rich flavour and smooth consistency, mashed banana mixed with cream (or soya cream), sugar, orange and lemon juice is a great alternative (see Banana Ice Cream page 205).

GENERAL RULES FOR MAKING CUSTARD-BASED ICE CREAMS

- Measure the amount of sugar accurately. Too much sugar will lead to a soft, over-sweet ice cream and too little results in hard, bland-tasting ice cream. Sugar generally makes up about one-third of the weight of the ingredients in ice cream.
- Add milk and cream (or soya milk and soya cream) in equal quantities to ensure the correct consistency.
- Use very fresh eggs (generally, 4 egg yolks per 570 ml/1 pint of liquid) as they are only partially cooked when the custard is made and could still carry the salmonella bacteria. Never refreeze custard-based ice cream once it has thawed.
- Cook the custard over a gentle heat, stirring continuously so that the egg thickens slowly and doesn't coagulate.
- Remove custard from the heat when it starts to steam and thicken and the base of the pan feels slippery as it is stirred with a wooden spoon.
- Taste buds are less sensitive to frozen foods. The ice cream mixture should therefore taste over-flavoured and too sweet, before it is frozen.
- If you do not have a food processor to churn the frozen ice cream, allow it to soften slightly before beating it with a wooden spoon until smooth but firm enough to hold its shape. Do not over-churn or the ice cream will melt.

NOTES FOR FOOD ALLERGY SUFFERERS

DAIRY-FREE DIET: Soya milk and soya cream are the most suitable dairy-free alternatives for making ice cream. Use good quality sweetened soya milk as the cheaper varieties tend to be watery and have a very beany flavour. The beany flavour of soya does come through in subtly flavoured ice creams such as vanilla but is masked by the addition of chocolate, fruit purées or coffee.

GLUTEN-FREE DIET: Homemade ice cream does not contain gluten unless ingredients containing gluten are included in a recipe for added texture and flavour.

EGG-FREE DIET: Custard-based ice cream is not suitable for egg-free diets. Instead, try making Banana Ice Cream (page 205).

NUT-FREE DIET: Basic homemade ice cream does not contain nuts unless they are included in a recipe to add texture and extra flavour. Read the labels of chocolate, and other products used to flavour ice cream as they could contain nuts.

SOYA-FREE DIET: Traditional homemade ice cream does not contain soya products. Soya cream and soya milk are, however, extremely useful for making dairy-free ice cream. If you are allergic to soya and dairy products Banana Ice Cream (page 205) can be made using rice milk or almond milk. The resulting frozen dessert is much lighter and tastes more like a sorbet.

RICH CHOCOLATE ICE CREAM

This ice cream is very rich, intensely chocolaty and just as delicious made with dairy-free soya milk and soya cream. Use a good quality dark chocolate for a really intense chocolaty flavour. Serve this ice cream with Meringues (page 199), pancakes or as a trio with Banana Ice Cream (page 205) and Raspberry Sorbet (page 202). This recipe contains egg – for an egg-free ice cream see opposite. **Serves 4**

INGREDIENTS

4 egg yolks

110 g/4 oz caster sugar

110 g/4 oz good quality dark chocolate with 70% cocoa solids, broken into pieces

● NUTS check label for traces of nuts
● SOYA check label for soya lecithin

290 ml/10 fl oz whole milk

● DAIRY good quality sweetened soya milk

290 ml/10 fl oz whipping cream

● DAIRY soya single cream

1 Stir the egg yolks and sugar together, in a medium sized bowl, until smooth.

2 Place the chocolate pieces in a saucepan and pour in the milk. Warm the milk over a low heat, stirring continuously, until the chocolate is completely melted. Remove from the heat.

3 Slowly pour the hot chocolate milk in a thin, continuous stream onto the egg and sugar mixture, stirring continuously, until thoroughly blended.

4 Pour the mixture back into the pan and stir over a low to medium heat until the custard starts to steam heavily and thickens to the consistency of double cream.

5 Remove the pan from the heat and immediately pour in the cream to stop it cooking or lumps of coagulated egg may form.

6 Pour the custard through a sieve (to catch any lumps of coagulated egg) into a shallow container. Allow to cool then place in the freezer for at least 3 hours, or until half frozen. Cut the freezing ice cream into pieces and beat until smooth in a food processor or in a bowl with a wooden spoon.

7 Return the ice cream to the freezer for another hour or so or until firm. Remove the ice cream from the freezer for 15 minutes before serving, to soften.

VARIATIONS

STRAWBERRY OR RASPBERRY ICE CREAM
Push 225 g/8 oz hulled berries through a fine sieve and stir into the cooled custard after the cream is added. Balance the flavour with lemon juice or a little more sugar before freezing.

VANILLA ICE CREAM
Replace the chocolate with 2 split vanilla pods. Add the pods to the milk and bring to a simmer. Remove from the heat, scrape the black seeds into the milk and pour the vanilla milk onto the egg yolk and sugar mixture. Follow the recipe from step 4 onwards.

BANANA ICE CREAM

This smooth and fruity ice cream is egg free and by replacing the dairy cream with soya cream, it can be dairy free, too. It's very easy to make and delicious served with fresh fruit, fruit pies and chocolate desserts or brownies. **Serves 4**

INGREDIENTS

4 firm but ripe bananas, peeled

juice of 1 lemon

juice of 1 orange

2 tbsp caster sugar

150 ml/5 fl oz whipping cream

soya single cream

● **DAIRY**

1 Break the bananas into pieces and place in a food processor with the lemon juice, orange juice, caster sugar and cream.

2 Purée the ingredients until completely smooth, pour into a plastic container, cover with a lid and place in the freezer for 3 hours, or until half frozen.

3 Break the half-frozen ice cream into chunks and churn in the food processor, or beat in a large bowl with a wooden spoon until smooth.

4 Return the ice cream to the plastic container, cover and freeze until firm.

5 Remove the ice cream from the freezer for 15 minutes before serving, to soften.

SWEET SAUCES

Sweet sauces add colour, flavour and texture to a wide variety of desserts and can make a simple dessert look and taste special. This section covers sweet sauces that complement the desserts included in this book.

CUSTARD

Custard is a smooth, creamy, pale yellow sauce made with milk, sugar and egg yolks or cornflour. Fresh custard thickened with egg yolks is also known as crème Anglaise and is served as a more interesting alternative to cream. It is also used to make custard-based ice cream. Cornflour is often used in crème Anglaise to help thicken it and to stabilize egg yolk as it is heated or in the case of custard powder, used alone to form an egg-free, smooth, slightly gelatinous milky yellow sauce best served with warm nursery puddings.

GENERAL RULES FOR MAKING CRÈME ANGLAISE

- Use very fresh eggs, as they are only partially cooked. To reduce the risk of salmonella poisoning, store the custard, covered, in the fridge, for no more than 24 hours and do not serve to very young children, pregnant women and the elderly.
- Cook custard over a gentle heat, stirring continuously so that the egg thickens slowly and doesn't coagulate.
- Remove custard from the heat when it starts to steam and thicken and the base of the pan feels slippery as it is stirred with a wooden spoon.
- To stop hot custard from cooking further, pour it into a bowl standing in cold water. As the custard cools it thickens to the consistency of double cream.

NOTES FOR FOOD ALLERGY SUFFERERS

DAIRY-FREE DIET: Although both custard made with custard powder and crème Anglaise are traditionally made with cows' milk, they are just as good made with dairy-free milk. Sweetened soya milk is best as it most closely resembles dairy milk in appearance and consistency. Rice milk and almond milk can also be used for making custard, however their thin consistency tends to make thin, watery custard. To enrich and thicken custard made with rice milk or almond milk, use 4 egg yolks per 290 ml/10 fl oz milk.

GLUTEN-FREE DIET: Crème Anglaise is ideal for gluten-free diets as it is thickened with egg yolks not flour. Where flour is needed to thicken a custard, cornflour is generally used.

EGG-FREE DIET: Although egg yolks enrich, colour and thicken crème Anglaise, a very similar egg-free sauce can be made using cornflour to thicken, a small quantity of custard powder for colour and milk or cream to enrich its flavour (see Vanilla Cream Sauce page 208).

NUT- AND SOYA-FREE DIETS: Crème Anglaise is entirely suitable for nut- and soya-free diets. Check custard powder for traces of nuts or soya flour before using to make cornflour-thickened custards.

CRÈME ANGLAISE

Fresh custard is a luxurious, creamy sauce to serve warm with hot fruit tarts, pies, crumbles and steamed puddings or chilled with mousses, ice creams and cold tarts and cakes. For an egg-free alternative see page 208. **Serves 4**

● DAIRY

INGREDIENTS

290 ml/10 fl oz milk

soya milk, rice milk or almond milk

1 vanilla pod, split along its length

2 egg yolks

40 g/1½ oz caster sugar

1 Slowly bring the milk to the boil with the vanilla pod.

2 In a bowl, stir the egg yolks and sugar together until smooth.

3 Slowly pour the boiling milk onto the egg mixture, stirring continuously. Pour the mixture back into the pan and stir over a low heat until the custard starts to steam and thicken.

4 When the custard reaches the consistency of double cream remove the pan from the heat. Strain the custard through a sieve to remove the vanilla pods and any lumps of coagulated egg. Pour the custard into a cold bowl – this prevents it from cooking further. Serve hot or chilled.

VARIATIONS

CHOCOLATE CUSTARD SAUCE

Allow the hot custard to cool a little before gradually mixing in 40 g/1½ oz chopped dark chocolate. Serve warm or cold with chocolate, coffee, banana, vanilla and almond flavoured puddings

ORANGE CUSTARD SAUCE

Add the finely grated zest of 1 orange to the milk with the vanilla pod. Add a tablespoon of Cointreau or Grand Marnier to the hot custard sauce for a dinner party. Serve hot or cold with rich chocolate, vanilla or almond puddings.

COFFEE CUSTARD SAUCE

Dissolve 1 heaped teaspoon of instant coffee in 1 tablespoon of boiling water and stir into the hot custard. Serve hot or cold with vanilla, coffee or chocolate flavoured puddings.

RUM CUSTARD SAUCE

Replace the caster sugar with 55 g/2 oz soft light brown sugar and mix 2 tablespoons of rum into the hot custard. This sauce is delicious served with Christmas pudding.

VANILLA CREAM SAUCE

This recipe is a wonderfully smooth, rich egg-free alternative to crème Anglaise. Vanilla cream sauce can be served as it is, hot or cold or flavoured with chocolate, coffee or orange (see the variations for Crème Anglaise, page 207, which also apply to this recipe). For a lighter sauce, use soya milk only. **Makes 290 ml/10 fl oz**

INGREDIENTS

2 tsp egg-free custard powder (Birds is egg free)

70 ml/2½ fl oz whole milk

● **DAIRY** soya milk

220 ml/8 fl oz double cream

● **DAIRY** 100 ml/3½ fl oz soya milk mixed with
100 ml/3½ fl oz soya cream

2 tbsp caster sugar

2 vanilla pods, split along their length

1 Place the custard powder in a heavy-bottomed saucepan and slowly incorporate the milk to make a smooth mixture.

2 Add the cream, sugar and vanilla pods to the pan and bring to the boil, stirring continuously. Simmer gently for 30 seconds and remove from the heat.

3 Serve hot or chilled. This sauce can be made in advance and reheated.

DARK CHOCOLATE SAUCE

This smooth, glossy sauce is wonderful served with dairy or soya vanilla ice cream. The chocolate sauce sets as it cools and can be used as a chocolate fudge icing on cakes and cold brownies. **Makes 290 ml/10 fl oz**

INGREDIENTS

110 g/4 oz good quality dark chocolate (70% cocoa solids)

● **NUTS** check for traces of nuts
● **SOYA** check for soya lecithin

85 g/3 oz butter

● **DAIRY** dairy-free margarine

100 ml/3½ fl oz golden syrup

1 Break the chocolate into pieces and place in a heavy-bottomed saucepan with the other ingredients. Melt the ingredients together over a low heat, stirring continuously until the sauce is glossy and smooth. Remove from the heat and serve immediately or gently reheat when required.

2 Alternatively, cook in a microwave for 15–20 seconds, then stir thoroughly and repeat until the sauce is smooth and glossy. Don't allow the chocolate sauce to boil or it will curdle.

SUGAR SYRUP

Sugar syrup is simply sugar dissolved in water – the greater proportion of sugar the thicker the syrup. It is useful for adding extra sweetness to fruit salads or softening the texture of sorbet. **Makes 290 ml/10 fl oz**

INGREDIENTS

200 ml/7 fl oz water

225 g/8 oz granulated sugar

1 strip lemon zest

1 Place the water in the pan, add the sugar and lemon zest and bring slowly to a simmer, stirring frequently until the sugar is dissolved.

2 Now boil the syrup until it is thick enough to coat the back of a spoon. Immediately pour the thickened syrup into a cold bowl to prevent it from cooking and thickening further. Allow to cool, remove the lemon zest and use as required.

FRESH SUMMER BERRY SAUCE

A versatile, vibrantly coloured and flavoured sauce made from fresh raspberries, strawberries or blackcurrants or a mixture of all three. Serve with fruit and chocolate puddings, ice cream, meringues and cakes. Pour into ice-lolly moulds and freeze for the most wonderful homemade ice lollies you have ever tasted. **Serves 4**

INGREDIENTS

110 g/4 oz hulled raspberries

110 g/4 oz hulled strawberries

55 g/2 oz topped and tailed blackcurrants

1 tbsp lemon juice

2 tbsp caster sugar

1 Blend all the ingredients in food processor, or with a hand-held blender, until smooth.

2 Pass the sauce through a fine-meshed sieve into a bowl to catch the seeds and any fibrous parts of the fruit. Use a wooden spoon to help press the puréed fruit through. The sauce should evenly coat the back of a spoon. If the sauce is too thick, add water tablespoon by tablespoon until the sauce is the correct consistency.

3 Taste the sauce and add more lemon juice or sugar if necessary. Serve as required or store covered in the refrigerator for up to two days.

Chapter 18 | BABY FOODS

Introducing your baby to solids is exciting, as it marks an enormous leap in your baby's development and the start of your baby joining the family at meal times. However, with the increased numbers of children suffering allergies, it can also be a daunting time as you may be unsure which foods are best to give to your baby. This chapter is about preventing food allergies, as well as catering for them, because it is at this stage that parents can do much to reduce the likelihood of their child developing food allergies or intolerances.

Irrespective of whether or not there are food allergies in the family, feeding your baby exclusively on breast milk or infant formula milk is recommended for the first 6 months. This allows your baby's immune and digestive systems to develop and prepare for processing solids. Before six months old a baby's intestine is porous and may allow molecules of partially digested food to enter the bloodstream. The immune system may see these molecules as foreign and dangerous, stimulating an immune (or allergic) response. If this occurs, the baby's immune system may react more and more strongly each time you feed your child that particular food, resulting in increasingly severe allergic symptoms. At six months, breast milk or infant formula should still make up the majority of your baby's diet, as it contains the perfect combination of nutrients your baby needs at this stage. The nutritional content of the purées you feed your baby becomes increasingly important as he starts to eat more and consumes less milk.

INTRODUCING YOUR BABY TO SOLIDS

In addition to delaying the introduction of solids until your child is at least six months old, it is advisable to avoid the common allergens – gluten, eggs, dairy, nuts, fish and shellfish – at least for the first month of weaning. An ideal starter food is flaked baby rice, mixed to the consistency of runny yogurt with a little breast milk or infant formula. Although the consistency of milk and baby rice is slightly thicker than plain milk, the taste is the same and your baby is unlikely to reject or react in any way to such a simple food. To begin with your baby may only eat one or two teaspoons but as he becomes more efficient at swallowing, his intake will increase. Once your baby is keenly eating 2 to 3 tablespoons of baby rice and milk a day, make the mixture slightly thicker and start to introduce your baby to other simple, mild flavoured purées. The question at this stage is do you buy ready-prepared baby food or make your own.

THE MERITS OF HOMEMADE BABY FOOD

Jars of prepared baby food are invaluable for providing your baby with an instant meal when you are away from home or when you are too tired or too short of time to cook. However, they are not as fresh, pure, varied or as inexpensive as the purées you can make at home. When you make your own purées you are in control of the quality and proportions of ingredients used, allowing you to tailor the consistency and flavour to your child's taste and to ensure your child is receiving the best possible nutrition.

By preparing a number of servings of purée in one go, cooking for your baby need not take up much time. Instant purées can be made with ripe avocadoes and peeled bananas, mashed separately or together with a fork. Freshly made purées made from cooked ingredients can be covered and stored for up to two days in the fridge or divided into portions and frozen. All you have to do is defrost and gently heat a portion of purée in a small pan or in the microwave.

MAKING
HOMEMADE
PURÉES

Start by making small quantities of very smooth purées from raw or cooked fruits and vegetables: mashed avocado or banana, or puréed apple, pear, root vegetables, sweet potato or butternut squash are ideal foods to start with as they have appealing flavours, are easy to purée to a fine consistency and are easy for your baby to digest. To get your baby used to a new flavour, mix a spoonful of purée into your child's baby rice and milk so that the consistency remains familiar and mild in flavour. You can also start to introduce iron-rich foods such as well-cooked, puréed beans and lentils, green vegetables, dried fruit (such as apricots) and iron-enriched cereal.

Introduce your baby to one ingredient at a time over a period of 2 to 3 days, so that your baby has a chance to get used to the new taste and texture. By introducing one food at a time it also allows you to associate any signs of allergic reaction, such as tummy aches, diarrhoea or rashes, directly with it. Your baby's reaction to a food will also help you decide which foods suit him and which do not. If he holds his mouth open for more and looks excited you're onto a winner! If there are no adverse reactions to that food, then you can give it to him again, either on its own or combined with another new or tried and tested food.

Recognizing an allergic reaction

When a particular food does not suit your baby, it may cause an allergic reaction either immediately or later on in the day in the form of diarrhoea, tummy aches and gassiness. Immediate allergic reactions can range from mild to severe. Mild allergic reactions include itchy redness and slight swelling around the mouth, nettle rash or hives, and the onset of eczema. More dramatic reactions include swelling around the eyes, nose and mouth, shortness of breath or, far more serious, anaphylactic shock.

If your baby suffers a mild allergic reaction to a new food, avoid giving it to him again for a few months. Giving your baby the food a second time, on its own or mixed with other foods, may well result in a more serious allergic reaction. When the initial allergic reaction is serious and threatens the health of your child, you may be advised by your doctor to avoid that food entirely until he is much older. In such cases it is important to see an allergy specialist and dietician to ensure your child is receiving a balanced diet and is developing normally. Sometimes it is unclear what is causing the onset of eczema, hives, asthma or other allergic reactions, as other factors such as allergies to pollen, house dust mites, pets and cleansing products may also be contributing factors.

When he is not sure of the flavour or the food is irritating him in some way, he'll soon make it clear by turning away. Respect this response as much as a positive one but do try again another time – as your baby grows and his digestive system continues to mature, his preferences and requirements will change.

INTRODUCING
MORE COMPLEX
FOODS

At around 7 to 9 months your baby will be used to eating simple purées made with fruit and vegetables and you will have a clear idea which foods suit your baby. He will now be relying on solids more, to satiate his growing appetite, and the nutritional content of his purées must now increase to compensate for his decreasing milk consumption. Start to mix a small quantity of gently poached and puréed chicken and fish or tender, slow-cooked lamb, beef and pork, into the savoury purées your baby enjoys. You can also slowly introduce each of the allergenic ingredients you have been careful not to use until now, such as bread and pasta, egg and dairy products, including mild flavoured hard cheese, baby yogurts and cows' milk. Nuts should be avoided until your baby is at least one year old. If there are nut allergies in the family, you may be advised to avoid giving nuts to your child until he is four or five years old.

As your baby becomes more proficient at chewing and swallowing, you can gradually increase the thickness of his purées and blend them more coarsely so they contain small, soft lumps. Your baby may also be ready to try simple finger food, cut into bite-sized pieces, such as bread, melon, ripe bananas and cooked carrots and sweet potato.

If your child appears to enjoy and thrive on these foods, you can have fun introducing a whole variety of foods to your child, but do it slowly and watch out for any adverse reactions.

SUBSTITUTING
INGREDIENTS
IN BABY FOODS

When your baby is allergic to particular foods, cooking fresh food for your baby becomes essential. Jarred baby food is very clearly labelled and may well be suitable for an allergic baby but it will never provide the variety and freshness of food that you can with freshly cooked food. There are many allergy-free substitutes available to use in the place of the most common allergens.

Dairy products: To thin purées and as a base for milky sauces, use breast milk or soya-based infant formula in place of cows' milk and dairy-based infant formula. After your child's first birthday, cook with calcium- and vitamin-enriched soya milk or rice milk. You can also introduce your baby to soya yogurt in place of dairy yogurts. See Substituting for Dairy Products, page 50.

Gluten: Use gluten-free cereals and flours to make breakfast cereals, baked goods and to thicken sauces. See Substituting for Wheat, page 40.

Eggs: Avoiding eggs is straightforward when your child is eating purées but as he starts to eat more grown-up foods, you'll need to be more vigilant. See Substituting for Eggs, page 34.

Nuts: As nuts commonly cause the severest allergic reactions, cooking fresh food from scratch for your baby becomes a necessity. As your baby grows you will want to introduce him to more complex foods. For ways of adapting recipes that contain nuts see Substituting for Nuts, page 55.

Soya: In particular, watch out for soya in ready-made purées and use cows' milk or rice milk in cooking. See Substituting for Soya, page 58.

PURÉES FOR BABIES 6 TO 7 MONTHS OLD

These recipes are gluten, dairy, egg, soya and nut free, and were great favourites with my boys when they were babies.

PARSNIP AND APPLE PURÉE

This purée has a delicate fruity flavour and light creamy consistency. It can be stored in the fridge for up to two days or divided into portions and frozen. **Makes 6–8 portions**

INGREDIENTS

4 small parsnips, peeled and cut into small dice

2 dessert apples, peeled, cored and sliced

1 Place the parsnips in a steamer or saucepan, and steam or simmer for 15 minutes.

2 Add the apple and continue to cook for another 5 minutes, or until tender. Drain the parsnip and apple and retain the cooking liquid.

3 Blend the parsnip and apple until smooth with 4 tablespoons of cooking liquid. Add more liquid to the purée, a tablespoon at a time, until it is just thick enough to hold its shape.

POTATO, LEEK AND PEA PURÉE

This is an ideal purée for introducing your baby to the aromatic flavour of leeks or onion. It can be stored in the fridge for up to two days or divided into portions and frozen. **Makes 6–8 portions**

INGREDIENTS

300 g/10½ oz floury potatoes, peeled and cut into small dice

1 leek, trimmed, washed and thinly sliced

2 tbsp frozen peas

water, White Chicken or Vegetable Stock (pages 64, 66) to cover

1 Place the potatoes in a pan, cover with water or stock and a lid and bring to the boil. Simmer for 10 minutes then add the leeks and peas. Simmer for another 10 minutes, or until the potatoes are tender.

2 Drain the vegetables, retaining the cooking liquid.

3 Using a hand-held blender or food processor, blend the vegetables to a smooth purée with 2 tablespoons of the cooking water or stock. If the purée is too thick, add more hot stock or water, a tablespoon at a time until the purée is just thick enough to hold its shape.

AVOCADO AND BANANA PURÉE

Instant and highly nutritious, this delicately flavoured purée is ideal to serve to your baby when you are out and about. It is rich in vitamin E and B complex vitamins, for growth, a healthy nervous system and for the maintenance of healthy body tissue. **Makes 1 portion**

INGREDIENTS

1 small or ½ large banana, peeled

½ a small ripe avocado, cut into slices

Place the banana and avocado in a bowl and mash to a smooth purée with a fork. Avocado discolours quickly so serve straight away or within a few hours.

APPLE AND PEAR PURÉE

Unsweetened apple purée, even when made with the sweetest dessert apples, can sometimes taste a little sharp for babies. Pear softens and sweetens the flavour of apple to make a purée your baby will love. Store in the fridge for up to two days or freeze in portions. **Makes 6–8 portions**

INGREDIENTS

2 dessert apples, peeled, cored and cut into dice

2 ripe dessert pears, peeled, cored and cut into dice

1 Place the apple in a pan and just cover with water. Cover with a lid, bring to the boil and simmer for 5 minutes.

2 Add the pear, cover and continue to cook for another 5 minutes or until both the apple and pear are tender, but not mushy.

3 Drain the fruit and retain the cooking water. Blend with 2 tablespoons of the cooking water and if necessary, add more, a tablespoon at a time, until the purée is smooth and just holds its shape.

CARROT AND BUTTERNUT SQUASH PURÉE

This sweet purée is rich in vitamin A, which is important for growth, the immune system, good vision and strong bones. It is particularly good made with stock and can be stored in the fridge for up to two days or divided into portions and frozen. **Makes 6–8 portions**

INGREDIENTS

1 butternut squash, peeled, deseeded and cut into large dice

2 large carrots, peeled and cut into small dice

Vegetable Stock (page 66) or water to cover

1 Place the vegetables in a medium pan, cover with stock or water and a lid.

Bring to the boil then reduce the heat and simmer the vegetables for 20 minutes, or until tender. Drain the vegetables, reserving the cooking water.

2 Using a hand-held blender or food processor, purée the vegetables with 2–3 tablespoons of the cooking water, until the purée is smooth and just holds its shape.

First finger foods for babies of 7 months plus

Between 7 and 9 months your baby starts developing an interest in feeding himself. Choose soft-textured, unseasoned foods that are large enough for him to hold easily in his hand while he chews and sucks them. Avoid hard foods that may crumble into small, sharp pieces and very small foods, such as raisins, as both may cause your baby to choke. Simple finger foods that are unlikely to cause allergic reactions include:
- Peeled cucumber sticks
- Carrot and sweet potato sticks and broccoli florets, steamed until soft
- Chunks of soft ripe, peeled, stoned or cored fruit such as pear, peach, nectarine, mango, banana and avocado

- Plain rice cakes
- Large pieces of soft dried fruit including apple rings, ready-to-eat stoned apricots and prunes
- Gluten-free toast 'soldiers' and breadsticks
- Gluten-free pasta shapes

Once you have established which of the more complex, allergenic foods, containing dairy, egg, gluten and soya are suitable for your baby, you can introduce him to:
- Strips of wheat-based toast
- Cooked wheat pasta shapes
- Breadsticks
- Lumps of mild flavoured hard cheese

PURÉES FOR BABIES 8 TO 10 MONTHS OLD

CHICKEN, POTATO AND CORN PURÉE

This nutritious meal can also be made using skinned fillets of mild flavoured white fish, such as cod, haddock and sole. This purée will keep in the fridge for up to two days or divide it into portions and freeze. **Makes 6–8 servings**

INGREDIENTS

¼ onion, finely sliced

½ tbsp vegetable oil

2 floury potatoes, peeled and diced

White Chicken or Vegetable Stock (page 64, 66) or water

1 chicken breast, cut into 2.5 cm/1 in dice

4 tbsp frozen sweetcorn

1 Gently fry the onion in the oil, in a pan covered with a lid, until very soft.

2 Add the potato, cover with stock or water and simmer for 10 minutes. Add the chicken and sweetcorn and gently simmer for 10 minutes or until the chicken is cooked through and the potatoes are tender. Do not overcook the chicken or it will become tough when puréed.

3 Strain half the cooking liquid into a bowl and coarsely blend or finely chop the remaining contents of the pan. If the mixture is too dry, mix in a little more of the strained cooking liquid.

CHICKEN AND APRICOT RICE

The soft texture of cooked risotto rice makes it an ideal base for smooth, coarsely blended or chopped meals for your baby. Once your baby is eating food with lumps, try making this meal with more fibrous, nutritionally superior brown rice. This dish will keep in the fridge for up to two days or divide it into portions and freeze.
Makes 4–6 portions

INGREDIENTS

¼ onion, diced

1 tbsp sunflower or corn oil

55 g/2 oz Arborio rice or other white rice

290 ml/10 fl oz White Chicken or Vegetable Stock (page 64, 66) or water

1 skinless chicken breast, cut into large cubes

55 g/2 oz dried apricots

1 Gently fry the onion in the oil, covered with a lid, until soft. Stir the rice into the onion, add the stock or water and simmer for 10 minutes.

2 Add the chicken and apricots to the pan and simmer for a further 10 minutes, or until the chicken is cooked through and the rice is swollen and tender.

3 Coarsely blend or finely chop the contents of the pan. If the mixture is too firm, mix in some water or hot stock, a tablespoon at a time.

RICE PUDDING

Made with flaked rice, this is a satisfying milk pudding to serve warm or cold. It's delicious flavoured with a tablespoon or two of your baby's favourite fruit purées. This dish can be stored for up to two days but should not be frozen. **Makes 4 portions**

INGREDIENTS

290 ml/10 fl oz cows' milk, infant formula or dairy-free milk fortified with calcium

45 g/1½ oz flaked rice

1–2 tsp soft brown sugar

1 Slowly bring the milk to the boil to prevent it scorching on the base of the pan. Add the rice, cover and simmer gently for 20–30 minutes, or until the rice is very soft.

2 Stir in the sugar and serve warm or cold.

FOOD FOR CHILDREN BETWEEN 9 AND 12 MONTHS OLD

Once your baby reaches 9 months old you will have a clear idea of the foods that suit him. At this stage cooking for your family becomes easier as you can start to give your baby some of the food that you serve to the rest of the family. If your baby is allergic to certain foods, you may be able to adapt recipes to suit his requirements so you can all eat the same things (see Part 2: Knowing How to Substitute…). Choose dishes that are soft in texture and require minimal chewing, such as soup or spaghetti bolognaise. Avoid using salt, pepper and spices in dishes your baby will be eating, until you have separated his portion.

The following recipes from this book are suitable for babies above 9 months old:
- Chunky Winter Vegetable Soup, puréed (page 69)
- Bolognaise, with spaghetti (page 122)
- Lasagne (page 122)
- Homemade Pork and Apple Sausages (page 94)
- Chicken and Mushroom Pie (page 128)
- Mediterranean Roast Chicken with gravy and vegetables (page 114)
- Salmon Fish Cakes (page 89)
- Mashed Potato (page 136)
- Oven Chips – avoid seasoning the chips until you have separated some for your baby (page 136)
- Crushed New Potatoes – peel the potatoes as the skins could cause your baby to choke (page 137)

There are also lots of baked foods and puddings your baby can try (although always remember that sweet foods should be an occasional treat not a regular part of their diet):
- Gluten-free Bread – substitute ground almonds in the recipe with more potato flour (pages 185–87)
- Victoria Sponge Cake (page 172)
- Plain Scones (page 174)
- French Crêpes (page 195)
- Buckwheat Pancakes with Caramelized Apple (page 196)
- Apple and Blackberry Crumble (page 201)
- Vanilla Cream Sauce – always make an egg-free custard for babies as the egg in crème Anglaise is partially cooked and could cause salmonella poisoning (page 208)
- Banana Ice Cream (page 205)

CHILDREN'S PARTY FOODS

Cooking for children's parties can be an unbearably daunting experience if you have a young child who cannot eat dairy, eggs, wheat, soya or nuts, as all these ingredients are commonly used in manufactured foods and in home-cooked party food. However, you'll find many of the recipes in this book are suitable for children – and for parties often all that is required is for them to be made in smaller pieces or sliced or cut into smaller portions. This chart offers an at-a-glance guide to which child-friendly recipes can be adapted for particular allergies (Y means yes the recipe can be adapted for that allergy and N means no it can't).

Party Food Ideas	page	Dairy	Egg	Gluten	Soya	Nuts
SAVOURY FOOD						
Mini Beef Burgers	92	Y	Y	Y	Y	Y
Mini Salmon Fish Cakes	89	Y	Y	Y	Y	Y
Crispy Fish Ribbons	104	Y	Y	Y	Y	Y
Mini Homemade Sausages	94	Y	Y	Y	Y	Y
Baked Homemade Honey Sausages	119	Y	Y	Y	Y	Y
Oven Chips	136	Y	Y	Y	Y	Y
Slices of Pizza Marinara	186	Y	Y	Y	Y	Y
Sticky Finger Chicken Drumsticks	123	Y	Y	Y	Y	Y
Sandwiches – ham, cucumber (use gluten-free bread)	185	Y	Y	Y	Y	Y
SWEET FOOD						
Chocolate Chip Cookies	180	Y	Y	Y	Y	Y
Shortbread Rounds	179	Y	Y	Y	Y	Y
Chewy Syrup Squares	178	Y	Y	Y	Y	Y
Mini Scones	174	Y	Y	Y	Y	Y
Squidgy Chocolate Brownies	176	Y	N	Y	Y	Y
Egg-Free Rich Chocolate Brownies	177	Y	Y	N	Y	Y
Victoria Sponge Cake	172	Y	Y	Y	Y	Y
Date and Orange Muffins	175	Y	Y	Y	Y	Y
Banana, Cinnamon and Honey Cake	167	Y	Y	Y	Y	Y
Jam Tarts	163	Y	Y	Y	Y	Y
Individual Meringues	199	Y	N	Y	Y	Y
Rich Chocolate Ice Cream	204	Y	N	Y	Y	Y
Raspberry Sorbet Ice Lollies	202	Y	Y	Y	Y	Y
Banana Ice Cream with	205	Y	Y	Y	Y	Y
Dark Chocolate Sauce	208	Y	Y	Y	Y	Y

INDEX